From Where Did You Come?

Bhagavan Sri Sathya Sai Baba

Charles P. DiFazio

A Sterling Paperback

STERLING PAPERBACKS
An imprint of
Sterling Publishers (P) Ltd.
L-10, Green Park Extension, New Delhi-110016
Tel : 6191023, 6191784/85; Fax : 91-11-6190028
E-mail: ghai@nde.vsnl.net.in
Website: www.sterlingpublishers.com

From Where Did You Come? Bhagavan Sri Sathya Sai Baba
© 1997, Charles P. DiFazio
ISBN 81 207 1928 x
Reprint 1997, 1999

Published by Sterling Publishers Pvt. Ltd., New Delhi-110016.
Printed at Saurabh Print-O-Pack, Noida, India.
Cover design by Adage Communications

Offering

This book is offered with devotion at the Lotus Feet
of the living Avatar,

Bhagavan Sri Sathya Sai Baba

Dedication

This book is dedicated, with love,
to my best friend
and my life's companion,
my wife, Patty Di Fazio,
who has lovingly encouraged and assisted me
in the writing of this book.

IN GRATITUDE

Several people graciously gave of their time to help me with the preparation of the manuscript for this book. Without their help, I could not have completed this work in time to take it to Sai Baba on our trip to His Lotus Feet in April of 1995. For their generosity, I pray that Bhagavan Baba will shower them with loving attention and His Grace, now and always.

Bob and Addie Grauch: Help in locating Baba quotations.

Charles and Edith Gregory: Critical editing.

John and Elena Hartgering: Outline organization and editing.
                                     Final book format.

Anthony (Tony) LoGrasso: Foreword.

Kevin Nelson: Computer advice and instruction.

FOREWORD

My friend Chuck felt compelled to write a book about his spiritual journey. When he asked me to read it, and write a foreword, I was reminded of Dante's words at the beginning of the *Divine Comedy*:

Nel mezzo del cammino di nostra vita
mi trovai in una selva oscura,
che la diretta via era smarrita

[In the middle of life's path,
I found myself in a dark forest
because the right way was lost.]

Dante Alighieri
Divine Comedy
Page 1

Like Dante, and many of us as well, Chuck found himself *nel mezzo del cammino di nostra vita* in unclear and less than serene circumstances. As Dante found the Expression of Life in Beatrice, Chuck found Hope, Beauty and Love personified in his wife, Patty. Dante found his spiritual guide in Virgilius [the Roman poet, Virgil], Chuck found his in BHAGAVAN SRI SATHYA SAI BABA.

We are born to this Earth at different times and in different environments. Some of us are black, some are white, some are yellow, some are red, others are brown. We grow up in different places, yet we each are part of the same planet. We are raised in different societies, cultures and traditions. Some are needy, others are well off, a few are opulent.

According to our traditions, we embrace a set of beliefs, and undertake a course of studies to learn a profession, a trade, or some way to eke out a living. Our needs vary, our goals are different, but we all strive to fulfill our desires. We embark on the adventure called Life.

If Life were an ocean, it would appear as if we were swimming in it. At times, the Wind of Destiny blows great waves, and we find ourselves in rough waters. Confused and exhausted, we cry for help, seeking a raft, a boat, a rock, or a rescuer. When help arrives, it feels good, reassuring. There is hope ... we can reach safety ... and sooner or later we all do.

We adjust, reconstruct our beliefs, change our way of living, and reorder our priorities until we reach a Comfort Zone. Now we are happy, relaxed, laid back ... until another blow stirs us up, and we find ourselves swimming in rough waters again.

This time we pray for guidance, strength, endurance, and courage. Now we become more aware that we are not alone. Regardless of race, status, age, nationality or culture, we all swim in the same sea, trying to reach the same shore. In the process, we start to recognise the Unity of All. Even though we are different individuals, we begin to see ourselves bound by the same Life Principle: LOVE.

Then Life takes on a different shape and meaning. Events unfold. Coincidences occur that are no longer meaningless. We observe, recognise, correct, connect. We rediscover our human values. We cleanse ourselves, and remove the dross from our personalities; we become more accepting of others. We no longer try to control, to oppress, or to abuse others. We shed our ego and show more compassion and love. Our feelings of superiority, the need to feel better than others ceases, and in humility, we accept everyone as they are, man or woman, straight or gay, poor or rich, young or old, mature or childish, sad or happy, intellectual or fool, and so on.

Tolerance becomes familiar and is practised frequently. Once only a bud, Love now blooms to full flower, opening its colorful petals, showing its beauty, emitting its fragrance, radiating joy and energy to all. As we progress on our journey [*nel mezzo del cammino*], we become more aware of Nature and the Universe; we begin to understand that the Winds of Destiny, the storms, and the big waves are really our own creation. Our thoughts, words and deeds caused this *maya,* or drama we call Life. So we search both without and deep within, looking for more understanding and light.

Chuck's book describes this process. He, along with many other swimmers, has seen in Sathya Sai Baba, the Light House of this age, the Perennial Light that takes physical form from age to age. This *Avatar* is here in order to rescue us, to help us and to guide us all across the ocean of life, so that we may reach the Unchanging Comfort Zone, where we are all destined to be self-fulfilled.
See you there, and have fun swimming

Love All - Serva All   Anthony[Tony]LoGrasso

INTRODUCTION

"What is the purpose of this book? Why are you writing it?" Charles Gregory looked at me intently, eyes unblinking. "For whom are you writing?" Embarrassed, I could only stammer because, in truth, I hadn't thought of a reason for writing this book nor had I considered who its readers might be. One day, it just occurred to me to write about my spiritual journey which has brought me after many left and right turns to the *Avatar* of the Age, BHAGAVAN SRI SATHYA SAI BABA. But Charles made me think. Is there an unconscious plan or design behind my inclination to chronicle the people and events that had crossed my path and heightened my awareness? And who was I writing for?

After much reflection, I now realise that I am writing this book because it is important to me to memorialise for myself the signs and symbols that kept me searching for something or someone that might grant me awareness and peace. First and foremost, I am writing this book for me. I need to record the little miracles and synchronicities that brought me to accept Sathya Sai Baba as an Incarnation of Divinity. In that sense, I am probably writing a spiritual journal rather than a book.

Secondly, I am writing for my children. In my life, the important milestones are spiritual and I want to leave a history of these milestones for them, so that they might know and share my insights. I want them to understand how I came to believe that the advent of Sai Baba is the most important incarnation in over two thousand years. It is my prayer that the stories related in the following pages will encourage them to study the phenomenon of Sai Baba and to practice His teachings.

Most of us, when we begin to inquire of God and matters esoteric, do not usually think of ourselves as being capable of deep spirituality. We do not see ourselves as saints or mystics. We do not appreciate that we are spiritual beings capable of soaring to great heights. Historical saints and *avatars* such as Krishna, Christ, St. Francis of Assisi, The Blessed Mother, and Saint Theresa of the Roses are as unbelievable to us as the sci-fi characters of the television show, Star Trek. It is difficult for us to believe that such beings really lived, exist now or could come in the future. Therefore, I offer this book to those of us who are spiritual seekers, early in our journey, as an introduction to a living avatar, Bhagavan Sai Baba. It is a primer for those who would like to begin an inquiry into the possibility that He is, like Christ, Buddha or Krishna before Him, a descent of Divinity come in human form for the purpose of raising mankind to an appreciation of the divinity inherent in humanity. This book is written by an average guy who is on the Sai path aspiring to understand the importance of the Sai Advent, His miracles, His teachings and His love. It is not a philosophical treatise meant to be studied by philosophers and theologians. It is not a mystical discourse setting out, in words, visions experienced in deep meditation. It is a writing about the ordinary people who have touched my life, and whose stories have taught me about Sathya Sai Baba. Hopefully, it will encourage others to affirm the truth that the spiritual quest is not just the path of the philosopher-saint or the mystic-saint, but eventually the final journey of us all.

I have written each chapter about people and events that have deeply influenced and touched my soul. These little stories have brought me closer to Sathya Sai Baba and it is with joy that I recount them here. Interspersed throughout each chapter are quotations from Sathya Sai Baba that highlight the message of the chapter story. It is my intent that this weaving of each chapter story with the teachings of Sathya Sai Baba will underscore my belief for the reader that Sathya Sai Baba has always been active in my life whether I was aware of Him or not. My spiritual journey is directed by Him.

Sai Ram!
Charles DiFazio

CONTENTS

CHAPTER 1

FEAR OF THE DIVINE

*"One should not fear God;
one should love Him so much
that all acts He disapproves are discarded.
Fear to do wrong; fear to hate another;
fear losing Grace."*

Sathya Sai Speaks
Volume VI
Page 179

I cannot remember a time when I was not concerned about God, saints, heaven and hell, good and evil and the unknown spirit world. Innately, I knew that another world lived and breathed all around me. It was a world of luminescent angels and vile devils, a hidden dimension where unknown entities both divine and demonic interacted with men to influence them and alter their course. As a young boy, I was in awe of this unchartered universe and its denizens. My overriding feeling of the spirit was **fear** and since I couldn't see, hear or touch spirit, I concluded that it must be terrifying!

I can recall one incident at age six, in the first grade at St. Augustine's School in Hartford, Connecticut. The school was administered by The Sisters of St. Joseph. With robes of black and starched bibs of white, they seemed at once clean and beautiful, yet commanding and powerful. At a school assembly, one of these awesome nuns spoke to us about the appearance of the Blessed Mother to the three children, Lucy, Jacinta and Francisco at Fatima in Portugal. She described a "lovely lady" and her shining robes, emphasising the awe and fear experienced by the children at the sudden vision of the heavenly visitor. I went home that day, after school, convinced that the Blessed Mother was going to appear to me that very night in my little bedroom and I was scared to death! I made sure that the night light was on in my room, as well as in the hallway, my door was open and my mother was "on call!"

I know that the sister who painted the scene of Fatima with such drama and flair, meant to instill in her young audience, an attitude of reverence and awe. For me, however, her descriptions of the "Lady in Blue," and the miracle of the sun dancing in the sky and plummeting towards the earth, evoked a feeling of fear and apprehension. I just **knew** that a vision was going to sneak up on me and frighten the living daylight out of me!

Soon after this incident, my father got the bright idea to bring me to the movies to see Gene Kelly in the "Three Musketeers." Toward the end of the movie, which I really couldn't understand, an executioner came to take away a treacherous woman in order to cut off her head. Not exactly the kind of event that a six year old child is going to be able to handle, and I was no exception. With all of the knowledge and experience of my six years on the planet, I thought that the executioner was the devil and that he was taking the woman to Hell! That night, not only did I demand the night light, the hall light and my mother "on call," I also petitioned for and received bodily protection against the devil by being allowed to sleep in a secret, hidden crevice between my mother and father in their bed where spirits were not allowed!

Even as I grew older, I didn't outgrow the fear of apparitions. I always felt that I would see a vision of the Blessed Mother or Jesus or one of the saints and I was sure that when it happened, it would be in the dark of night when I least expected it. I remember returning home from a friend's house at night with my heart pounding. Never did I think that some human degenerate would pounce on me. It was always a spirit that activated my imagination. So, I'd race home, with my feet barely touching the ground. I guess I thought that Jesus and Mary couldn't run. The fear of spiritual entities was so great, that even in my high school years, I would never enter a church alone. I imagined statues talking to me or Jesus coming down from the cross. And the church was Jesus' house, so if He were anywhere, He would be in there and I didn't want to bump into Him.

During my high school years, I spent less time thinking about apparitions, unless of course, I was alone at night. But fear arose in other ways. Six of us would usually eat together at lunch and have deep theological or philosophical discussions on such topics as whether the Catholic Church was the only true repository of God's truth or whether non-Christians could get to Heaven. Of course, I took the Catholic point of view (as far as I could understand it) and gave simple arguments supporting the legitimacy of Catholic preeminence, even among Christians. I advocated an exclusivity that kept us as Catholics in the Grace of God and all others outside of His love and care. Of course, I realize now that my narrow opinions were building walls around God and limiting His effulgence. Usually, it is fear that motivates people of one religion to suspect others and to exclude them from God's love and grace.

> *"Therefore, if anyone finds fault*
> *with another's faith,*
> *he is casting a slur on his own faith.*
> *If anyone defames another religion,*
> *he only reveals his ignorance*
> *of the nature of religion*
> *and the glory of God."*

Sathya Sai Speaks
Volume V
Page 333

Soon thereafter, I was off to Georgetown University in Washington, D.C., a Catholic school run by the Jesuits. I was older, a little more mature, certainly more educated and fast becoming less naive. So, one would think that I might begin to shed my fear of the spirit world and my belief that only my religion was the one true religion. However, both ideas were intensified during those college years. Although I was one of the few who enjoyed and even relished the heavy load of theology and philosophy courses required for graduation, the emphasis on Thomistic theology and Catholic doctrine, narrowed the scope of possible positions on any issue and therefore limited my understanding.

One of the theology courses was called "Comparative Religions," and was supposed to give an overview of each major faith discussed. However, the real bias of the course as presented, was that other religions were not as real, deep or true as the Catholic Faith. The legitimacy of Catholicism was emphasised, rather than how to live that faith in love and righteousness. It was important to be right. It was important to hold all other religious persuasions as false.

> *"Each religion defines God within the limits it demarcates*
> *and then claims to have grasped Him.*
> *Like the seven blind men who spoke of the elephant*
> *as a pillar, a fan, a rope or a wall,*
> *because they contacted but a part*
> *and could not comprehend the entire animal,*
> *so, too, religions speak of a part and*
> *assert that their vision is full and total."*

Samuel H. Sandweiss, M.D.
<u>The Holy Man and the Psychiatrist</u>
Chapter 17
Page 191

And my fear of the Divine and of the world of spirit continued during those years without respite. I remember once attending a retreat run by the Jesuits in Virginia. It was required that all of my class attend. The leader for the retreat was a magnificent speaker, a Jesuit, whose oratory and theatrical skills were awesome. His main presentation started innocently enough as he spoke to us in the chapel about some innocuous subject. Suddenly, he screamed: "No, no, I'm not ready!" and began pleading with the spirit of death, who, he led us to believe by his one-sided conversation with the specter, was there to claim his soul as his time had come!

We looked at each other and then at him and then up the aisle. We believed that he really was seeing and talking to someone or something. It was frightening! And, of course, the subject matter, death, wasn't exactly a peaches and cream topic. It is hard to fathom how he did it; how he made it seem so real; how he made us believe it, but we did! We really were convinced that he was seeing something or hallucinating big time. Either way, his performance was very scary. Once again, my inordinate fear of the unknown was fertilized, watered, pruned and tended. The spirit world was not friendly, it was terrifying!

On another occasion, I decided to go to Dalgren Chapel in the Quadrangle to pray for God's help on a particular exam that I was worried about. True to my history, I gingerly opened the door to make sure that someone else was in there and when I saw a man kneeling in a pew five or six rows from the entranceway, I breathed a sigh of relief, and went in. After praying for about a minute from a pew directly behind him, I thought: "What if this guy turns around and **looks** just like Jesus? What if he **is** Jesus?" I bolted out of there so fast that my soul was waiting outside for my body to catch up!

Once, while on holiday from school, I was sitting with my family around the dining room table. It was late and my brother, also home from school, decided to sleep in my grandmother's bedroom because it had a large bed. She had gone to visit a relative and the room was available. About five minutes after he left us, we heard a scream and he came running out of the room holding rosary beads. "What are these?" he yelled. At first we didn't know what he was talking about. "These beads were glowing in the dark!" We all broke into laughter. My grandmother had left the beads hanging on her wall. They were phosphorescent; when the light was on, they absorbed the light and when the light was extinguished, they glowed in the dark. I'm glad I wasn't the one to have seen them blazing on the wall in that darkened room. They would have had to scrape me off the ceiling!

And yet, during those early years, and in spite of my fears and my parochial education, I was building my own spiritual devotion and beginning to walk a spiritual path. That path was directed toward the Blessed Mother. I don't know why she was so comfortable for me, but I really enjoyed talking to her in my mind and feeling that she listened. So, even though I was not at ease with the unknown spirit world in general, I was content with my relationship with Mother Mary in particular. For that time in my life, she was gentle; she was forgiving; she was motherly love.

> *"The devotee of God must become as a little child,*
> *with God as Divine Mother*
> *and with the fullness of love*
> *flowing from the devotee's unguarded heart*
> *to Divine Mother.*
> *This open, unrestrained and unmodified love,*
> *spontaneously embracing Divine Mother,*
> *is devotion to God."*
>
> **John Hislop**
> My Baba and I
> Page 67

CHAPTER 2

WHO AM I...REALLY?

*"The attempt to know about the Knower
is called Sadhana (spiritual discipline).
Knowledge about the Knower
is Atma Vidya
(understanding the divinity within)."*

Sai Avatar
Volume II
Paragraph 710
Page 320

Where I grew up fearful of the Divine, my wife Patty's experience was very different. She sought the Divine. Her earliest remembrances of a spiritual nature were from the age of eight years. There was a television show that was popular around this time in her young life called :"This is Your Life." Patty would imagine being the guest whose life was to be spotlighted. Teachers and little friends from the past would speak from a microphone backstage and Patty would imagine trying to guess who they might be. With a life that short, it wouldn't have been too difficult.

But her imagining wasn't really daydreaming. It was an early step, a first step into the life of the spirit. "I always felt that I was just playing the role of Patty Montanaro and someday I'd get to view my life as Patty Montanaro, in much the same way as if I were the honoured guest on that television show," she said. "I always knew, deep down inside of me, that I wasn't just this little kid named Patty, but that I was much, much more. I just couldn't pinpoint who I really was. I imagined that all the different people in my life would have played a role in helping me to know who 'I' was."

*"Man is a spark of the Divine;
he must manifest in every activity of his,
the Divine."*

Voice of the Avatar
Part 1
Page 3

Even at that early age, Patty used to meditate on the question: "Who am I, really?" Oh, she didn't know at the time that it was meditation, but it was. She would sit in front of a mirror for several long minutes staring into her eyes looking back at her and ask: "Who am I? Who is deep inside? Who is behind these eyes?"

While other children were playing jump rope and running around the playground, hopping and skipping and expending their youthful energy, Patty would organize one or two girlfriends and wander down to the meadow beyond the school yard at recess. There they would flatten the long grass and make an imaginary convent in their minds where the little girls would pretend to be nuns devoutly worshipping God. "I was always Sister Maria and I'd take care of the altar," she remembered. " I'd kneel and pray in that field until the bell rang for us to come back to school." Patty recalls that her interest in the religious life continued as she grew a little older. She would pray for a vocation to be a nun: "Please, dear God, help me to know if this is the right path for me." Thankfully, for me, it wasn't.

In her early teens, Patty found comfort in the devotions of the Catholic Church. One year during Lent, she attended mass in the morning before school for forty consecutive days. "I am grateful to my mother for dropping me off at the church so early each morning," Patty recalls. She would attend the mass and then walk to school at seven a.m. Patty was the only one in her family interested in this devotion. Although she wasn't consumed with spirituality, in these little ways, she maintained her spiritual connections.

Patty and I grew up in the same town, and attended the same church. Our parents knew each other casually, but were not friends. And, through our teen years, Patty and I never met or at least we don't remember having met. I am five years older than she, and when I was in high school, she was in junior high, and of course, when she was in high school, I was off to college. Even later, as we became young adults, our paths never crossed.

Patty was married on August 8, 1965, the same date as my marriage the year before. She was married in the same church as I was; she went to the same honeymoon spot as I did, she just did all of these things with someone else, not me. But the syncronicity is amazing. In order to marry on the same day one year apart, she had to get married on a Sunday, which is unusual in the Catholic Church. She did that because Saturday was a big business day at her father's

store and he needed to work. Although we had not met; although our
lives were seemingly going in different directions, the symbols and
signs of our eventual meeting were starting to appear. We were
beginning our journey to each other, a journey that would bring
spiritual discovery to both of us, together.

Patty's marriage ended in divorce. With divorce came new
challenges: Single parenting and a career she has grown to love. But
there seemed no answer at all to her question repeated and repeated
over the years: "Who am I...really?"

"There is no such thing as failure in the universe.
A hundred times a man will hurt himself,
a thousand times he will tremble,
but in the end he will realise
that he is God."

Part of a letter
from Sathya Sai Baba to John Hislop,
reproduced on page 233 and 234
of Hislop's <u>My Baba and I</u>.

CHAPTER 3

THE DOOR CLOSES

"This is my blessing to you
and I hope you will be able
to get good company always."

A Recapitulation
of Baba's Divine Teachings
Page 345

On August 8, l964, I married Carol, a young woman whom I had dated since the end of my senior year of high school. The marriage was in trouble from the beginning. We had little in common and we both felt, and correctly, that the other person blocked our way. Perhaps we married too early or were too naive to understand our obligations, but in any event, we never became friends. We could disagree on anything. And yet, nothing happens by chance . We had three children in a little over three years and I believe that these three kids had to be born to Carol and me. They had to have our genes; they had to experience the social setting that our marriage afforded; they had to suffer through our eventual divorce. It was their Karma. It was their destiny. But, they were the gold in that marriage. They were its reward.

Our first born, Marc Paul, was born crying and cried every night until he was six years old. I remember walking him in my arms, night after night, wondering why he was so unhappy or sad, or fearful or hurt. After all, those tears came from somewhere. Very slowly, I came to accept that Marc must have lived a prior life or lives and the tears and crying were the residue, from another age, of a soul who had been hurt or tormented with some fear or grief.

I chose Marc's name during my junior year in college, before he was born, before there was a marriage, before I knew that I would marry anyone for that matter. In prayer, I promised St. Mark, that if he would intercede on my behalf and help me graduate from college, I would name my first son after him. I had the better of that deal. After all, if I graduated, I would be the beneficiary; if I had a son, I would be blessed; and if I named him, "Marc," I would be using a name that I liked anyway. I wonder if St. Mark ever caught on?

Andrew Paul came along next and was just the opposite of Marc. He was born laughing. Everything made him smile, especially Marc.

He was outgoing and friendly and people oriented from the minute he began to walk. Even now, Andy is the family picker upper. He has a sense of other people's feelings and can always raise their spirits.

I didn't know why I chose the name, "Andrew." Before he was born, I was set on the name "Alexander," after Carol's grandfather, who I really liked. But, at the last minute, he was "Andrew" and "Andrew" fit him well. It was only later, after my divorce, when I met Patty that I realised why I had chosen the name, Andrew for him, but more of that later.

After two boys, I wanted a baby girl and when we realised that Carol was pregnant again, I prayed that this child would be a healthy, little girl. One evening, Carol started contractions and we rushed to the hospital. We were greeted by a nurse with a wheel chair and Carol was brought into what I thought was the labor room. A nurse came out of that room a few minutes later and I started to go in. The nurse barred my way. "Where do you think you're going?" She asked. "In there to wait with my wife." I responded. "No you're not, she's having the baby right now!" In those days, men didn't participate in childbirth as much as they can today. I looked at her stupidly until the import of what she said hit me. We were only in the hospital five or ten minutes. If we had left our apartment later or been delayed by traffic, I would have had to help deliver my daughter in the car!

Luckily, Carol delivered a cuddly, baby girl in the hospital, not on the corner of Woodland Street and Farmington Avenue. I saw her just after she was born, before she was washed or weighed. They were wheeling Carol down the hall and the baby was beside her. We had not agreed upon a name before going to the hospital, but as we talked in the hall with the baby looking up at us, we decided on "Leslie," and so, Leslie Ann entered my life and my heart.

Even with the blessing of the three kids, the marriage continued to unravel. We had so little in common. We were two good people who were just not on the same path. Whatever the reason, the marriage finally ended in divorce. Because I am basically a homebody, the divorce was difficult. Losing my family and living apart from my children was a scenario that had never occurred to me. The reality was crushing.

Another significant part of my life ended with the divorce. For several years, I had directed and channelled my interest in spirituality into service within the Catholic Church. I taught high school seniors in the Catholic Youth Organization(C.Y.O.), led the folk music group and was elected to our parish council. I was particularly happy with my work with the folk group which grew from an initial four or five members to over forty teenagers. We had a drummer, guitarists, a flutist, a base player, a violinist and some great singers. Some of these kids even wrote some of our songs. I was very proud of them. With the divorce, all of that ceased. The rules of the Church, as I understood them, were that being a divorced Catholic, I could still attend Mass and receive the sacraments, but if I ever remarried, I could not. This conditional acceptance highlighted my feelings of alienation from my religion and all the work that I had been doing within it. In the eyes of the Church, marriage to anyone else would mean I was living in sin so I did not feel that I could continue working with the folk group or teach C.Y.O. The divorce seemed to me to be a moral failure and I couldn't bear the negative judgment of other parishioners, whether real or not.

My disaffection from the Church was underscored by a chance meeting that my mother had with the pastor of my parish about a year after the divorce. She was dining at a restaurant and when she saw him across the room, she went over to his table, introduced herself as my mother and said innocently: "I guess you miss him working with the folk group." He looked up at her and said: "No, not really." She didn't know what to say. It was a very embarrassing moment for her caused by a very insensitive man who happened to be a priest. Yet, it does highlight the feeling of separation caused by the Church's attitude toward divorce.

Even my relationship with my best friend came to an abrupt halt when my marriage ended. He had been a friend since the eighth grade. We were students at Georgetown together. Later, when he became engaged, he asked me to be his best man. After graduation from law school, I represented him and his wife on a few small matters. We were close socially, often getting together with our wives and other mutual friends. He was responsible for my becoming involved with the Curcillo Movement in the Catholic Church and we taught C.Y.O. together as a team. With my divorce, all that ended. Although he was the one that I had spilled my guts to, and the only one who knew all the problems that I had experienced in my marriage, when the divorce was final, the friendship, too, was over. He told me that he believed that divorce was wrong and against his morality. I knew that he believed that, so I could not fault his decision to cut our ties, but I was devastated. I realised that I was losing my marriage, my children, my church and my friends. I felt alone and adrift, not knowing where it would all wind up, but at that time and in that space, my life, even my spiritual life was crumbling down around me.

> *"It is good to be born in a church,*
> *but it is not good to die in one.*
> *Grow and rescue yourself from the limits*
> *and regulations and the doctrines that*
> *fence in your freedom of thought;*
> *the ceremonies and rites*
> *that restrict and direct.*
> *Reach the point where churches do not matter,*
> *where all roads end and from where*
> *all roads begin."*

<u>Sathya Sai Speaks</u>
Volume VII
Page 85

CHAPTER 4

THE FIRST STEP

"God is so merciful that
He will come ten steps towards you,
if you but take one step
towards Him."

Sathya Sai Speaks
Volume VII
Page 307

In the early seventies, I began to read books on spiritual esoterica and new age subjects. I read about reincarnation, psychics, Nostradamus, the prophecies of the Great Pyramid, and Edgar Cayce. But this study was mind stuff and not experiential. I wasn't **knowing** the subject matter, I was just thinking about it. Looking back, I realise that each subject, each study, advanced my beliefs and expanded me a little, but the first quantum leap in my spiritual growth was my introduction to Curcillo, a special retreat program of the Catholic Church.

A dear friend had gone on this retreat and encouraged me to attend the next programme. The Curcillo is a three day weekend retreat devised by a panel of Spanish Catholics for spiritual renewal. Retreatants are cut off from the world without newspapers, radio, television and telephone. The three days of isolation are meant to be symbolic of the three days that Christ spent in the tomb. The goal of the experience is to help the retreatant to realise that the spiritual journey is an intense inward renewal of one's spirit; a conversion of one's spiritual energy from the outer rites and forms of the mind to a deeper emphasis on the inner substance of the heart.

I made my Curcillo retreat at the old Convent house of St. John's Roman Catholic Parish in Middletown, Connecticut. At first, I experienced withdrawal pains from the lack of television, radio and newspapers. I was fidgety and unfocused because I didn't have my daily dose of baseball highlights, the news and Star Trek.

"Do not get too much attached to the world,
and too involved in its tangles".

<u>Sathya Sai Speaks</u>
Volume VII
Page 269

But after a while, the programme, the team leaders and the imposed separation from the world, all helped to quiet my mind and quicken my spirit. I found myself participating fully in the discussions and the devotions. One reason for my plunging in feet first was a team leader that I'll call "Bill." Bill turned out to be a man who helped change my life. He was direct, open and honest in his interaction with the retreatants, and I think that his honesty is what endeared him to me.

During the first night of the retreat, the team brought us all into the chapel for prayer. Several members of the team prayed out loud, speaking from their hearts. It was a very emotionally charged evening of devotion. When Bill began to pray, the tone of his prayer was different than all the others who had prayed before him. Where they had been reverent, he was friendly; where they had spoken to a God above them and apart from them, he was intimate and personal. After a minute or two, he said: "Lord, I know that I've been a bastard..." and his prayer went on, but I didn't hear it all. My mind had stopped and focused on the word, "bastard." How could he have been so disrespectful, so irreverent? After we all left the chapel, I went to Bill and asked him why he felt he could talk like that in prayer. He looked at me and said: "Chuck, this is my way of talking every day with my friends, and associates. Why should I change how I speak when I talk to the One who should be my best friend, my closest confidant? He hears me every day. He would know that I wasn't being me if I changed my way of talking when I spoke to Him!"

At the time, I was speechless. I had approached Bill to challenge him and maybe embarrass him, but he made me realize that our approach to God is very personal and we should talk to Him the same way we would talk to our best friend or want our best friend to talk to us. We should be able to be ourselves when we come before God, not somebody that we think God will accept. For the first time in my life, I had an image of God as friend rather than as the distant, unapproachable, fearsome Lord of all!

"God is the best friend for man."

Sathya Sai Speaks
Volume XI
Page 117

I don't condone irreverent talk in prayer. For me, using such terms as "bastard" while praying would not be comfortable, so I don't use them. And Bill's logic isn't perfect either. After all, he could work to change his every day language so as not to use any profanity. Yet, I think Bill was close to the truth when he spoke to God from his heart, with words and idioms that he used every day. The real Bill was sharing his own reality with God. Most importantly for me, Bill taught me the concept of God as Friend, as Nearest and Dearest. I could **begin** to look at Divinity as loving, not threatening.

On the following day, a young priest who was a member of the team, gave a talk on sex and money. His thesis was that sex and money were evil. I looked around me and realised that most of us in that room were married, with jobs and children. We needed money to support our family and we had to have sex in order to have a family, so obviously there was something grievously wrong with his presentation. I stood up and angrily denounced his blanket condemnation. Looking back, I realise that even though he had approached the topic narrowly, I was all too happy to gain the limelight by putting him down, and for that I am sorry. But the episode made me think. I concluded that, for me, the correct path in these matters is the path of the Buddha: The middle way; moderation, balance and harmony. Sex and money are not evil per se. Misuse of them is!

"Of course, money is desirable.
But, only as much as is essential."

Sathya Sai Speaks
Volume XI
Page 257

"Misuse of money is evil."

Sathya Sai Speaks
Volume XI
Page 49

For me, the central teaching of the Curcillo was its emphasis on a harmonious life of piety, study and action. It holds that man should approach Divinity with devotion (piety), with inquiry (study), and with selfless service for others (action). Curcillo made me ponder the proposition that righteous living requires that all that we **think,** all that we **say,** and all that we **do,** should be offered or dedicated to God. These three tracks of piety **(worship)**, study **(wisdom)** and action **(works)** make up the Royal Road toward enlightenment and oneness with God. Curcillo directed me toward that path.

"You can hold fast to God
either through ***Jnana*** *(Wisdom or Knowledge),*
Bhakti *(Worship or Devotion),*
or ***Karma*** *(Good Works or Service)...*
The destination is the same."

Kristina Gale-Kumar
The Scriptures Are Fulfilled
Chapter 5, Page 216

At the end of the retreat, others who had made a Curcillo previously and were now trying to live their lives consciously in devotion, awareness and service, came marching into the main hall, about four hundred strong, singing: "De Colores," which, in Spanish, means: "From many colours" and signifies that God's people find unity in diversity, and a holy brotherhood in the many talents, traits, cultures, races, religions, and nations that form humanity. What a wonderful feeling of love surged through my heart when I saw that army of love parade into the hall! In one moment, I became aware that I was not alone. There were many who were walking up the mountain seeking divinity and they wanted to encourage me, to urge me to go up higher. It was one of the most important and thrilling experiences of my life and it exhilarated my soul!

"There is only one religion;
the religion of love.
There is only one language;
the language of the heart.
There is only one race;
the race of humanity.
There is only one God;
and He is Omnipresent."

Mark and Barbara Gardner
Sai Baba and You
Practical Spirituality
Introduction

Whereas the Curcillo is a three day programme, symbolic of Christ's three days in the tomb, the Fourth Day is the rest of your life, symbolising resurrection and ascension to God.. In that Fourth Day, each Curciesta meets regularly with other Curciestas to pray together and share their successes and failures in the areas of piety, study and action and to encourage each other up the mountain of Grace toward Divinity.

I began to meet with several others on a weekly basis and it wasn't long before I and some others from our small group were asked to serve as part of a team for a Curcillo retreat. Being on a team is an uplifting experience. Each team member is greatly concerned about the well-being of each of the retreatants and because of that concern, are themselves, blessed with a sense of love and joy. The team meets for several weeks in prayer and devotion to prepare themselves for the weekend and a strong bond of community builds among the team members.

During a Curcillo, a team member will volunteer to pray in the chapel on behalf of another team member who is in the main hall giving a talk on some aspect of piety, study or action. It is the duty of each volunteer to remember a speaker in prayer, continuously, while his talk is in progress. At one point, I had volunteered to pray for another team member. As part of my devotion, I meditated unsupported on my knees for the hour or so that it took my colleague to complete his speech. After about half an hour, I fell deeply into a meditative state, oblivious of everything around me. My only awareness was of peace and great joy. I stayed in that space until the speaker had finished his talk and came into the chapel to pray with me in thanksgiving for his opportunity to serve.

I was in such a deep, blissful, contemplative state, that I never heard the speaker enter the chapel and was unaware of him until he gently tapped me on the shoulder and embraced me in love and peace. I have never experienced such a deep state of prayer either before or since. All awareness of my surroundings evaporated and I was at one with the Object of my prayer, never feeling any discomfort from kneeling for such a long period of time. That blissful experience taught me the truth that the journey within is the divine journey to the soul, to the Indweller of our heart.

> *"The three colours,*
> *Wisdom, Worship and Works,*
> *are different only when*
> *The White Light of God*
> *is passed through the prism*
> *of human reason and mind.*
> *Activate them in deed,*
> *they are but parts*
> *of One Ray."*

Kristina Gale-Kumar
<u>The Scriptures Are Fulfilled</u>
Chapter 5, Page 216

CHAPTER 5

SMOKE GETS IN MY EYES

"The Atma is ever disentangled.
It is...not bound by flux.
Its nature is purity, wholeness, joy,wisdom;
where Ego is, there bondage persists.
Where there is no 'I', there freedom holds sway.
The 'I' is the real shackle."

Sai Avatar
Volume II
Page 478

Several months later, Father Angelo Fazio, a Passionist monk living at the Holy Family Monastery in Farmington, Connecticut, called to ask me to speak at a weekend retreat. The monks usually ask a lay person to give a presentation on the last day of each retreat, held each week at the monastery. The person who was supposed to deliver the talk had to cancel because of a death in the family, so I was called to fill in. When I asked him for the date of the talk, there was a short pause and Father Angelo answered: "Tomorrow!" There was a long pause and then reluctantly I said: "Sure." Angelo was a Curciesta, a dear friend and a spiritual brother. How could I say no?

I sat down and quickly wrote an outline of what I wanted to say, practiced it in my mind one or two times and went to bed. The next morning I drove to the monastery, arriving about an hour and a half early. I hadn't been very spiritual for about six months and I felt separated from God. I don't remember if I felt that He had abandoned me for a while or that I was just lax in my own devotion, but the truth was that I had not had many heart to Heart talks with Him for a long time.

When I arrived at the monastery, I walked through the grounds, which are quite beautiful. There are outside Stations of the Cross, statues of the saints and little grottos for prayer and reflection. In that peaceful setting, I took the time to have a little talk with God. I told Him that I hadn't felt very close to Him for several months, and yet, I had to ask Him for His help. I told Him that I had to give a talk to about one hundred men who were expecting an uplifting presentation, and they deserved one. My estrangement from Him shouldn't be their problem, and so, I asked Him to speak through me that day.

However, I wasn't confident that He would be so willing to take time from His other duties, and come to my aid, so I switched tactics and talked to the one that I knew would listen to me, Mary, the Blessed Mother. I told her that I needed help and if she could put in a good word with her Son, I'd appreciate it. It never entered my mind that she wouldn't listen to me or be understanding. I walked back toward the retreat hall, with my head down, still talking to her. As I entered the hall, I looked up and there on a table, looking back at me was a statue of Mary! I felt intuitively that was the sign that my prayers had been heard and that I would be assisted in my talk. Putting my concerns about my estrangement from God away, I put the results of my talk into His hands. I knew that He would talk through me and everything would work out fine. After all, His Mother was in my corner!

"Make Me your Charioteer!"

Sathyam Sivam Sundaram
Part III
Page 50

I delivered a great talk! I spoke from the heart and **felt** everything that I said. Even my jokes were perfect, my timing splendid! I could feel the audience paying attention, almost hear them listening! I knew that God was in control. I spoke confidently, with an air of authority because I sensed God's grace flowing fully. I found myself speaking words and phrases that I had not prepared myself to say; that weren't in my outline and came from I know not where. For instance, I found myself expounding an idea that I never had before. I said that each of us should "let the Christ in our heart knock on the door of the heart of another, and greet the Christ in that heart." Since I had never thought of Christ residing in our hearts before, I realise now that statement was brought from a subconscious awareness of the teaching that the Atma, or the God force, is in everyone!

"The Atma is the source, the sustenance of every being...
It is the One and only Source, Substance and Sustenance.
The Atma is God; the Particular is the Universal, no less.
Therefore, recognise in each being, in each man, a brother,
the child of God and ignore all limiting thoughts and prejudices
based on status, colour, class, nativity and caste."

Voice of the Avatar
Part I
Page 3

As soon as the talk was completed, several retreatants and many of the monks that were in the hall came up to compliment my talk and thank me for speaking. I basked in their praise and **never, never** thought to retire to the chapel or some secluded spot on the grounds to thank God and the Blessed Mother for their intercession and loving help. I forgot them completely. I was so wrapped up in my own ego, that I never stopped to consider that this success was theirs, not mine!

The following week, Father Angelo called again. Same problem! The speaker couldn't make it. Would I fill in? Sure I would. I was the greatest speaker since Cicero! I even had a speech prepared from the prior week; I didn't even need to practice or rehearse it. On the day of the talk, I drove down to the monastery early again, but instead of going out on the grounds to chat with Jesus and Mary, and to pray for guidance and strength in presenting the talk, I went from monk to monk, receiving their praise for the talk the week before and indulging myself in idle chatter.

"Praise feeds the fire of egoism
and fogs genuine faith."

Sathya Sai Speaks
Volume V
Page 189

But, after I had been introduced and had begun my presentation, I became immediately aware that something was wrong. The talk was not going well. My jokes went flat, and my audience drifted somewhere a million miles away. I gave the same talk, used the same outline, incorporated all the words and phrases that worked so well just one week earlier, but I saw only hollow eyes looking at me, reflective of minds that weren't really paying attention. The talk was awful.

I had kept Him **locked** behind the steel doors of my heart. He had no opportunity to come forth and knock on the doors of the hearts of the retreatants. It was my ego! My ego!

> *"Knock; the doors of Grace will open.*
> *Open the door;*
> *the sun's rays waiting outside*
> *will flow silently in and flood the room*
> *with light"*

Sathya Sai Speaks
Volume V
Page 189

The lessons for me from that experience were many. No matter how far away I am from God at any one moment, He is as close as my call. If I surrender my will to His, He responds. When I act as if I am the doer, not Him, I fall flat. When I open my heart, He sallies forth, shines His Light on others and raises the consciousness of all!

> *"The Lord alone is the Saviour*
> *of the helpless and forlorn.*
> *Do not waver in your faith in the Lord*
> *in any circumstance.*
> *Go ahead with your tasks with faith*
> *and determination."*

Sanathana Sarathi
September 1993
Page 233
Line 10

CHAPTER 6

GIRL OF MY DREAMS

"True love expands the self
Attachment contracts it."

Sathya Sai Baba

While the divorce process dragged on, I felt terribly isolated. The embarrassment of it all often kept me from my friends and social interaction. After a time, I began to venture out, attempting to rebuild relationships with friends and acquaintances, but it wasn't easy and I often felt alone even in the presence of others. It was within that aura that a friend, Matt, a former Catholic priest still practicing his faith, invited me to attend a weekend retreat with him at the Holy Family Monastery, and I agreed.

On the first night of the retreat, there was a short talk and then a "get to know each other" hour with coffee and doughnuts. Even though I didn't know any of the other retreatants except Matt, I did know several of the monks, and I was embarrassed talking with them because of the impending divorce. I decided to retire early and went up to my room around 8 a.m. I guess I was hiding out.

That night, I had a very vivid dream. I found myself flying horizontally, parallel to the ground like Superman, with my arms stretched out in front of me. I felt free and exultant. Thinking about it now, my feeling of freedom very much tallies with the experiences of others who have had out-of-body experiences or OBEs as they are popularly called. Suddenly I saw a woman holding a spray of flowers in her hand, standing in front of a background that looked like a clam shell glittering with sparkling lights of many colours. I noticed the cut of her hair and how it framed her oval face. She appeared calm and stood silently as I flew in front of her. I tried to fly behind her but try as I might, the glittering shell seemed to rotate, so that it was always behind her. Then, clearly, I was aware of words that I neither heard nor saw written, but rather felt: "Be patient, I am coming!" And then, I awoke.

I can remember standing next to my bed in the middle of my small room, holding my head, trying to remember the dream. I knew that it was important for me to remember, but I couldn't pull it from the dim recesses of my dream state into my awakened consciousness. Finally, I gave up the effort and dressed for morning prayers.

The chapel at the monastery has a solemn aura and design. The ceiling is quite high and at the back wall is a huge mosaic of Christ hung on the cross with God the Father looking on from above. The Crucified Saviour stares toward the altar at the front of the chapel which is simply decorated and accented by a large cross on the wall behind it. The layout of the chapel pews is unique. Instead of facing the altar, they face toward the pews on the opposite side, across a wide center aisle. So, one does not face the alter when seated, but rather the opposite wall and the earth toned stained glass windows above the pews. The altar is viewed over the shoulder.

When I got to the chapel, I sat with Matt in the first pew. Morning prayers had not yet commenced, so my eyes wandered over that large room, scrutinising every nook and cranny of the simple chapel. I gazed at the stained glass windows on the opposite wall, reading the names of the saints or the Stations of the Cross depicted there. When I examined the last window, I stood up startled, eyes open wide, mouth agape! There in that window was the lady I had seen in my dream! She had the same brown robe, clutching the same flowers, with her hair framing her face in much the same way as I remembered my dream lady. And, I remembered the unspoken, unread, but clearly felt message: **"Be patient, I am coming!"** Saint Maria Goretti of the stained glass window appeared shockingly similar to the lady of my dream and it was obvious that I was supposed to recall that dream. Matt walked me out of the chapel in a daze.

For several months before Matt and I made the retreat, Susan Connors, a friend of mine, had been visiting a psychic named Aida Bellerose of Glastonbury, Conn. Aida was in her late seventies, with a gentle matronly look that reminded me of my grandmother. She had one leg missing from the knee down and wore a prosthesis in the shape of a leg. If you didn't know her condition, you wouldn't be able to detect it at first glance. Aida had many psychic gifts. She was clairaudiant and clairvoyant; did readings for others by automatic writing, by psychometry and by mediumship wherein spirits allegedly spoke through her, using her body and vocal apparatus in order to communicate.

Sue and her friends met with Aida regularly. Aida taught them and demonstrated her abilities to them, explaining her gifts as best she could. She tried to show them how they could develop these gifts and how to use them correctly for the good of others. On one particular night, about two or three days after my retreat, Aida was acting as a medium, and without provocation or question from Sue, and while in a trance state, looked at Sue and said: "I have a message for your friend, Charles. Tell him that his dream is true. Tell him to be patient!"

Although Sue was my friend, and an employee, I had not told her of my dream at the monastery. In fact, I don't think I saw her or spoke to her between the time of the retreat and the evening of Aida's message in trance. So, Sue didn't know what Aida was talking about. After the session, Sue told Aida, now in her conscious state, what Aida had said about me while she was in her trance state. Sue asked her if she would like to see me. Aida thought a minute and said "No, they don't tell me that I should." The "they" that she was talking about, were her spirit guides and at the time, she felt no further message from them that necessitated her meeting with me. However, several days passed and on one of Sue's next visits to her, Aida told Sue that she had been given a message that I should come to her for a reading.

Sue delivered the message to me and asked me if I would go. I told her that I was delighted over the prospect of meeting Aida and yes, I would definitely contact her. That evening I called Aida, arranged an appointment and a few days later I was sitting with this unusual woman in her living room. She was shorter than I had pictured her, and her features were heavier and larger, but she exuded a warm, grandmotherly air and I felt immediately at ease. It was almost as if I had known her for years. She wasted little time in the formalities of getting to know me and jumped right into the reading. She told me that she could divine that I was in the middle of a divorce and that I had three children, two boys and a girl. She spoke of many other things that had occurred or were occurring in my life, all of which were true. Finally, she revealed the reason that she wanted to see me. Her spirit guides wanted me to know that a special lady was coming into my life. Aida described her exact height, the colour and style of her hair, and the roundness of her face. The description, as it unfolded, was not only detailed, but matched, exactly, the lady in my dream. She said that this lady had two children, a boy and a girl; that she was partially of Italian ancestry and that I would meet her in strange circumstances within six months. Aida emphasised that this lady was the soul that was meant to come into my life at that time and in that space, from all time.

Aida's ability to accurately read my past, led me to be open to the possibility that she could know my future or a part of it. Of course, I know now that my wife, Patty, who I had not yet met at the time of Aida's reading, was the lady of the dream and the soul described by Aida. Patty's hair was styled in the same way as the lady of my dream and matches Aida's description. Her face is round, she has two children, a boy and a girl and is partially of Italian descent. Her family owns Cherrystones Restaurant in Old Lyme, whose logo matches the shell which sparkled behind the lady of my dream. I felt then and I know now, that some force was guiding me and pointing me forward. Meeting Aida was not a coincidence. She was both an instrument to lead me to Patty and an instrument to teach me that there are inexplicable miracles beyond man's knowledge in the world; there are spiritual gifts allotted to some and there is a deeper universe that man has not yet discovered. Aida made me aware of an unknown force or consciousness greater than myself, which was active in my life, concerned about me and guiding me.

"The Lord, alone, is aware of the Plan,
for His is the Plan!"

<u>Voice of the Avatar</u>
Part II
Page 148

CHAPTER 7

A WINDOW OPENS

"Treat Me not as one afar, but as very close to you.
Insist, demand, claim Grace from Me;
do not praise, extol and cringe.
Bring your hearts to Me and
I shall give you My Promises.
But first see that your promise is genuine, sincere;
see that your heart is pure;
that is enough."

Sai Avatar
Volume II
Paragraph 285
Page 144

Several months later, I was driving to the golf course to meet friends for a round of golf and I was running late. Passing was impossible on the winding secondary road. As luck would have it, I was following a big car being driven by a little old lady who was peering over the steering wheel which she gripped solidly with both hands. She was travelling extremely slow and I was riding on her bumper. With each passing second, I became more frustrated, and finally, unable to contain myself any longer, I pulled off the road on to the grass bordering the pavement.

To my surprise, I began to cry loudly and uncontrollably. The months of separating, divorcing, living apart from my children most of the time and being lonely all of the time got to me. I erupted in one, huge, emotional burst of sadness. The lady who had been driving slowly in front of me had nothing to do with my tears; she was simply the catalyst, the trigger, that released my frustration and feelings.

Looking up toward the sky through the open sun roof, I found myself pumping my fist toward Heaven, challenging God and shouting: "Why am I so lonely? Why haven't you sent me someone? I can't take this loneliness anymore!" The whole episode was shocking to me. I realised how much I needed someone, but who? I had dated, but none of the women qualified as companion and friend. So, there I sat, for several minutes, angry, defiant and demanding that I be sent a special someone, a special soul to walk and talk and share with me.

"Whatever you hold, once you have held it
hold on to it, till you win.
Whatever you've asked, once you've asked it
ask aloud for it, till you win.
Whatever you wish, once you have wished it
wish deeper for it, till you win.
Whatever you've planned, once you have planned it
plan firmer for it, till you win.
He must grant the victory to stop the wail.
Wail, weep and pray, till you win."

<u>Sathya Sai Speaks</u>
Volume X
Page 248

The next day, Friday, I represented a client in court against his ex-wife. He wanted to reduce the child support that he was obligated to pay. For some reason, I had imagined that his ex-wife would be tall, skinny, with bleached blond hair, wearing wing tipped sunglasses and chewing gum. I certainly had no reason to think of his former bride in that fashion, but that is the image I had of her. I asked my client if she had arrived. He nodded and pointed. My gaze followed his arm and finger to where he was pointing and to my astonishment, I was staring at a lady with a warm, bright smile. I thought to myself: "This guy is crazy!" She was lovely! I realise that I was judging a book by its cover, but I had a hard time keeping from looking at her!

I went into the sheriff's office to use the phone. It was a small room with a metal table and a chair. A sheriff was sitting on the chair, so I sat on the table and was looking out the open door into the hall. My client's former wife, wearing a lovely dark green summer dress, was walking down the hall toward me. When she noticed me looking at her, she smiled a beautiful smile and I was mesmerised! She walked down a corridor to the left and into the main waiting room outside the court. Finishing my call and pulling myself together, I joined her attorney in the office of the family relations officer who was going to try to mediate the dispute so that we could go before the judge with an agreement. As we talked, I couldn't keep the image of that smiling lady out of my mind. Luckily, I convinced the officer and her attorney, and I carried the day. The child support that my client had to pay was reduced. If I had lost, I think I would have had to question my commitment on behalf of my client. It was difficult to picture his former wife as the "enemy!"

Needless to say, she was angry and disappointed with the result. She stormed out of the courtroom and, I thought, out of my life. On the way back to my office, I asked my client why the marriage had broken down. He took the blame. I blurted out that she was someone I would love to see socially. He said that he had no objection. Although I realised that he was serious, I never intended to call her. It seemed too bizarre. I could almost see headlines: "Lawyer dates ex-wife of client!"

On Saturday, I had a golf match scheduled at Glastonbury Hills Country Club with three friends. They were all pretty good golfers and the competition was keen. My partner was Joe Felony, and as we played, I bent his ear talking about the lady at the court; how lovely she was; what a nice smile she had; and how I wished I could get to know her. After nine holes, Joe and I were losing the match and were in serious trouble. He took me aside and said: "Look, why don't you call this girl; its obvious that you're not concentrating on your game. We're getting killed! Call her, maybe you'll concentrate better on the back nine."

Well, I did. I walked into the clubhouse, called several people that I thought might know her in order to get her telephone number. Taking a deep breath, I dialed her number and surprise, surprise, she was home!

"Hello, Patty?"

"Yes."

"This is Chuck DiFazio."

"What do you want?"

"Well, if I'm not out of line, I'd like to ask you to dinner."

She broke into peals of laughter. Ordinarily, I would have just hung up, but for some reason, I didn't. When she finished laughing, I repeated myself, saying again that if she "...didn't feel that I was acting out of line," I would like to ask her out. There was a moment's hesitation, a moment's silence, and then she said:

"What did you have in mind?"

Bingo! I knew from her question that she would consent. That night we met at my partner's beach house and then all four of us went to the dog track for a few races and dinner. Pretty romantic, huh? Anyway,

I had a wonderful time. Later in the evening, we stopped at her family's restaurant where her aunts and uncles, and mom and dad were sitting around a table together. Of course, they knew that she was going out with me that night and when we arrived at the restaurant, they did a friendly number on me. "Do you often date your clients' ex-wives, Chuck?" My embarrassment brought howls of laughter from all of them. Anyway, I liked everyone, and didn't feel intimidated by any of them. In fact, it was a fun evening.

The next day, my cousin, Linda Lech, had a party at her home in Point O' Woods Beach on the Connecticut shore. I arrived early and immediately began talking to Linda about Patty and our date the prior night. Then Father Angelo showed up and gave me the opportunity to retell the same "Patty" stories to him. Finally, Linda said that she was going to call her. "Call whom?" I asked. "Patty," she responded over her shoulder. "What for?" I asked. "Because I'm sick of hearing you talk about her. I'm inviting her over here for you!" I grabbed the phone out of Linda's hand and told her that I would make the call. It was another beautiful day and I expected that Patty would be out, but once again, she was home. I invited her to Linda's party, she quickly agreed. Linda lived only five miles away and when Patty heard she could bring her kids, the deal was made.

Linda's place soon became filled with people. Kids were running everywhere. Food was brought out to the deck and everyone was thoroughly enjoying themselves. But the whole scene was too busy for me. I wanted to be alone with Patty and at the house there was no escape; people kept coming in and the chatter just became noise to me. I asked Patty if she wanted to go with me for a boat ride. Little did she guess that it would be a rowboat! Linda's beach house sits on a high stone cliff overlooking an inlet of the ocean between Point O'Woods Beach and Giant's Neck Beach. The inlet, although part of the Connecticut Sound, is usually calm and so a little rowboat ride was not difficult.

When we were alone in the little boat, I guess I talked too much and Patty got scared. I must have been coming on pretty strong. She told me that her divorce had hurt her and that she was in no rush to get serious again. She went on and on about how another marriage wasn't in the cards for her right away. I listened, slightly annoyed. After all, I hadn't thought that I was being forward and I hadn't mentioned marriage. But her little monologue touched a raw nerve and finally, I pulled in the oars and let the boat rock and flow of its own accord. "Look, my marriage didn't work out either, but I'm not going to lock myself in and the world out. I know that I can love again and some day the stars will shine for me, flowers will bloom around me and **fireworks** will shoot into the sky!" I can't believe how "schmalatzy" I got, but I was wound up.

Suddenly we heard a loud "poof" overhead, and when we looked up, fireworks were exploding above us and showering down upon us. Both of us were staring skyward, totally incredulous!. From the deck at Linda's house, up on the cliff, we could see Leo, Linda's husband, shooting Roman Candle fireworks at us. Leo and the kids were playing "fort," and were pretending that Patty and I, in our little rowboat, were invaders from the sea attacking their land so they were firing their "cannons" at us!

Sitting in that bouncing rowboat, I couldn't believe it! The timing could not have been better if Leo and I had planned it...and we had not! To this day, Patty still suspects that we had rehearsed the scenario, but even if we had, there was no way those Roman Candles could have exploded **precisely** as I spoke the words: "Fireworks will shoot into the sky." Till the day I die, I'll always believe that a Higher Power was playing with us that day, sending us little signals that we were on the right path, toward each other.

'Pray to Him and He reveals Himself.
He is the yarn in the cloth, the gold in the jewelery;
He is the mud in the pottery;
He is the water that sustains all these waves.'

Sathya Sai Baba

Three days later, I called Patty and proposed that we have dinner together. She suggested that she would arrange for a babysitter and pack a picnic dinner for us that we could share at Harkness Memorial Park. Harkness is a beautiful, scenic estate that was left to the State of Connecticut to be maintained as a public park. There is a stately old mansion with sculptured gardens that sets back from the beach overlooking Long Island Sound. We set our basket on one of the picnic tables scattered across the vast lawn. Aida was on my mind, so I started telling Patty about her prediction of a special lady coming into my life. I had not planned to talk to Patty about it, in fact, I had not thought of Aida's prediction for a while and I certainly hadn't thought about Patty being the fulfillment of that prediction, but there I was telling Patty the story and realising **as I spoke** that Patty was the one! She was the lady in my dream and she was the lady about whom Aida had prophesied!

Patty listened, fascinated I think, but unsure of whether she was being treated to one of the all time "lines." But as I got further into the story, the more I **knew** that the dream and the prediction were true. Patty was "it!" Patty, on the other hand, thought I was "nuts!" "You don't even know me," she said. I had no real response because I didn't know her, really, but I was aware of who she was. She was the "lady!" Patty persisted. "Look at how differently we are dressed," she said. I looked at myself. I was walking on the beach in my suit, pants rolled up, patent leather shoes in my hand, white shirt and tie, my work clothes. Patty, on the other hand, was wearing casual summer pants and top. "We're so different! You're very conservative, but I could walk right out into the ocean, clothes and all." "Go ahead!" I answered, not thinking that she was wearing my suit jacket to protect herself from the evening coolness. The next thing that I knew, she was in the water, my suit jacket and all! I stood on the shore. She was right, I wouldn't run in dressed as I was, but I was smiling. She was fun and I knew then that I loved her. She walked in the water away from me and then bolted across the sand toward the mansion. I ran after her, laughing all the way. When I caught up to her, we walked to the patio of the mansion, sat down on lawn chairs and talked. I elaborated on the dream and Aida's prediction and I told her that she was the fulfillment of both stories. I told her that I wanted to marry her. She emphatically responded: "No, I still think you're nuts!"

Our picnic at Harkness was on Monday. On Tuesday, Aida Bellerose called me and asked me to come to see her. Aida was an actress in the Patty drama, which was being directed by an unknown entity who was dancing with delight at my wonder.

> *"Shiva, or the Eternal Absolute Person,*
> *in His desire to attract the world of matter,*
> *engages Himself in the..Cosmic Dance.*
> *The dance is a Divine plan to attract the material creation...*
> *...both the soul and the world of matter*
> *dance together to the immense delight of the Gods*
> *and of all creation."*
>
> <u>Sathya Sai Speaks</u>
> Volume 10
> Page 201 and 202

Aida had never called me before. I knew that whatever she wanted to see me about must be important and I didn't hesitate to make plans to visit her that very evening. She met me at her front door and led me into the parlour. Aida sat across from me and wasted no time in telling me that the lady that she had predicted would be coming into my life, had arrived! "You met her across your desk," she said. She went on to say that she didn't literally mean that we had met at my desk, but by that phrase, Aida wanted me to understand that she knew that Patty and I had met through my work. "This woman," she explained, "has been coming into your life karmically, since she was born."

Aida's prediction and my dream were not the only signs that Patty and I were destined to find each other. After we met, we became aware of many synchronicities, many meaningful coincidences that highlighted our awareness. I have already pointed out that we had been both previously married in the same church on the same day one year apart and that we went to the same place on our honeymoons. It was also true that I had been engaged, once, to a girl whose birthday, August third, was the same as Patty's birth date. Patty had a daughter by her prior marriage named Andrea. I had a son named Andrew. Andrea had the same due date as my daughter, Leslie. Patty has a mother, Virginia and an Aunt Lucy, while my mother's name is Lucy and I have an Aunt Virginia. The birth dates of Patty's Aunt Lucy and my mother, Lucy, are the same. Patty's brother, Drew, (also really an Andrew) has the same birth date as my father. Patty grew up at a home numbered 111. When we married, our first home together was my beach house also numbered 111.

But the strangest coincidence began to unfold a long time ago. In 1939, my father's first cousin married my mother's first cousin and they had a baby girl, born on the same day, in the same year in the same town as I. That baby's name was "Patricia DiFazio!" Was my cousin's birth, simultaneous with mine, a presaging of my wife, now also known as Patricia DiFazio, coming into my life?

"Even an atheist must accept a superior
or mysterious power which guides things and events...
There is a limit to the capacity of man to control events.
You may call it Destiny,
another may call it Providence and a third, God.
Names do not matter.
Ii is the humility that matters, the wonder, the sense of awe
that matters."

Voice of the Avatar
Part II
Page 197

CHAPTER 8

THE LIGHT

"Love alone gives light."

<u>Sathya Sai Speaks</u>
Volume VII
Page 345

One day, after Patty and I had been married about four years, she spoke to me about her need for spiritual community. She missed being a part of and participating in a church made up of like-minded people. Just prior to the Easter Lenten holidays, she read in the paper that our local Catholic church, St. Patrick's, had scheduled an Easter Vigil Retreat. It sounded good to her so she signed up to participate. The vigil was to run for one week during the evenings and was hosted by a charismatic priest. Patty asked me to go with her, but I declined. Because of my divorce and remarriage, I didn't feel that I was welcome in the Catholic Church and didn't feel that I belonged. Yet, since Patty was so intent on finding a spiritual community, I wasn't inclined to dissuade her from attending, even though I was very concerned that she might not be accepted because of our divorces.

Patty's intention was to offer her retreat, her vigil, her prayers to God for our five children and our blended family. During the week, she prayed for God's Grace to help her to be a good mother to all five children and to be able to give them what they each needed.

Her week went well and Patty truly enjoyed the programme and the spiritual services. She rushed home each night to fill me in on what she had been doing. Although I was pleased that she was enjoying herself, I was still concerned that the topic of her divorce and remarriage might surface and cause her embarrassment and pain. On the next to last evening, there was to be a charismatic healing service. In the Catholic context, charismatics usually have gifts of the spirit such as healing touch, speaking in tongues or some other spiritual power. During a charismatic healing service, healers lay hands on those who want or need a healing, pray over them, and if the faith of the healer and the ill person were intense enough, there often would be a healing. Sometimes there would be healing of the spirit, and sometimes nothing noticeable at all.

Patty was not physically ill, but she felt that she wanted to experience the heightened awareness from being prayed over by the charismatic healer. She went up on to the altar. Two charismatic healers prayed over her and placed their hands on her head and shoulders. During the prayers, Patty did not experience any particular energy or become aware of the activity of the Holy Spirit. When the praying was finished, she left the church to return home. She casually walked to the parking lot, opened the car door and sat inside. As she went to start the car, the entire inside of the car's cab filled with a brilliant white light! She was immediately caught up in a blissful state and experienced rather than heard the words:

"Chuck's children are your children!"

Upon experiencing those words, Patty had an instant insight or awareness of what the words really meant. You see, in Patty's prior marriage, she had lost three babies in childbirth. Within this aura of light, she realised that those three children could not be born because there were no souls for them. The souls already existed in the materialised bodies of my three children: Marc, Andrew and Leslie!

When the light subsided, Patty drove home. She was so overcome with emotion, she couldn't talk. She went to her desk in our room and wrote out the experience in full, including her conclusions about my kids. She asked me to read her account. I was very moved. The story of the bright light was amazing and her awareness of the meaning of those words touched my heart. Patty now felt that her "family" was complete and "together again." She remained ecstatic as her heart was burning with joy. In fact, she was bursting with a need to share her revelation with everyone. So, she decided that on the final night of the retreat vigil, a night when retreatants were going to attend a final mass ending the program, she was going to ask the priest to read her testimony about her vision of light and the insight it had brought her. After all, she had been prayed over and had been obviously moved by the Holy Spirit!

I tried to explain to her that the priest might have trouble using her story because of the fact that we were divorced and remarried Catholics. She wouldn't listen to me. She was so full of love, she couldn't comprehend that the priest, the retreatants, the Catholic Church, the whole world, in fact, wouldn't want to hear her story of the vision of light and the insight it brought her. She didn't believe it would matter that she was divorced and remarried. I decided that I would attend the Mass with her. I didn't want her to be there without me if her plan backfired as I believed it would.

Upon arriving at the church the next evening, Patty handed her written account of the vision and its meaning to the priest. He took it with him and read it as he reached the altar. My eyes never left him as I waited for his reaction. When he finished reading, he walked from the altar, down the center aisle to our pew and asked Patty if we had been married in the Catholic Church. When she shook her head in the negative, he told her that he couldn't read her letter. Patty froze. I wouldn't have been surprised if she had fainted dead away. She had been so elevated and was brought down so quickly! The mass began. After a few minutes, we both felt conspicuous although no one else in the church knew our predicament. We couldn't just leave and we didn't want to stay. We felt so awkward. Finally, as other people rose from their seats and entered the aisles to walk toward the altar to receive the sacrament of Holy Communion, we got up, walked down the side aisle and left the church by the side door. Patty was devastated and my heart was torn. I felt such hurt for her disappointment. Her experience had been real, but our circumstances didn't fit the rules of the church. The priest really had no choice. We no longer were part of that society.

But the Lord works his wonders in strange ways. In spite of the huge disappointment and disillusionment caused by the rejection of Patty's spiritual insight, good things came out of this event. My children were thrilled with the vision and moved by the message. They realised that Patty wanted them in her life and that she wanted to be in theirs. But more than that, Patty believed that they were **destined** to be part of her life. A great healing took place as Marc, Andy and Leslie realized the bond that Patty recognised existed among them all. Patty was right. We were a family, blended perhaps, but blended with love.

And finally, the incident made Patty and me realise that we would not find our community of like-minded people by looking back. Our community still had to be found, and our spirituality would take a different road, another path. The past was behind us and over. It was now time for Bhagavan Sri Sathya Sai Baba.

*"Life is a pilgrimage where man drags his feet
along the rough and thorny road.
With the Name of God on his lips; he will have no thirst;
With the Form of God in his heart, he will feel no exhaustion.
The company of the holy will inspire him
to travel in faith and hope.
The assurance that God is within calling distance,
that He is ever near, and that He is not long in coming,
will lend strength to his limbs and courage to his eye."*

A Recapitulation of
Sathya Sai Baba's Divine Teaching
Pages 48 and 49

CHAPTER 9

HE IS PURSUING ME!

"Let Me tell you one thing;
However you are, you are Mine.
I will not give you up.
Wherever you are, you are near Me;
You cannot go beyond My Reach."

Sai Avatar
Volume II
Page 163

Bob Iantoni and I have been friends for many years. Sometime around 1983, he and I began having lunch together in order to discuss politics, history, philosophy, psychic phenomenon, religion and spiritual matters. On one occasion, Bob asked me if I had ever heard of **Bhagavan Sri Sathya Sai Baba**. Until that moment, I had not. He told me that **Sai Baba,** as He is most generally known, is a great miracle worker who lives in India. Bob told me that He is believed to have duplicated all of the major miracles of Jesus Christ, including raising men from the dead!

I was mildly interested, but about the time that we were discussing **Sai Baba**, there had been some adverse publicity and stories of alleged holy men who had come from India to the United States and become embroiled in questionable methods of raising money and in suspect relationships with their followers. So, I lightly dismissed Indian holy men in general and **Sai Baba** in particular. My mind was not willing at that precise moment to place anybody, even an honest holy man, in the same miracle producing category as Jesus Christ.

Well, the very next day, a client of mine, Santo Perruccio came into my office. "Sam" is a good man who is very interested in spiritual matters and is a spiritual seeker. I don't know why, but I asked him if he had ever heard of **Sai Baba**. I guess I was more interested than I believed I was. Anyway, Sam told me that he was a devotee of **Sai Baba!** I was really taken aback. The synchronicity was amazing. The following day Sam brought me a little red book about three inches tall called:

Sai Avatar **Volume I**. It was a compilation of the sayings of **Sathya Sai Baba**. As I thumbed through the little book, Sam reached over and handed me a plastic bag filled with a gray ash which he called **vibhuthi**. He said that the ash comes out of the palms of **Sai Baba** when He wills it. I stopped looking through the book and took the ash. I was intrigued, but certainly not believing. The enormity of an entity who could make something from nothing didn't quite sink in and smacked more of movie fiction than of reality. Sam explained that **Sai Baba** often used the **vibhuthi** as medicine for curing illness.

Sam also gave me a copy of a letter from **Sai Baba** to a devotee encouraging him in some aspect of devotion. Later that morning, I clipped off the signature at the bottom of the letter and showed the body of the letter to Bob Iantoni. Bob had taken several courses in handwriting analysis, so I asked him if he could tell me anything about the personality of the writer. Bob looked at the writing and quickly said, "Is this **Sai Baba**?" I couldn't believe it! "How did you know that," I asked. "I don't know, maybe from the spiritual teaching in the letter and because the handwriting shows a strong character, " he replied.

On Friday of that week, Patty went to visit her mother at her beach house on the Connecticut shore. Her mom was going to host a large family party that Sunday and Patty went down to help her prepare. So, for a few days, I was home alone. The first evening, I bought one of those weekly newspapers that shout out outrageous headlines such as: "Dog has two heads!" Some headline had intrigued me and being home alone, I was bored. As I turned one page and then another, a photograph and its caption caught my eye. The picture was of Sathya Sai Baba! It finally dawned on me, that somehow, in some inexplicable way, Sai Baba, the Man of Miracles was continually entering my orbit and grabbing my attention. In fact, He seemed to be pursuing me!

Some people might laugh at my conclusion that Sai Baba was somehow orchestrating events in order to get my attention, but I began to believe that He was. Further, this strange, alien man from India whose five foot height, outrageous, afro-styled hairdo and orange-red robe, did not appear to be typical of a messiah. But I wasn't laughing. Like Karl Jung, I have a healthy respect for repeated, related occurrences that happen in my life. I believe that in some unexplained way, these random and yet connected events are happening in my life in order to teach me or in the very least, to draw my attention to their underlying message. "Synchronicity" is what Jung called this phenomenon of meaningful coincidences which, when considered together, tell a larger story than the sum of the events themselves. In one week, this Holy Man from India, about whom, I had never before been aware, entered my life through my best friend, through a client, and through a newspaper photograph. I became alert to the "synchronicity" multiplying around Sai Baba and me.

I began to read about and study this man who claimed to be an Avatar, a vertical descent of Divinity into matter, and who explained that He has come in these perilous times as did Krishna, Buddha, Pythagorus, Zoroaster and Jesus before Him, in their time, to show mankind a way of living, a way of being, a way to travel towards Divinity. The readings multiplied my questions and increased my thirst for the answers. Books like Howard Murphet's Sai Baba, Man of Miracles, Dr. Samuel H.Sandweiss's, The Holy Man and the Psychiatrist and John Hislop's My Baba and I were read and reread. I questioned: "Who is He? Is He the Cosmic Christ? Is He the Second Coming? Why is He here? Is He really Incarnated Divinity? Why is He here now?" I was determined to learn as much as I possibly could about Sathya Sai Baba and more was not enough!

At one point during this time of inquiry, Patty and I decided to entertain three couples at dinner. Our purpose in planning the gathering was to bring a group together for a discussion of spiritual, paranormal, esoteric or religious events, philosophies or phenomena. The guests invited were a Congregationalist minister and his wife, Scott and Joy Raeburn; a couple interested in and students of UFOs, Pythagoras, Ancient Egypt, and many areas of the occult, Tony and Peggy Gonsalves; and Igor and Diana Sikorsky, teachers of The Course In Miracles, a Christ-oriented way of living.

Patty, who had been encouraging my investigation of Sai Baba, asked me not to talk about Sai Baba that night, as she didn't think that any one else would know about Him and I would wind up monopolising the conversation and boring everyone to tears. I promised that I wouldn't bring up the subject. I didn't, but Scott Raeburn did. Scott had been reading about Sai Baba for about a year, and after much study, concluded that He could not be an incarnation of God in the same way as Jesus is. I don't remember why or how he had come to that conclusion, but what struck me that evening was that I had lost a possible cohort in my investigation of Baba. Scott had made up his mind that Sai Baba was not an Avatar. I had just begun my inquiry. His reasons for disbelief were based upon study, and I respect that, but on that particular night, he was tough on me, challenging me by talking the Sai phenomenon down.

Tony, the student of all things esoteric was even stronger in his feelings against Sai Baba. He went to great and comical lengths to "prove" that Sai Baba's miracles were just magic; nothing more than sleight of hand. He claimed that he could do similar "tricks," and offered to exhibit several "magical" deceptions. For instance, he covered a small juice glass with a napkin, moved the glass and napkin to the edge of the table where he obviously dropped the glass to his lap. Of course, when the napkin was removed, the glass was nowhere to be seen. It was a difficult evening.

But after dinner, Igor walked with me into the living room and quickly convinced me that if I really believed that Baba might be an Avatar, then I should go to India and personally experience Him.
" There is power there, Chuck," Igor said. "I don't know if the power is good or bad, but there is power there. You have to decide what it is for yourself. You need to go to India."

"In this world which is impermanent and ever transforming,
the Immanent Power of the Lord
is the only permanent and fixed entity.
*In order to realise the **Nithyam** (the Eternal)*
*and the **Sathyam** (Truth),*
one has perforce to attach oneself to that Source and Sustenance.
There is no escape from this path.
It is the destiny of one and all irrespective
of age or scholarship, clime or caste,
sex or status."

Sathya Sai Speaks
Volume I
Chapter 3
Page 23

CHAPTER 10

DREAMING

*"Whenever I appear in a dream
it is to communicate something to the individual;
it is not a mere dream as it is generally known.
It is a real appearance."*

Rai
Sathya Sai Avatar
Glimpses of Divinity
Chapter 9, Page 46

Because of Igor's encouragement, Patty and I began to plan a trip to India. Amid the effort to obtain new passports, purchase tickets and gather information from Sai devotees on what to pack and bring with us, I decided to have a complete physical before we left. As part of the physical, my doctor ordered a stress test to be administered by his partner, a cardiologist from India. While I went through the different procedures of the test, I had the opportunity to talk with the doctor about India, Hinduism and, of course, Sathya Sai Baba. Although he had heard of Sai Baba, he didn't know that much about Him and was personally a follower of another guru who was the spiritual leader of several million people in India. After he realised my sincere interest in Sai Baba in particular and all things Indian, in general, the doctor told me that his guru was coming to the United States in a few weeks and would be staying at his home. He would be giving *darshan* (the seeing of a holy man which confers grace) there and talking with devotees. He asked me if I would be interested in coming to his home to meet the guru. I told him that Patty and I would be delighted to come and would look forward to an invitation when the dates for the guru's visit were firmed up. In truth, I thought he was just being friendly and I really didn't expect him to call.

Soon thereafter, I had a dream that didn't seem to have anything to do with the doctor or his guru, but would be very much connected to them as events unfolded. The dream was one of those vivid, in colour dreams that are so striking, you remember it upon awakening and then consciously try to analyse it. In the dream, I entered a science lab lecture hall where the seats for students rise upward arena style, so that the students can observe the instructor as he lectures and works in the lab below.

The lab was located at Georgetown University where I had attended college many years ago. There was a registry desk halfway up the tier of seats. I walked up from the floor of the lab and approached the lady behind the desk who was registering students for a lecture to be given by Sathya Sai Baba. The lady's name was Sheila. After we had introduced ourselves, she asked me why I was signing up to attend the lecture since I was obviously too old to be a student. I told her that I was a Georgetown graduate and that I was interested in hearing the presentation. She seemed quite skeptical, and persisted in questioning my reasons for being there.

Finally, I left her and continued up the aisle between the seats and through a door at the top of the lecture hall. I entered a lobby and encountered a Jesuit priest in a black cassock who was pacing nervously. I asked him when Sai Baba would be arriving. He answered that Baba was late and that he was very worried because he wanted Baba to say Mass before the lecture. I was surprised that the Church would allow Baba to say mass. I remember that as I talked with the priest, I thought that the Jesuits were certainly becoming very open and inclusive if they were going to let an Indian Holy Man say mass.

I then reentered the lecture hall and walked down the stairs between the rows of seats to the floor of the lab. I picked up the rug and hid under it so that I could be close to Sai Baba when he gave His lecture. I was peering from under the rug, looking up the aisle, expecting Baba to enter through the door at the top of the hall. Suddenly, I became aware that He had entered at the lab floor level and from behind me. I was immediately struck with how old and frail he appeared. He was so feeble that two helpers had to carry Him in to the hall. I became confused and didn't know what to do. Finally, I came out from under the rug and voluntarily fell at His feet. He began to pat my back and addressing the audience said : "I have a message for this young man, but it is too disgusting to tell him in public. I shall tell him at Diane's house." Then the dream ended.

A few days after this dream, I received a call from the doctor who had performed my stress test. He gave me the date that his guru was coming to visit his home and he wanted to know if Patty and I were still interested in attending. I was surprised and certainly pleased that he had remembered me and so I happily accepted his invitation.

On the evening of the guru's visit, Patty and I arrived before the guru. As soon as we entered the home, events occurred that seemed augured by my dream of the lecture in the science lab at Georgetown. There were fifty to sixty guests which approximated the number of students in the lecture hall of my dream. I asked our hostess where the guru was. She told me that her husband had gone to pick him up at the airport and they were late returning. She was upset because she wanted the guru to have time to hold a prayer service to bless her home. This real-life scenario matched, very closely, my dream wherein the priest was worried that Sai Baba's tardiness might delay or cancel His saying mass before the lecture. Oh, by the way, the doctor's wife's name was "Deena," which was very close to the "Diane" mentioned by Baba in my dream.

The doctor's home was constructed in multi-levels. I realised that configuration mirrored the science lab lecture hall of my dreams which had at least three levels: The floor level lab, the tier of seats and the lobby above the seats. The similarities between what was happening at the doctor's home and what had occurred in my dream were fast becoming too coincidental.

When the guru arrived, we all ran to the front door to greet him when he came in. Our intent was akin to my going down to the floor of the laboratory in my dream to await Sai Baba. While we were all waiting for the guru to come to the door, he walked up the stairs from behind us. He had come in from the lower level garage area. This entry was analogous to Sai Baba coming in from behind me in my dream.

Later that evening, an Indian meal was served . A woman who had been watching Patty and me all night asked Patty to sit with her. After filling my plate, I joined them. We were the only westerners present and she was very interested in our reasons for being there. She wanted to know how we had come to be aware of this guru or the Hindu religion. We explained that we had been investigating Sathya Sai Baba and that we were trying to absorb as much about India, Hinduism and the Indian culture as we could so that the knowledge that we accumulated would help us as we explored and inquired into the phenomenon of this possible Avatar. This episode correlates to the woman at Georgetown, in my dream, who asked me many questions because she couldn't understand why I was registering for the lecture. Further, our curious dining companion at the doctor's house had the same name phonetically as the inquisitive registrar in my dream. The lady registrar was named "Sheila" while the lady at dinner with us told Patty and me to call her "Sheela!" Like the Sai Baba of my dream, the holy man was quite elderly, After dinner he was given a seat on the couch in the living room and all the guests, including Patty and me, lined up, and in turn, touched their forehead to his feet. I was a nervous wreck. I certainly didn't want to touch his feet and didn't know what to do. Finally, when my turn came, I folded my hands in the *namaste* pose of hands together at my chest, and lightly bowed in respect. My reluctance to touch his feet and my ignorance as to what was proper as a substitute for that sign of respect was very much like my state of mind in my dream when I had no clue as to what I should do as Baba entered the hall.

Later, the guests were allowed to sit at the guru's feet and have their picture taken with him. I watched as a man took a picture of his wife and the guru. I took his camera and volunteered to take a picture of both of them together with the guru. Afterward, the man took a picture of Patty and me sitting on the floor next to the guru. He promised to send us the picture after it was developed. As we sat for the photograph, the guru gently patted my back just as Baba had done in my dream, and in both the dream and at that time in the doctor's house, I was sitting on the floor.

When I had the opportunity to approach the guru alone, I asked him about Sai Baba. Maybe that was not very polite, asking one holy man about another, but I did it. He began to rant and rave, screaming that Baba was a magician and a charlatan! Baba was certainly no *Avatar* to him! He kept yelling that Baba was a fake. I was so shocked at his reaction to my question, that I silently backed away. His attitude related to Baba's words in my dream about His having a "disgusting" message for me, in that, if Baba were a magician and a fake, that would be "disgusting." If Baba is not a charlatan and the guru was jealous and spiteful, that fact too would be "disgusting."

Patty and I decided to wait for the earliest moment that we could gracefully depart. The guru's outburst had made me uneasy. As I opened the front door to leave, I looked over my right shoulder toward the guru and found him looking over his right shoulder at me. I will never forget his look. I knew that he was aware that I had been repulsed by his negative outburst. There was no *shanti* or peace in his action. He was agitated. He was envious of Sathya Sai Baba.

There was no question in my mind that my dream had been prophetic. The events at the doctor's home clearly reflected the contents of my dream. The whole episode made me reflect on many things. I wondered if an *Avatar*, as Baba claims to be, had the power to influence dreams and I wondered if that is what had happened to me. The *guru* at the doctor's house was not Baba, but had Baba used him and the dream to show me his power? Was Sathya Sai Baba not only the creator of my dream but also the arranger of each step that led us to experience the guru's visit at the doctor's home? The answer to each of these questions is: Yes! I believe that He was controlling all of these events and because of this belief my desire to see Baba intensified. I felt that Sai Baba was calling me to His side. Soon thereafter, we finalised our plans to travel to India.

There was one more meaningful dream before we left for India. I dreamt that the Indian God, Shiva, in the form of the four-armed, dancing God, Nataraja, was dancing in front of me. At that time, I had no knowledge of Nataraja, although I had seen pictures depicting this Indian deity. In my dream, Nataraja was dancing on a cubed platform and as He danced, the cube rose higher and higher into the air until He was almost out of sight above my head.

For many years, I could not figure out what that dream meant . I knew that it was a dream that related to Baba because Baba claims to be an incarnation of Shiva. A friend, Jay Borden, told me that Nataraja dances on a raised platform (a cube), the four corners of which represent Love, Righteousness, Peace and Bliss. Still, I couldn't understand the significance of the dream. Then recently, in March of 1994, our Sai Baba Center did a study circle on the Indian holiday, MahaShivaratri. From that study, I learned that the cosmic dance of Nataraja, the Dancing Shiva, is a dance to attract mankind to Divinity. I finally understood my dream! Baba was trying to attract me toward him! He had been pursuing me, trying to get my attention. And, if I would live my life by the four cornerstones of Love, Righteousness, Peace and Joy, I could rise higher and higher, thereby approaching God and finally merging in Him.

"I am the Dance Master
I am Nataraja, the Lord of Dance
You are all my pupils.
I, alone, know the agony
of teaching you each step of the Dance."

Sathyam Sivam Sundaram
Part IV
Page 173

CHAPTER 11

OFF WE GO

"If anybody thinks, that he will go himself and see a Saint,
that will be a mere boast.
Unless the Saint wills it,
no one is able to go and see him."

Shri Sai Satcharita
Chapter XXX
Page 160

The word got out. Patty and Chuck, nutty Patty and Chuck, were going to India! Our friends and family thought that we were out of our minds. Their first reaction to our telling them that we were travelling to see Sai Baba half way around the world was a vacuous stare. Their second reaction was a question steeped in disbelief: "Why would you want to go there?" And the third reaction was a generalised statement based on hearsay, not experience: "People are starving there." Our parents didn't want us to go and although they never said it, we knew that they were worried that we would never come back. I am sure they had images of disease, and parasites and fights between Muslims and Hindus which frightened them and made them fear for us. No matter what we said, they tried to discourage us from going. My dad's favorite line of attack was heavy sarcasm: "I can think of a **million** places I'd rather go to than India."

My brother is a staunch, conservative Christian who has studied the Old and New Testament intensely and is knowledgeable about the prophetic literature concerning the awaited Second Coming of Christ. I have had many enjoyable discussions with my brother about the predictions of Daniel and Isaiah concerning the return of Jesus. Based on his studies, he believes that Jesus will come again in our era. I suggested to him that Sathya Sai Baba might be the fulfillment of prophecy regarding a Second Coming and could be the One that he was expecting, but he rejected that idea as Baba did not seem to fit what he believed were the signs that were foretold. He was openly disdainful of Sathya Sai Baba. "There is only one Son of God, and that is Jesus Christ," he said. "That's what is meant by the term, 'the only begotten son!' he insisted. But at the time that Patty and I were ready to set off to India, I wasn't so sure that the Cosmic Christ could only appear once in the form of Jesus and then never appear again.

Since God is omnipotent and can do whatever He wills, He can incarnate in human form whenever He deems it appropriate. He has no restrictions. I had even come to believe that Sathya Sai Baba was prophesied in the Bible, in fact, I was convinced that He is the "King of Kings and Lord of Lords' mentioned in Revelations 19, Verses 11 through 16:

"**And now I saw heaven open, and a white horse appeared** (An allusion to the *Kalki Avatar* of Hinduism who is supposed to come in this era riding a white horse); **its rider was called Faithful and True** (Sathya, Baba's first name, means truth); **He is a judge with integrity, a warrior for justice.** (Baba's life of righteousness and selfless service to others does seem to fit that description); **His eyes were flames of fire, and His head was crowned with many coronets** (A reference not only to Divine Kingship, but possibly a symbolic description of Baba's huge head of hair); **the name written on Him was known only to Himself** (If He is an Incarnation of God, His full reality could not be knowable by the mind of man); **His cloak was soaked in blood** (A colorful allusion of Baba's red-orange robe); **He is known by the name, the Word of God** (An expression of God into the material world, an *Avatar*); **Behind him, dressed in linen of dazzling white, rode the armies of heaven on white horses** (Baba's close followers, especially the students attending his school, dress in pure white clothes); **From his mouth came a sharp sword to strike the pagans with** (A symbol of the destroying "word," Shiva the Destroyer in Hindu mythology, who cuts away the resistance of unbelievers); **He is the One who will rule them with an iron scepter and tread out the wine of Almighty God's Fierce Anger. On His cloak and on His thigh there was a name written: The King of Kings and the Lord of Lords.**

I read that excerpt to my brother, but he couldn't accept my interpretation. I can't fault him; he has chosen a path that is comfortable for him and he actively pursues it. That is more than most people can claim. But it does hurt when those that you love most walk a road different than yours. At least my brother's final statement about my developing interest in Sai Baba was positive, although he meant it as a rebuke: "I will pray for your soul!" He said.

But when devotees of Sai Baba heard that we were planning to go to India to see Him, they came to the rescue and supplied some of the support that was so lacking from family and friends. Art and Edna Yuile of the Windsor, Connecticut Sai Center helped us immensely. They gave us a book to read about planning a first trip to Baba, The First Pilgrimage to Sathya Sai Baba by Dara Irani, which outlined many of the things that we should bring with us, what to expect on our travels and how to prepare for the Ashram. Edna gave us little hints like suggesting that we bring a rubber shower hose and nozzle to attach to the spigots at the ashram, since the showers at Prasanthi Nilayam were nothing more than a faucet on a wall with a bucket under it. You filled up the bucket, and dumped it over your head! Then, after lathering up, you emptied another bucket of water, rinsing yourself off. It is effective cleansing, but not what we westerners are used to.

Edna suggested that we bring certain kinds of food with us. Sometimes Indian dishes are too spicy for western palates. She encouraged us to bring certain snacks to help us when we became tired of the Indian food. But most of all, Edna educated us on ashram rules and mores. Silence or at least quiet reflection is encouraged. Frivolous or careless behaviour is not permitted. Women could not sit with the men during *darshan* or at meals, as the energy from the two sexes is different and can be unsettling when mixed together. Baba wants all your attention directed spiritually with no sexual distraction. Women are required to dress modestly at all times while at the ashram.

Other devotees helped us prepare too. Ashok Kumar arranged our tickets and travel through his brother, Ram, a travel agent living in India. Ram Kumar made arrangements for people to meet us at the airport and to transport us by taxi to the ashram. He also contracted with airlines and taxi services to move us around the subcontinent so that we could experience India after we had visited Baba's ashram.

The Indians whom we had come to know also helped us . Devesh and Kajal Jain invited us to their home so that we could sample Indian cooking and spices. They introduced us to Nathan Kollingode, whose parents and brother lived at the *ashram* and who regaled us with stories about Baba and made suggestions to us about our conduct at the *ashram*. Kajal and others gave Patty saris to wear, teaching her how to put them on and how to wrap them properly. Looking back, we were real novices but the advice and tender love of these devotees was exactly what we needed. Not only did they help to educate us on what to do, eat and wear, but by their excitement over our trip, they propelled us forward. As the time drew near for our departure, our interest was high. We **wanted** to go!

Many of our friends warned us that Baba always seems to create some stress or tension just prior to leaving on a trip to see Him. In one sense, I guess that means we have to earn the privilege of visiting him by overcoming obstacles that He puts in our path. In another sense, the hurdles that we must jump prepare us for the culture shock and inconveniences of travelling in a third world country. We were no exception to the rule. We had our little anxiety attack over whether our visas would arrive from New York on time. All other arrangements had been made and except for the visas, our preparations were complete. Finally, the day before our early morning flight, Ashok Kumar called to tell us the visas were on hand. As fearful as we had been that the visas would not arrive, somehow, deep down, we knew that Baba was drawing us like a magnet, pulling us across the ocean to the other side of the world and nothing could halt our journey.

We travelled Air India and although the plane was crowded, it was very comfortable and the airplane attendants were very friendly. The Indian food served on the aircraft was not as spicy as we had expected, but it was tasty and a good introduction to the native Indian food that we would encounter in India. The flight was high energy for us, not only because we were excited about our adventure to see a person that might be an Incarnation of God, an *Avatar*, living in a land half way around the globe, but also because the plane was packed with at least one hundred people travelling to India to see their Guru. There was a spiritual aura that permeated the entire plane.

Our flight brought us first to London for a few hours where we were able to shop in the duty free area, then on to Bombay, crossing time zones and seeing the sunshine at hours where we normally might see the moon. We landed in India in the wee hours of the morning and had to wait about two hours for customs and entry into the country. I was not happy about the delay and in a typical tourist fashion attributed it to what I perceived to be disrespect for Americans, since most of us arriving on that flight were from America. In reality, I had no reason to presume that to be the case. I was just travel weary and irritable. Looking back on the episode, it was probably just Baba testing us again.

When we finally manoeuvred through inspections, questions, paper-rustling and document-stamping, we walked around a corner and faced a row of windows looking out into sweltering Bombay. Pressed up against those windows were hundreds of brown faces with large eyes peering at us, hands waving at us to give, to buy, to rent, to ride. There were beggars, short ones, skinny ones, dirty ones, maimed ones, females, men and children, lots of children and it was well past midnight! As we gazed at the hundreds of people, all talking and waving and gesturing at once, I spotted my name, **DiFazio,** in bold letters on a sign being held up by a neatly dressed man, who was smiling warmly.

What a relief, our travel agency had not forgotten us. Ram Kumar, Ashok's brother was there to meet us and bring us to our hotel. Patty had done our packing and we had enough clothes, food and supposed necessities, to outfit an army division. Ram and his people quickly gathered our five overly laden bags and herded us into our cab. Just before we drove away from the airport, a woman beggar holding a baby stuck her face and the baby in toward the window next to Patty. She was horrified! The woman had a sorrowful look; made feeding gestures to the baby's mouth and then held out her hands for money. Ram's people shooed her away and we drove off, but Patty was appalled. We had been warned of the beggars by our devotee friends back home, but nothing they say prepares you for the emotional tearing that occurs when these sad faced, pathetic looking people approach you and make you feel that they are seconds away from death unless you reach into your pocket for a hand full of dollars or rupees. Although many are truly in need, living amid dire poverty and squalor, begging is an industry for many others who have made the seeking of alms their career. As we drove through the streets of Bombay, Patty was asking herself why she had ever agreed to come to India.

The ride to our hotel took forty-five minutes through the heart of Bombay. We drove along in silence, eyes gaping at the rickshaws parked on the side of the road and the bodies of men and women sleeping on the pavement. There were some cows standing asleep in the streets and dogs roamed freely. The air was heavy with the smell of burnt cow dung; the pungent odour accosted our nostrils. Cars coming toward us were being driven with their lights off. We were told the drivers did that to save the bulbs. I couldn't believe it. Aren't you supposed to put your car lights on in the dark of night? We drove down narrow streets with barely enough room for one car let alone two. A car suddenly appeared out of the night with no lights on to warn us of his approach! Our taxi driver, seemingly oblivious to the danger, simply turned our cab to the left into a one-way street and stopped abruptly in front of steps leading into our hotel.

Carrying some of our bags and followed by a phalanx of porters vying to carry the rest of them, we walked up the stairs into a lobby that looked like a scene from Casablanca. There were men in white dhotis wrapped around their waists and loins, standing on a scaffold, ostensibly repairing the air-conditioning. There was a counter in front of a small cubicle and the desk manager, upon greeting us and ascertaining that we had reservations, opened a large guest book and entered our names in much the same way a guest would have been registered at a hotel in the Unites States, a hundred years ago.

I was tired, not having slept for very long since leaving the United States. I know that I looked even worse than I felt. But when I looked at Patty, I knew that I was in serious trouble. There she was, exhausted, looking totally bedraggled. Her lips were drawn into a thin line so tightly they were white not red! Her hands were resting on her hips and one foot kept tapping on the ground. She never said a word.

There was a wide flight of stairs to the upper floors, but thankfully, we didn't have to drag our tired bodies and luggage over each step. We were brought to the third floor in an ancient elevator with a clanging, metal grated door. Our room was large with twelve foot ceilings, and great French doors which opened on to a little balcony overlooking the street below. We never figured out how to open those doors. The double bed was covered in a blanket that looked like army surplus. The mattress was horse hair and very hard. The room, however, was clean and the bathroom was the best thing we had seen since our arrival. It was all marble, had a "geyser," which was an overhead water tank for flushing and had a hot and cold tap for the shower.

While Patty was washing up after our long trip, I tried to find the air conditioner controls. There were several buttons on the backboard of the bed. I pushed one and a light came on. I pushed another and nothing seemed to happen. In a few minutes there was a knock on the door and a bell hop called through the door: "You rang, sir?" I was startled. "No, no, I didn't call for anyone," I said. Minutes later, I again pushed the buttons trying to locate the air conditioner. Again, a knock on the door. "Sir, what do you need?" came the call through the door. "Nothing, I didn't call for you, there must be a mistake, " I yelled! Patty came out of the bathroom and I went in. She went to the headboard and did the same thing, fiddling with those buttons. It was only after this poor guy ran up those three flights of stairs the third time that we realised that the buttons on the bed signalled the main desk for room service! Management of the hotel wouldn't let the employees use the "lift," as the elevator is called, so every time we pushed the buzzer, the bell hop had to run up the three flights of stairs. The poor fellow must have lost five pounds.

We slept well on our rock like mattresses. I think the jet lag, the sleepless hours of travel, the sights and smells of Bombay and the tension of our early morning arrival at our hotel, had left us totally exhausted. We needed the sleep. Early the next morning, we were awakened by a telephone call from the lobby. Our travel agent had sent us a guide for our day of sight seeing in Bombay before heading on to the ashram at Puttaparthi. Our guide was a thin woman in her thirties who we came to know was of the "Parsi" faith, the religion of Zoaraster. She explained that the religion originated in Iran or Persia, but persecution had forced relocation of most of its followers to India. She told us there were only about two hundred fifty thousand adherents left. I knew that Baba considered the Parsi faith, a major religion of India, and had incorporated its symbol of "Fire" in His "Sarva Dharma" logo along with the "Cross" for Christianity, the "Om" for Hinduism, the "Star and Crescent" for the Islam, the "Wheel of Life" for Buddhism and in the western countries, the "Star of David" for the Jewish faith.

"Cut the 'I' feeling clean across
and let your ego die on the Cross
to endow on you Eternity.
Offer all bitterness in the Sacred Fire
and emerge Grand, Great and Godly.
Remember the wheel of cause and effect,
of deed and destiny, and the wheel of Dharma
that rights them all.

Be like the Star that never wavers from
the Crescent, but is fixed
in steady faith.
Listen to the Primeval Pranava (sound)
resounding in your heart,
as well as in the heart of the Universe."

Ron Laing
Sai Baba, the Embodiment of Love
Book Two
Chapter 10, Page 207

She brought us by boat to Elephanta Island from the Gate of India, a huge arch built at the water's edge in the 1920s to greet the then Prince of Wales when he travelled to India. On the island we saw Bhuddist monasteries and temples carved into the side of a mountain. The walls of each room and giant pillars, all decoratively carved out of the solid rock, were the carrying walls, beams and supports that supported the tons of mountain above. As we ascended up from the boats to the temples and then after our viewing the monastery, as we descended down to the boats, dozens of wild monkeys glared or laughed at us as they scurried about amid the tourists, the trees and the rocks. Three young women walked around with large gold coloured pots balanced precariously on their heads. They allowed you to take their picture for a price, so that you could bring back "authentic" native photographs to friends and relatives back home.

Inside the temples, our guide pointed out huge linghams which were worshipped and used in the spiritual rites of the Buddhist monks. A lingham is an ellipsoid usually made of stone or marble. It represents the unknown, omnipotent, omnipresent, omniscient God because there is no beginning or end to the egg-shaped lingham. You can travel around it in any direction and you never come to an ending. Hence, it is a symbol for the eternal Deity. Our Parsi friend showed us a lingham that had cracked, and could therefore no longer be worshipped as a symbol of God, because it now had an imperfection. God has no imperfections.

Our official tour was scheduled to end at noon. But we liked our guide so much, that we asked her to stay with us for the afternoon.

She agreed and showed us much more of Bombay. As our taxi darted to the left and right, just missing passing vehicles which were constantly blowing their horns, she led us to view the farmer's market where individual shopkeepers sold their oranges, mangoes and other fruits and vegetables. Each shopkeeper neatly piled their produce in precise pyramids, squares or circles. The design and colour of these stalls were rich in their variety, but when we realised that many of the shopkeepers slept under their tables at night, the poverty of so many in India was, once again, obvious.

Our taxi driver drove us through an area inhabited mostly by lepers. We saw these unfortunates, sitting and staring back at us, making us both uncomfortable and filled with compassion for their plight. Then, in contrast, we drove through a park, where a huge monument in the form of a shoe told the story of the fairy tale, "The Old Woman Who Lived in a Shoe."

We stopped at a Jain temple where silver doors with raised figures depicted stories of the Jain faith. Women were chanting and singing spiritual songs as we looked on and many people wore what looked like sterile surgical masks. Our guide explained that the Jain faith teaches that all life is sacred, even microbes invisible to the eye. Therefore, the masks are worn to keep the wearer from inhaling and thereby destroying microscopic life.

One of the sights that has left an impression on me was the view of the Parsi towers, which are enormous pillars, maybe 150 feet high, upon which sit huge grates. When a Parsi dies, his or her body is brought up to the top of the tower and laid upon the grate where scavenger birds such as vultures dine upon the corpses until nothing is left but bone, which falls through the grates and is eventually burned. The Parsis believe that all life must be recycled and therefore they do not bury their dead, but offer their lifeless bodies back to nature as food for these large birds.

After paying and thanking our lady guide, we went back to our hotel exhausted. The travel agency sent a driver early the next morning, before the sun was up, to transport us to the airport. We flew from Bombay to Bangalore where we were again met by a representative of our travel agency waiving another "DiFazio" sign. We were whisked off in a cab and began our three and one half hour journey over land to Puttaparthi and Sai Baba. The sights that we saw as we traveled over the narrow, bumpy road were amazing. We watched in awe as road crews of men and women dug out a four foot deep hole in the road, into which others, working in assembly line fashion, were dropping baskets filled with crushed stone. These baskets were carried on the heads of both male and female workers. There were others who gathered the stone from several women whose job it was to break up and crush the stone by hand using primitive tools.

Almost everybody was barefoot and many men were dressed just in dhotis. All the women wore saris, even those engaged in the road work described above. Young children could be seen herding goats and cows, many of which had their horns gaily decorated with bright colours. Wagons carried loads of hay or twigs or dung and rolled on wooden wheels, pulled by slow but steadily moving oxen. As we passed through small towns, roadside stands selling lemon "Limca" soda and coconuts were filled with people sitting together and socialising.

But the outstanding image of that drive to Puttaparthi, in my mind, is of a dead camel in the road being torn apart by three feet high vultures gathered around it. The taxi driver pulled to a halt. "Do you want to take a picture?" he asked. I couldn't believe it! It was a grotesque sight! Why would I want a picture of that? "Get us out of here," I yelled! He shrugged and drove on.

"This universe is as unreal as the dream.
It is only relatively real;
it is not absolutely real."

Voice of the Avatar
Part 1
Page 126

CHAPTER 12

PRASANTHI NILAYAM
THE FIRST ENCOUNTER

"Everyone has to be asked to approach me and experience me.
In order to get an idea of a mountain,
it is not enough if you show a stone and say,
'The mountain is a million times the size of this.'
You will have to see an actual mountain,
at least from a distance."

> Samuel H. Sandweiss M.D.
> <u>Sai Baba</u>
> <u>The Holy Man And The Psychiatrist</u>
> Chapter 2, Page 28

"It is on account of the store of merit in past births
that we have attained the feet of Sai Baba"

> <u>Shri Sai Satcharita</u>
> Chapter X, Page 62

We drove for hours on dusty rural roads through the beige and brown Indian countryside and rustic villages teeming with people. There were trucks and buses honking their way through sheep, cows and bicycles. Finally we approached the squared arch that announces the entrance to Prasanthi Nilayam, the *ashram* of Sathya Sai Baba. We drove on for another five minutes, to the village of Puttaparthi, the birthplace of Sai Baba. Soon we entered the *ashram* separated from the village by a tall wall. Our driver stopped in front of a building that housed the "office" where new arrivals could inquire about lodging. We had been warned by our devotee friends at home that reservations are not an option and rooms might be scarce. Sure enough, there was "no room in the Inn." At least there were no private rooms. We were offered space in the only shelter available, large   sheds which were concrete block buildings with windows open to the elements and metal roofs protecting residents from the hot sun or the cool rain. There were no partitions and the floors were poured concrete. We were very tired from our flight, our sightseeing excursion around Bombay the day before and our early morning drive for over three hours to the *ashram*. At that point, the shed accommodations sounded just fine, not only acceptable but a welcome haven.

Our taxi brought us to the "married couple's shed." There were already a few families who had set up residence there and had delineated their space with bed sheets suspended from the rafters. We were standing there in the open and realised that we needed to build some kind of cubicle for privacy, so Patty went into the village to buy four or five sheets that we could use to build the partitions of our sleeping area. The drape-like partitions would be the only barrier between us and the other residents of our shed. When she returned, we tied string to the sheets and then tried to throw the string over the rafters so that the sheets could be hung. I was so tired, I couldn't figure out how to throw the string over the rafters. Every time I threw the string into the air, it would rise up, hover in the air for a moment and then waft gently to the ground. I was so frustrated. Finally, another denizen of our concrete shelter, a young man from France walked over to me, took the string from my hand, tied it around a sandal, threw the sandal over the rafter and caught it as it came down. The attached string was now hanging down ready to receive a corner of one of our cloth partitions. I was so embarrassed and exhausted, that I started to laugh loudly. My benefactor couldn't understand English and I couldn't understand French, so all of his help came in his action, not in words. There is a lesson there, I guess. Anyway, following his lead, we quickly erected our eight foot by eight foot "room," adding mosquito nets strung from the four corners of the cubicle. As the sheds have windows open to the outer air, mosquito nets are a necessity as a protection from the dive-bombing mosquitoes that seemed several times larger than our New England, U.S.A. variety.

Thanks to the advice of Edna Yuile, we brought two air mattresses. We filled them with air by huffing and puffing into a nozzle. I'm an old softy and the thought of tossing and turning on the concrete was not appealing. The air mattresses gave us hope for restful sleep. Since it was only about four o'clock in the afternoon, we decided that tired as we were, we would go for a walk to get the lay of the land. We carefully retraced our steps back to the office near the Mandir or Temple where Baba lived.

In front of the office, we saw a sign announcing that N. Kasturi, Baba's chief biographer was going to speak in the lecture hall down

e married couple's shed — Our cubicle is marked by the brown sheet straight ahead.

Here we are in our cubicle in the married couple's shed.

by the main gate. I was overjoyed at our good fortune! I had to attend. I considered Kasturi to be Sai Baba's "St. Peter!" It would be an opportunity to listen to a saint. But Patty was so exhausted, she didn't want to go. She just wanted to turn around, head back to "Chez Shed," drop down on her air mattress and sleep, sleep, sleep. But, being the insensitive clod that I can sometimes be, I insisted that we stay the course and attend the lecture. She reluctantly agreed and after removing our shoes, we entered the hall.

Patty was further upset when she found out that men and women were separated and made to sit on opposite sides of the room. She didn't want to be there in the first place and was not very happy at being corralled into the ladies side of the building away from me. She was just so tired, everything irritated her. Meanwhile, there was a row of chairs along the wall facing Dr. Kasturi. Everybody in the room was sitting on the floor looking at him. No one was sitting in the chairs, but I didn't take notice of that fact and casually sat down on one of the empty chairs. At that time, I didn't know that it is a sign of respect to sit lower than a holy or revered personage. No one had ever told me that was the Indian custom and so, I was oblivious to what must have seemed like an act of disrespect to the many Indians sitting cross legged on the floor in front of me.

Kasturi began to speak. I leaned forward. He was frail, and quite elderly, in his nineties I think. His voice was so soft, almost a whisper. I really tried to listen, but my exhaustion plus Kasturi's soft murmuring combined to lull me into a deep sleep. Abruptly, I was awakened by one of the men sitting on the floor, tugging at my pant leg. As I became aware of my surroundings, I realised that he was pointing to the door on my left which was open to the outside. There in the doorway stood Patty, madly gesturing to me to get off the chair and come outside. I jumped up and ran to where she stood. She had lost her shoes and her sense of direction and was totally out of control. She was so tired and disoriented that she couldn't find her way back to the shed alone. Crying and yelling at me at the same time, she wanted to go home and leave the *ashram* and all of India behind. She had been wandering lost and bare footed through the sands and was just hysterical. I took her by the arm and led her up the hill to the shed, and along the way, I told her that I would call the taxi company in Bangalore and ask them to come and get us. I promised her that we would leave the *ashram* the next day after a good night's sleep. That seemed to comfort her as she slumped against my side. I guided her steps as we walked slowly back to the shed.

The next morning, we rose early, showered in a shower cubicle attached to the shed, and then set off for the *Darshan* of Sai Baba. *Darshan* is seeing the form of a great and holy man. But true to my promise to Patty, after *darshan*, I went to the post office to use the one telephone available to devotees at the *ashram*. First I tried to get an operator in Bangalore so that I could ring up the taxi company. However, try as I might, I couldn't even raise up the operator, let alone contact the cab company. For three hours I dialed and dialed in between calls that other devotees made. But Bangalore seemed to have vanished! A city of millions, and I couldn't find an operator to talk to! Patty was sitting patiently on the steps of the building and every few minutes or so, I would go out and report my lack of progress. She just looked at me quietly, not really saying much. I began to feel guilty, I wondered if she thought that I was purposefully not making the connection, so that we would stay at the *ashram*.

While making another call, I heard a cry: " Baba's coming, Baba's coming!" I hung up the phone and ran outside. The cry got louder, as the news spread from one devotee to another. Patty was still sitting on the steps. I stood beside her as Sai Baba was slowly driven past us in the back seat of a small red car. He didn't look in our direction but I had the feeling that He knew we were there and in some way acknowledged us. As His car disappeared in the direction of the dormitory construction near the sheds, I sat down next to Patty and said: "I guess we're staying." She replied quietly: "I know."

Later, after retiring to our cubicle for another night's sleep, I was awakened by Patty getting up and walking away. It was still dark. I glanced at my watch. It was three a.m. "Where are you going? " I asked. "To the shower," was her reply. She had been awakened by others rising and leaving the shed. We had no idea of the routine at the Nilyam and didn't realise that many people rose early to attend *Omkar* (early morning chanting of the mantra, *Om*,) and to partake in *Nagarasamkirtan* (singing bhajans and the names of God in procession through the streets.) With the disturbance and still suffering from the time dislocation of jet lag, Patty was wide awake. She decided to shower and dress.

As she entered the shower building with her trusty rubber shower hose, an English woman with a heavy accent told her that there was a "turd" in the shower stall. At least that is what Patty heard. Patty ran back to our bags, and pulled out an aerosol can of Lysol. Armed with the can, she returned to the shower stall and sprayed the "turd." She was going to clean the shower stall. The "turd" had other ideas. It jumped about two feet! It was a "toad!"

Early that morning, just around dawn, I found myself leaving my sneakers with hundreds of pairs of footwear near the *mandir* area. The *mandir* is the temple at the *ashram*, the spiritual hub of the place, which at that time also housed Baba's living quarters. Following the direction of a Seva Dal worker (one of the volunteers who help direct the devotees), I walked to the end of a row of devotees and sat down. There were already several rows of men sitting, Indian style, on the gravel waiting for the signal to enter the *mandir* area for morning *darshan*. Several people turned to stare at me. Some laughed, some just shook their heads and turned away. What had grabbed their attention was the full sized-pillow that I was sitting on. Most of the Indians sat directly on the sands; many had small cushions and some had meditation pillows, but none of them had the full-sized bed pillow that I tucked under me. At first I was a little self-conscious, but after sitting cross-legged for about forty five minutes, I was grateful for my soft seat.

I decided to meditate while waiting for Baba. I hoped to quiet my mind and prepare myself for His appearance. I had never been a strong meditator, but I was amazed how easily I was able to get into that space where the world was blocked out. I am sure that part of the reason was the relaxation that comes just from being away from the pressure of work and family, and I am confident that part of it was my resolve to be in the right mind set to receive His Grace. Yet, I was also aware of an aura of the place, a feel, an unseen but deeply felt calmness that pervaded Prasanthi Nilayam, making meditation easy.

Then, as the realisation dawned that I might soon be in the presence of an *Avatar*, a vertical descent of the Godhead into our world of matter, I became frightened! I started to talk to Him in my mind, pray, I guess, but a crazy kind of prayer. I asked Him not to look at me. You see, I was suddenly very aware of certain shortcomings of mine and I was ashamed. These "sins" were heavy on my mind and I found it difficult to face Him. I felt that these personal failings were embedded in my personality. "Please Baba," I begged, "please don't look at me. I'll just look upon You and that will be enough."

After a while, the waiting made me a little restless. There was shifting of seats, movement of legs, daydreaming, whispering until Sathya Sail Baba walked out through the portal of the *mandir*. When He first emerged, I hadn't been looking in the direction of his appearance, but in a split second, I knew something had changed. A sense of awareness and attentiveness permeated the crowd as all eyes looked in one direction. As I followed their gaze, I saw a small man in a bright orange-red robe, walking slowly across the sands. His movement was fluid and His walk smooth. I couldn't take my eyes off of Him. I didn't **want** to take my eyes off of Him!

Soon, I realised that I was not only paying attention to Him as He walked in front of devotees, talking to some, taking letters from others, allowing *Padnamaskar*, the devotional touching of the feet of a Holy Man, to very few, I was also paying attention to my reaction to Him. I didn't think that I was very excited or emotionally high. In fact, everything about my feelings were very natural, very calm, I thought. It wasn't until I had returned home to Connecticut and crashed, that I realised the intense joy that I experienced at Prasanthi Nilyam. Yet, at the time, I wasn't aware of my heightened emotions, but I was aware that I wasn't as excited as many others obviously were. Their eager faces straining to look at Him as He passed; their sometimes comical attempts to get His attention by standing, kneeling, calling His name or reaching across the sands to touch His elusive "Lotus feet," were visible testimony to their exuberant love and devotion. They were expressing themselves from their heart. I was still in my mind, thinking and reflecting on what Sai Baba was and who He was.

At that first *darshan*, I was struck with how blue-black his complexion appeared. He looked ferocious and I thought He had the outward look of the Destroyer God, Shiva. But on other days at other *darshans*, His complexion was lighter and He seemed friendlier, more approachable. I learned from devotees, that these observations were normal. They told me that Baba often changes in appearance, colour, mood, look, and that these changes and their significance, though lost to many, are symbolic and meaningful to some and purposeful in Him. He wills to change color. But whether He looked friendlier didn't matter to me. I still prayed for Him not to look at me. I felt that

Sathya Sai Baba was a manifest expression of the All-Knowing God, and I was fearful of His confronting me and gazing into the depths of my sinful nature.

While at Prasanthi, I had no interviews with Baba; I saw no miracles, except the creation of *vibhuthi* or holy ash which he manifested by waving His hand in a circular motion and then catching the ash as it descended from His palm. Once, He waved His arm and hand from left to right in a big sweeping motion over His head. *vibhuthi* poured out of His hand in a wide arc, showering part of the crowd with the holy ash.

One event at *darshan* really struck me. I couldn't figure it out for a long time. Baba was walking back toward the *mandir*, and a young boy, possibly five or six years of age, ran up to Him, but Baba waved him to stop. He wouldn't let the boy get close to Him, nor did he allow the boy to touch Him. I was surprised. I expected Baba to scoop the child up into His arms, but that didn't happen. After thinking of that event over and over again across the years, I realised that Baba was maintaining respect and discipline. In a setting of thousands of adoring devotees, anything less would have surely resulted in chaos and danger to many. In this case, the child's parents probably sent him up to Baba. They were taught a lesson about discipline on the spot. If everyone sent their children scurrying to Him across the sands, bedlam would ensue, as other devotees devoutly attracted to Him, would most surely follow suit. So, as in all else, He sets the example. Decorum and respect must be followed by all.

And for the entire time that we were in the presence of Sai Baba on that trip, I prayed for Him not to look at me. And...He didn't.

"Bring me the depths of your minds,
no matter how grotesque,
how cruelly ravaged by doubts or disappointments.
I know how to treat them.
I will not reject you.
I am your mother.
No matter where you go, I am there.
I can work with you everywhere."

Samuel H. Sandweiss
<u>Sai Baba</u>
<u>The Holy Man And The Psychiatrist</u>
Page 203

CHAPTER 13

WHY DID I SAY THAT?

"Let your words be few, fair, and felicitous.
Soft speech adds sweetness to living."

Sathya Sai Speaks
Volume X
Page 48

The *ashram* of Sathya Sai Baba, Prasanthi Nilyam, lies next to the little village of Puttaparthi, where Sai Baba was born. Puttaparthi sits on the banks of the Chitravathi River and is surrounded by desert and hills. Like most Indian villages, it is poor and primitive by western standards. It bustles during the day with people, wagons, cows, dogs and goats. Yet, once you enter the main gate of the *ashram* and set foot on the walkway that brings you toward the *mandir,* a sense of peace pervades the atmosphere. Brightly coloured stone signs, inscribed with pointed statements of Sai Baba on morality, love and service, line the walk and further set the tone of quiet reflection.

One quiet afternoon I walked up the hill behind the *mandir* to the gravel and sand platform around what is called the Meditation Tree. From that vantage point, I could look down on the roof tops of the *ashram* and the ramshackle buildings of the village and up to the brown and gray hills protecting the *ashram* on all sides. The hills were patched with some vegetation, but were mostly stone and sand baked by the hot Indian sun. I remember thinking that what I was viewing must be a lot like the parched sands and hills of Palestine at the time of Jesus Christ. The silence wasn't absolute but it was calming. This was a place for prayer and restful meditation, not for sound and nervous movement. You would not yell out at Prasanthi Nilayam.

But amid the silence, which I like to call "**SAI**-lence," there are pilgrims to the feet of the *Avatar*, living their lives within the boundaries of the material world, with all of their human frailties. Although I enjoyed the quiet of the *ashram*, I was still enmeshed in the tug and pull of my mind and the everyday world. In 1985 there was no western dining hall at the *ashram*. Most devotees ate at least one meal each day in a huge canteen where only Indian food was the offered fare. There were many stone or marble tables and I was told that the hall could seat 1500 people. The windows of the hall were open to the outside and the smell of cooking spices was always in the air.

I don't like most of the Indian food. However, I must admit that I have relished certain dishes that our Indian friends have prepared at home for Patty and me. Anyway, I had trouble with the odor of spices at the canteen and so couldn't eat in that hall. I would run in for a cup of water or a bottle of Limca soda, then leave quickly before I began to fell sick. I drank bottles and bottles of lemon Limca and ate ice cream purchased at a kiosk in the center of the ashram. But, basically, Patty kept me alive with peanut butter, granola bars and other packaged food items brought from America.

Once, I left our shed alone to visit the book store. On the way, I met an Italian lady who was on her way to the canteen for lunch. Baba had materialised a ring for her and she showed it to me happily, explaining how it had fit perfectly when He put it on her finger. She had lived at the *ashram* for over a month and was planning on staying for a substantially longer time. She told me that she was going to the canteen for a bite to eat. I asked her if she enjoyed the food. She said that she did. I asked her how she could enjoy the Indian food when she had been brought up on Italian food. She just shrugged. I then complained about the Indian food at the canteen and told her how much trouble I had with the spicy odours in the hall. I vividly described how they made me feel quite ill. She looked at me in disbelief and simply said that she had no such problem and in fact, rather liked the food.

We parted company, I, to the book store and she, to the canteen for dinner. About fifteen minutes later, having finished my shopping tour of the store, I walked out into the street and found the same Italian lady, sitting on a basement window sill of the building opposite me. She had her head in her hands and didn't look well. I greeted her and said: "I thought you were going to eat." She just looked up at me with a pained expression on her face and said: "I wish that I had never met you!" I am sure that she couldn't eat "spicy" food for months after that. How sorry I was that my careless talk had influenced her in this negative way.

Now Patty didn't mind the spices at all and ate in the canteen regularly. She had purchased some camping gear and western utensils and brought them to India with her. The first time that she went to dinner in the canteen, she brought them along, so that she wouldn't have to eat with her hands, Indian style. She took them out of their package and started eating with them. Very quickly, she had the feeling that something was wrong. She looked up and realised that every Indian lady in the place was either staring at her in disbelief or smiling at her indulgently. All chatting had stopped. Suddenly, they all began to laugh and giggle. Surprisingly, their reaction to her using the western utensils tickled Patty and she laughed right along with them. She was a good sport and...a good ambassador.

That afternoon, there was another well-known follower of Baba that was scheduled to speak in the lecture hall. I decided to attend. Patty took a rain check. I really wanted to hear the lecture, so I made up my mind that this time, I wouldn't fall asleep, nor would I fail to hear the speaker even if he spoke as softly as Kasturi. So, when I got to the hall, I sat right at the speaker's feet. I do not remember who the speaker was, but he, like Kasturi, was on in years. As he began to speak, I realised that I couldn't make out a word that he was saying. A gentleman sitting cross-legged behind me about three or four rows, raised his hand, got the speaker's attention and said: "I can't hear you, Doctor." The speaker said nothing in reply. I looked at him and said, "I can't hear you either, Doctor." He looked at us with a gentle smile, shrugged and simply said: "That is how I speak."

"Words can confer strength; they can drain it off;
words can gain friends; they can turn them into enemies;
words can elevate or lower the individual.
One must learn the habit of making one's words
sweet, soft, and pleasant.
A person is judged by his words;
words inflict damage in other ways too.
Whenever we talk disparagingly or defamingly
or sarcastically or hatefully of others,
they get recorded on the tape,
which is our own mind."

Thought For The Day
1008 Gems From The Sri Sai Manasasarovar
Page K 95

CHAPTER 14

THE PUPPETEER

"Be wherever you like, do whatever you choose,
remember this well, that all you do is known to Me.
I am the Inner Ruler of all and seated in their hearts.
I envelop all the creatures, the movable and immovable world.
I am the Controller, the Wire-Puller of the show of this universe."

Shri Sai Satcharita
Chapter III
Page l4

On the afternoon of the next to last day of our stay at Prasanthi Nilyam, I went to the Poornachandra Auditorium. There are no visible partitions or columns holding up the huge roof overhead. This building is considered to be the largest free span auditorium in all of Asia. I was told that about twenty thousand people could be accommodated in that hall, if they were seated Indian style on the floor. It is a place that Baba often uses for discourses and *darshan*, and was designed with roll up doors on the side, to accommodate those devotees who could not get into the hall. At least with the doors rolled up, they could see and hear Baba. Inside the auditorium, on either side of the stage which sits about three feet above the floor, there are large brightly coloured paintings of the major faiths of India: A picture of Zoaraster for the Parsis; of Jesus Christ for the Christians; of Buddha for the Buddhists; of Krishna for the Hindus and for the Muslims, a depiction of the holy book, the Koran.

As I walked slowly through the hall, admiring the paintings, I met a young man who reminded me of Patty's cousin, Gino. I stopped him, introduced myself and began what turned out to be a delightful conversation. He was dressed all in white and was sixteen years of age. He was a student at Baba's school in the *ashram*. I was struck with his manners and courtesy and his adult way of talking. I had the impression of speaking with an adult rather than a teenage boy. Just before we parted company, he asked me if he might have a favour of me. It seemed that the boys at the school were preparing special projects as a school assignment. I was surprised to learn that Baba approved every project. This young man's project was a collage of coins from foreign countries and Baba had given him permission to ask foreign visitors at the *ashram* for coins for the collage. He asked me if I had some small coins from America that I might share. I wasn't sure whether the kid was sincere or whether I was being hit up for money. At the time, I didn't have any money on my person, so I told him that I would give him some coins if I ran into him again during our short stay. I knew that we were leaving on the following morning at ten o'clock.

We parted with a smile and I went on up toward the *mandir* for afternoon *darshan*. It is a Hindu custom to leave your shoes outside when entering a temple or holy place and a large area was set aside for that purpose. It is meant as a sign of respect not to track in the dust and dirt of the roadway in holy precincts. As I deposited my brand new Puma sneakers with everyone else's shoes and sandals, I saw a man from the village eyeing them covetously. My heart sank. Although the *ashram* is the earthly abode of an *Avatar*, that fact does not stop non-believers or cloudy-minded people from doing exactly those evil things in the *ashram*, that they do outside the *ashram*. Anyway, I just knew those sneakers would be gone when I returned from *darshan*.

Sure enough, when I approached the spot where I had left my sneakers, they were gone. Knowing that shoes don't walk without feet in them, I sadly realized that someone's feet other than mine had put my sneakers into high gear. I didn't know what to do. I kept looking for them or for someone wearing them, but they were no where to be seen. I did have a pair of black dress shoes back at the shed, but formal footwear couldn't be worn comfortably on the sands of the *ashram*. I had a vision of spending the rest of my stay bare footed.

Suddenly, the same young man that I had been talking with at the Poornachandra Auditorium appeared on my left. "Can I help you, sir?" he asked. I told him quickly of my predicament. He listened and then suggested that I go to the *ashram* store at 6 p.m., and purchase rubber thongs. He agreed that good shoes should not be worn on the sand and gravel of the *ashram* and explained that you had to be careful of your possessions as the villagers often took things that didn't belong to them.

The *ashram* store was like a general store, selling little things like cushions and sandals to devotees at very reasonable prices. At six o'clock, I was waiting for it to open, but it didn't! I didn't know what to do, and once again, my young friend appeared. "Can I help you, sir?" I didn't know how he could. The store was closed. "Wait here," he said, and ran off. A few minutes later, he arrived with the shopkeeper who opened the doors and for a few rupees I bought a pair of rubber thong sandals. I thanked the young man profusely and then left to meet Patty at the ice cream kiosk.

As we sat on the curb in front of the kiosk, I told Patty about my meeting three times with my young benefactor. "Something is happening," I said. Patty grimaced. "You want to believe that something is happening," she said. "You're reading too much in to it." I understood what she meant, but still, I felt something was out of the ordinary.

I had brought five photographs to India with me of members of our families. Some pictures had only one person in it, while others had large family groupings. I brought the photographs to India with the hope that Baba would take them and bless each person shown. If I couldn't hand them to Baba personally, I intended to leave them on the altar of the Shiva temple marking the spot where Baba was born. The temple is about a mile and a half into the village. The reader might recall that I had been praying that Baba would not look at me, so the only way I could "give" Him the photographs was symbolically. By placing them on the altar, I would be presenting them to Him.

As we finished our ice cream, at the kiosk, Patty suggested that we walk to the temple while it was still light. Although I wanted to leave the pictures there, I didn't want to take the trek through the village. In fact, I was very nervous about entering the village. It was a different world. The cultural differences were incredible and I was a little afraid of what we might encounter. The streets are all dirt and after an afternoon shower, all muddy. Young children run around almost naked while chickens, cows, goats and dogs roam the streets without restraint. Bullock carts piled high with anything from dung to branches rumble by on solid wooden wheels, pulled by oxen, who look tired and worn. There were women carrying pots on their heads and men sitting at the open doors of shops, dangling their legs and bare feet over the thresholds. It was like a scene, I thought, out of ancient history. If Roman soldiers had come around the corner dragging Jesus under the cross, I might not have been surprised. To me, the village had the feel of another place and another time.

Well, a Panamanian lady from the Baba Center at the U.N. in New York came along and walked up to us. We had met Maxima Bond earlier in the week. She and her son were also camping out in our shed. She asked what we were doing. When Patty told her that she was trying to convince me to go into the village to the Shiva Temple to deposit our photographs, Maxima got up and took Patty with her, saying that she had been there many times and would be happy to lead us there. I had to go. I couldn't let Patty go into that unknown without me, but I wasn't too happy about it. Yet, as we moved along, I began to really enjoy the walk. Every new step brought another scene that was colorful and so different from what we were used to in Middle Haddam, Connecticut.

When we reached the temple, there was an old man washing the marble floor to our left. He wore a turban and a dhoti wrapped around his middle. He had a white beard and was a fairly big man with long arms and large hands. Looking back, I have to admit that the fellow reminded me of Shirdi Sai Baba, the first of the tripartite *Sai Avatara*. Shirdi has appeared to many in this age and is revered today as an *Avatar*. Well, I don't know who that old man was, but, his presence at that place and his resemblance to Shirdi Sai became a sign or a symbol for me that our prayers for our families would be heard by Bhagavan Sri Sathya Sai Baba.

I took the envelope containing the photographs out of my pocket and counted the five pictures to make sure they were all there. They were. I sealed the envelope and placed it reverently on the altar. I stood there and prayed for a blessing on each of the people in the photographs and then turned to walk away. After three or four steps, something told me to look back and as I did, there was the old man pouncing on the envelope. He looked up at me and smiled guiltily. I gave him a disappointed look, bade him leave the envelope, turned and walked back with Patty and Maxima to our shed.

Who was that old man? Was he just a villager charged with keeping the temple clean? Was he grabbing at the envelope looking for money? Or, was he Shirdi Sai Baba? I had prayed to **Sathya** Sai Baba that He not look at me. Did He send His **Shirdi** form to the temple and was it He who took the pictures as a sign of blessing on my family? I guess I will never know and Patty thinks that I sometimes let my imagination conjure up what I would like to believe. I don't know about that, but I do know that I cannot get the old man out of my mind. I see Him today almost as clearly as I saw Him that day nine years ago.

When Patty and I arrived at the shed, I began to get ready for bed. I put my hand into my pocket and there in that pocket were two of the photographs that I had left at the altar! I couldn't believe it! How could that be? I had counted the five pictures in the envelope before I left it on the altar and they were all in the envelope. Then I became very angry, not amazed at all, just angry! After all, miracles or special happenings always seem so normal when they occur. The pictures appeared to have been apported back to my pocket, but I was more concerned over the fact that I had asked for a blessing on all the people in those photographs. I imagined that the apport of the two pictures meant that Baba would not bless the two people in those photographs. One photograph was of my brother's son, Daniel, and the other was of my wife's ninety-year old godmother, aunt Lou. I could not see any significance to these two being the subjects of the photographs that were apported back to me. Daniel was only a few months old and aunt Lou was a kindly old woman in her nineties.

The next day was our last at Prasanthi Nilayam. I decided to go to early morning *darshan* and bring the two pictures with me to try to hand them to Baba. I wanted those two people blessed by Baba. Patty decided not to make *darshan* but rising early with me, she took a walk up the hill toward the University Administration Building. She wanted to be alone and to meditate. She brought her camera with her, planning to take some snapshots of the environs around the *ashram* from that high vantage point.

At *darshan*, I was seated about seven rows back and had no opportunity to hand over the pictures to Baba. I had prayed that He would not look at me and my prayer had been answered. In my eagerness to have little Danny and aunt Lou blessed by Baba, I had lost my fear and was intent only on giving Him the photographs. I was never closer than forty feet or so from Baba and His eyes averted mine. *Darshan* was soon over and I was left with the two snapshots still in my hand.

As ten thousand people got up and filtered out of the *mandir* area, I stood in that open courtyard and talked to Baba in my mind. I mentally told Him that I wasn't going to leave until He took the pictures. I told Him that I had travelled nine thousand miles to ask for a blessing on **all** the people in the five photographs that I had brought

with me to India and that included Danny and aunt Lou. I told Him I
was standing pat. He had to do something. So I stood there, with my
eyes closed talking to Him in that fashion for several minutes.
Almost no one was left in the area and I stood there like a pillar. I was
very self-conscious of where I was and how solitary I must have
looked, but I wasn't moving. I began to wonder what I would do if I
were still standing there at ten a.m., the time when our taxi was
planned to arrive from Bangalore to drive us back to the airport for
departure to other parts of India. Once again, I didn't know what I
could do. Suddenly, an idea came to me. "Send me that young man,
Baba, " I shouted mentally. There was an immediate tapping on my
left shoulder. I turned and looked into the eyes of my young
benefactor for the fourth time in less than nine hours. I never saw him
walking toward me; he must have done so, but I never saw him or
heard him approaching. I began to cry and wrapped my arms around
him. Immediately, I became embarrassed by my show of emotion.
Yet my actions didn't seem to bother him. Through tears and sobs, I
explained my story to him. I told him that I was leaving soon and
Baba did not have the photographs. I asked him if he would take
them and leave them at a holy place like an altar or shrine.

He wasn't amazed at my story; not of the apport of the
photographs or the synchronistic encounters with himself. "These
things happen here all the time," he said. He took the snapshots and
assured me that he would take care of them and make sure that they
were left at a shrine. I felt better. I realised that Baba had sent him to
me just for this purpose and I was grateful. Baba hadn't looked at me,
as I had requested, but He hadn't ignored me or my prayer. Often,
when I recounted this story to family, friends or acquaintances, they
would look at me and indicate with a nod, that yes, it was a nice story
but "maybe" I only **thought** that I had put all five photographs into
the envelope and "maybe" it was just **coincidence** that I ran into the
boy so often and "maybe" it wasn't really surprising that the young
man met me in the temple area just when I called for Baba to send
him to me, because, after all, I was standing there, all alone, easy to
see...

Yes, my little story could be "maybed" away, but in my heart, as
I stood there, I **knew** that I was in a controlled situation, because
those events moved me deeply. I just **knew**! To me, Baba had spoken
to my heart with this little *leela*, His Divine Play, and I **knew** and

believed, possibly for the first time, that He is *Avatar*, the Full Christ Consciousness on earth!

> *"Some persons have said in their ignorance*
> *that I am divine sometimes and*
> *that I become human after that!*
> *They say I alternate between*
> *Daivathwam (God) and Manavathwam (Humanness).*
> *Do not believe this.*
> *I am always of one Thwam (Universal) only.*
> *The Lord will never undergo a fundamental change..."*

Sathya Sai Speaks
Volume I
Page 180

The young man was very patient with me and by his quiet acceptance of the events, calmed me and after a while I regained my composure. Then he asked me again for the coins for his collage. I was immediately disappointed. I had felt him to be Baba's messenger and here he was again talking of money and begging from me. With a heavy heart, I made an appointment to meet him at ten a.m., our departure time, with some money and left to find Patty and tell her of my experience.

As I approached our shed, I saw Patty walking quickly, almost running toward me. Before I had a chance to say anything, she blurted out that she had just had a "miracle" occur and she was just bursting to tell me all about it. Just like a little boy, as all grown men really are, I almost pouted. I wanted to tell her **my** story! But, like all husbands, I let her tell hers first. She said that she had walked up the mountain toward the University Administration Building after she had left me that morning.   As she approached the top of the little mountain, she noticed a black man, that she recalled we had met in the Bombay Airport on our way to Puttaparthi and Sai Baba.

Having recognised him as an American, we had introduced ourselves to him and to an American lady that was standing with him. It seemed that she was flying that day to Bangalore on the same plane that we were. He had asked us if we would travel with her as she was alone. He had plans to stay in Bombay just a day or two longer. We

were delighted to have another companion on our flight and we
assured him that we would look after her.

The next time Patty saw the man was on the mountain. When she
recognised him, she was pleasantly surprised, and called out a warm,
"Sai Ram" greeting to him. He turned toward her and shouted at her.
"Stay away from me! I'm a dead man!" Patty froze. Something was
terribly wrong. He looked hysterical and his clothing was soiled and
torn. "They're coming to kill me!" His ramblings led her to understand
that he believed that the Indian devotees at the *ashram* and Sai Baba,
Himself, wanted to hurt him. "Baba's men are coming with machine
guns," he shouted. Inexplicably, Patty didn't turn and run. She tried
to gently encourage conversation. Obviously, some demon in his
own mind had brought him to the preposterous conclusion that he was
in danger of being injured by Baba in mind or body.

Whatever was tormenting him, Patty realised that he needed help
and that there was no one around to help except herself. Cautiously,
she sat down on a rock and continued talking quietly, but firmly to
him. She patiently explained that Baba loved him and has never hurt
anyone. She spoke affirmatively and tried to help him to understand
that Sai Baba was the *Avatar* of love, not a devil of discord. She
assured him that his life was not in danger. He listened.

Patty told me, at that moment, she found that the "right words"
just flowed out of her and that she felt that she was being "guided" by
Baba in what she was saying, Ordinarily, the situation would have
been frightening to most people, but not to Patty. She knew that she
was being directed by a Higher Power. She wasn't thinking of what
to say. The words seemed to speak themselves.

The man became quieter, but he still insisted that he would
never leave that mountain alive. Patty told us later that he had
attempted to take his own life because he could not "control the evil
spirits" that came to him during meditations. It took all of Patty's
strength and spiritual awareness to talk him into blocking the evil and
surrounding himself with white light. She told him that the white
light would serve as a protective shield and wouldn't allow evil spirits
or any negative energy to approach him. Obviously, having him
believe her was no easy task. His clothing was dirty and torn. He had
hammered his body with rocks and stabbed his own chest with sticks,
and yet, he seemed to listen to her.

After a lot of discussion, Patty took him by the hand and told him that she was taking him down from the mountain and that he would be okay. We were leaving on that day and, if he liked, she promised him that we would take him to Bangalore with us. He let her take his hand and she led him, bare-footed, over the stony pathway down the mountain toward the sheds. As they walked along, Patty kept talking to him about Baba, about the white light energy protecting him and assured him that he was safe. By the time they reached the Meditation Tree, Patty breathed a sigh of relief. The *ashram* was in sight. Still, she realised that she had one more challenge. She had to walk the troubled man through the crowds of devotees and she was afraid that he would panic believing that the Indian devotees would harm him. Patty felt that she needed to prepare herself for that last leg of their journey down the mountain. She told him to sit quietly as she wanted to do a meditation. Surprisingly, he did. When she was finished, they continued their walk down the mountain, past the *mandir* to the shed where he was staying. She left him there to gather his belongings and she went on to meet me coming up from *darshan*.

When she had finished explaining what she had just experienced, we set out immediately for the office in order to solicit help for Patty's friend. A couple of Seva Dal workers were sent to find him and to make sure that he received the assistance that he needed.

Later, when Patty and I reflected on this adventure, there was no doubt in our minds, that Baba had directed Patty subconsciously and sent her on her walk up the mountain. After all, what are the odds that having met this American in the Bombay airport, Patty would encounter him at that important moment up on the mountain? And why had Patty decided to skip the last *darshan* of our stay at Prasanthi? Finally, it seems that Patty was the "right" person to help this devotee. She was a woman, and therefore less to be feared at a moment when he was frightened of almost everyone. She was American, not Indian, and his spoken fear was that **Indian** devotees were out to get him. And, Patty had no racial hang-ups; she only saw a man in trouble and she reached out. She wanted to help and I believe he sensed that.

After the Seva Dals had taken over and we were comfortable that he was being assisted, I told Patty of my episode with the young man and the photographs. She was amazed that the young student had come to my aid once again and in those strange circumstances. And, try as we might, we couldn't figure out why the photographs of Danny and aunt Lou had been apported back to my pocket.

Ten o'clock was approaching and we gathered up our baggage and brought it down in front of the office where our taxi was expected. My young benefactor was there waiting for us. I told him I had money for his school "project," and pulled a five dollar bill out of my pocket and handed it to him. I was still disappointed that this fellow who had been Baba's instrument to touch me spiritually, was so materialistically inclined. He took the bill and looked at it quizzically. "What is this?" he asked. "Well, you wanted American money," was my reply. "Sir," he said, Baba has only authorised me to ask for **small coins** of different nations not large amounts!" To my embarrassment, he refused the bill. I was angry at myself for being so judgmental of the boy's intent. I should have taken him at his word, and presumed that Baba's students could be trusted. He hadn't let me down, I had let him down.

I apologised, muttering something about "misunderstanding," knowing fully well, that this intelligent young man knew exactly what I had been thinking. I gave him the coins that he needed and hugged him goodby. As we prepared to enter the taxi, we could see Patty's friend from the mountain top, sitting quietly in the office. He looked exhausted. We left him in Baba's care and drove off the *ashram*.

I'd like to share a short postscript about the two people in the two snapshots that were aported back to me from the envelope which I left at the altar. Aunt Lou was about ninety-years old when we had left for India. She was alert and still driving an automobile, but within a year of our return to the States, aunt Lou had so deteriorated mentally, that she was unable to recognise family and had to be placed in a convalescent care facility.

Danny was only about a year old when we set off to visit Sathya Sai Baba and seemed to be a beautiful, healthy baby. By the time that he was three years old, it became obvious that Danny was not developing normally. Soon thereafter, Danny was diagnosed as being autistic. When Patty and I reflected back on our experience with the two pictures of aunt Lou and Danny, we could only surmise that Baba was telling us that with these two, there were to be problems, karmic or otherwise, that could not be changed.

During our flight back to America, Patty was very quiet and reflective at one point. When I asked her what she was thinking, she said that she thought that the two events, the man on the mountain and the student and the photographs, were controlled events that we had no power to direct.   Those events were Baba's drama. He was the playwright and the director. We had been simply the actors in His play.

"You are only actors on the stage, before the footlights.
The Director who knows the play, who assigns the rolls,
who gives the cues, who calls you in
and puts you on--He is behind the curtain.
You are a puppet; He holds the strings.
If He must be seen you have to be His Sakha (friend)
or Bandhua (kinsman)."

Sathya Sai Speaks
Volume VI
Page 294

CHAPTER 15

THE STONE

*"Without His Will,
No single blade of grass can quiver in the breeze"*

My Baba and I
Dr. John Hislop
Page 171

As part of my preparations to travel to Prasanthi Nilayam in India, I had intended to bring a stone with me, any old stone, taken from our yard at home. I had planned to drop it on the ground amid the gravel of the *ashram* in exchange for a stone that I would select there, to be brought back to our home in the United States. My intent was that the exchange of stones would be a sign of unity between Baba and me and a symbol of blessing upon my home and family. On the surface, it seems a silly exercise, but to me, it was important. It would be an overt act with a material object that would help to remind myself of my connection to the *Avatar*.

Well, in the hustle and bustle of getting ready to travel to India, I forgot to bring a stone with me. When we had boarded our 747 and were on our way to India, I realised that I had no stone to leave on the sands of Prasanthi Nilayam. I was very upset with myself. After reaching the *ashram*, I was besieged with an attack of scruples about what to do. Should I take a stone **from** the *ashram* even though I didn't bring one **to** the *ashram*? Should I simply not take one? Would I create negative *Karma* by taking one? Would Baba want me to take one anyway? Oh, how I wanted to take a stone! I agonised over the decision. I felt that if I didn't take this symbol of Baba's Grace, it would be an affirmation that Baba would not bless me. Finally, I decided that I was being silly. I wanted the symbol of Baba's blessing and I couldn't bear to think that I couldn't have it. I searched for a small stone on the ground in front of the *mandir* and selected one. I brought the stone back to the shed and placed it in one of our bags. Later in Bangalore, I purposefully stored the stone in a compartment of one of our bigger suitcases for transportation home.

When we returned to the United States, I went to the bag, opened the compartment and searched for the stone. It wasn't there! I searched again. I looked through the other bags. No, I ransacked them! The stone was nowhere to be found. I tried to remember if I had put the stone somewhere else, but I knew that I hadn't. I knew where I had placed the stone in the bag. No, it was gone and I was terribly depressed. Finally, I faced the only explanation of what could have happened to that stone, as incredible as it seemed. Baba had somehow taken the stone back. He had dematerialised it, apported it, whatever; it didn't matter how He did it, I just believed that He did take it. He took back the stone! I had not lived up to my end of the bargain. I had not **brought** a stone from home. I had no right to **take** a stone from Him.

> *"Practice what you preach;*
> *be what you profess to be.*
> *Your word and your work*
> *have to tally.*
> *Keep your senses and the mind*
> *under rigorous control..."*

Sai Avatar
Volume II
Page 201

CHAPTER 16

HIS COMPASSION

*"It is the Compassion
of the Avathar
that prompts His every Activity"*

Sathya Sai Speaks
Volume VII
Page 292

At Prasanthi Nilayam, we had designated our shed the "westerners family shed" because, at first, the residents were mostly western families and couples. There was a mother and her adult son from the United Nations Sai Center in New York, a French couple, a mother, father and two little girls from Germany and many more from the United States and Europe. But as it got closer to Baba's birthday, more and more people arrived and had to be housed where practical. Soon the population of our shed was augmented by the arrival of many Indian families, who like the earlier occupants, set up little cubicles or marked off space for themselves on the concrete floor.

Speaking of concrete floors, we were delighted that we had listened to Edna Yuile and others who had encouraged us to bring air mattresses to sleep on. It took quite a while to fill them puff by puff, but it was worth it. Because of those mattresses, we had a chance at a good night's sleep in spite of mosquitoes, mosquito netting, partitions made of sheets and the hard concrete floor.

A day after we had constructed our cubicle, a young mother from France arrived with her young son, Stephen (not his real name), and laid out blankets or mats on the firm concrete floor. Rumour had it that the young woman intended to reside permanently in Prasanthi and wanted Baba to accept her son in the school at the *ashram*. Patty and I thought the little guy was adorable. He couldn't speak English and we couldn't speak French, but he communicated to us with the most angelic smile and luminous eyes. We were concerned about his sleeping on the concrete, softened only by a reed mat.

When we were breaking down our cubicle on our last day at the *ashram*, we decided that we would leave our mosquito netting and sheets with the German couple who occupied an area across an aisle from us. They and their daughters had been in the shed for a while but had no protection from the monstrous mosquitoes. We hoped that they would set up the nets for their two little girls. I don't remember them being in their space when we left the material for them. We simply folded everything up neatly and placed the netting on their blankets.

We decided to take our air mattresses home. I don't know why we didn't just resolve to leave them there with someone as we had with the mosquito netting, but we didn't. I pulled out the nozzle on the first one, squeezed the air out of it, folded it up and packed it in our bag. Then, I took the second one, pulled out its nozzle and tried to press the air out of it but no air came out! I checked the nozzle; it was open and yet no air was escaping. I pressed again. Nothing. I squeezed. Nothing. I folded it in two and compressed it. Nothing. I walked on it. Nothing. The air just would not come out. I was dumbfounded. There was no reason why the air should not have escaped into the atmosphere. The nozzle was wide open!

Finally, Patty said: "Maybe, Baba wants us to leave it here for someone, Chuck." I looked at her blankly as her words sunk in. "Yes, you're right!" I agreed. "But for whom?" I asked her. "Maybe for little Stephen?" she mused. "Yes, yes, that's perfect, " I happily concurred. I brought the mattress over to where Stephen and his mother had set up camp. She was nowhere to be seen, but Stephen was sitting on his mat. When he saw me, he smiled broadly. I made him understand with primitive sign language that we were leaving the mattress for him. When he grasped our intent, he literally beamed from ear to ear. Giving him that gift and seeing his pleasure in receiving it was a great joy to both Patty and me.

Yet, Patty and I can't take credit for thinking of leaving the mattress with Stephen, after all, we couldn't take it with us, not fully inflated as it was. We had to leave it. No, it was all Baba's doing. In the purest sense, He took the mattress from us and gave it to Stephen, who had a real need for it. We were awed by Baba's omniscience. He **knew** we had no further use for the mattress and he **knew** that this young child was sleeping, separated from the concrete, only by a flimsy mat. We were moved by His **compassion**. He was obviously concerned about the well-being of that little boy.

What struck Patty and me, as we thought of what had happened with that mattress, was the realisation that Baba controlled our thoughts, making us think of little Stephen and He controlled an inanimate, material object like that mattress making it impossible to release the air contents, even though the nozzle was wide open and air should have been swiftly flowing out!

Although we left Stephen that mattress, we didn't leave the other one for his mother. We took it with us. Why, I can't explain. The thought just never entered our minds. Looking back at it now, the best explanation that I can come up with is that Baba did not intend that she should have that little comfort. I certainly make no judgments, but I am amazed that somehow we never thought to give her the other mattress. I am convinced that our thoughts were being controlled, otherwise, I am positive that just handing the one air mattress to Stephen, would have triggered an impulse in us to leave the other one for his mother.

> *"I am the Master,*
> *the Sakthi (power)*
> *that overpowers everything else."*

> Sathya Sai Speaks
> Volume III
> Page 24

CHAPTER 17

OPEN MY EYES LORD

*"God makes the dumb speak
and the lame leap across the mountains."*

<u>Baba: Sathya Sai Part 1</u>
Page 390
Ra. Ganapati

Sometime during the winter of 1986, just a few months after
Patty and I had returned from India, I came home after work to find
our son, Garrett, sleeping on the couch in the family room. Patty came
home a few minutes later and we agreed to let him sleep until dinner
was ready. When the meal was set on the table, Patty asked me to
rouse Garrett. I called to him and got no response. I went over to him
and gently shook him. No response! Immediately frightened, I shook
him violently. No response! I shouted to Patty. She rushed to the
phone to call 911 or an ambulance, I'm not sure which. Feeling that
he might be dying, I scooped him up in my arms, ran to the door and
asked Patty to forget calls, I was taking him to the emergency room
in Middletown. She followed after me. I asked her to sit in the
passenger's seat and I placed our comatose fourteen year old in her
lap.

As we drove to the hospital we kept the radio blaring, the
windows open to the cold winter air and Patty kept slapping Garrett's
face to try to awaken him. He was breathing and alive but not
responsive to any action to revive him. We got him into the hospital
and the hospital staff immediately wheeled him to an examination
room where a doctor was able to awaken him. Garrett was groggy
and confused, but alive and we were greatly relieved.

Now the question was: What had caused his blackout? The
doctor told us that he suspected drugs or alcohol. We told the doctor
that we didn't believe that was the problem as we had never had any
evidence of Garrett using any mind altering substances. The doctor
stood his ground and blood tests were ordered. Patty and I were
dumbfounded when the tests came back showing a 3.0 alcohol level!
In Connecticut, a 1.0 rating is legally drunk.; 2.0 is serious inebriation
for an adult. 3.0 is dangerously close to death and our son was no
adult. Even for a fourteen-year old, Garrett was very slight, weighing

less than 100 lbs. He could have died! In fact, I have often wondered what would have happened if we hadn't rushed him directly to the hospital that night.

At once, the parent in both Patty and me reacted strongly. We were both relieved that he was okay but livid that he had been drinking. We questioned him intensely about why he drank and how he had gotten so drunk? Garrett was adamant that it had never happened before. This was the first time, he said. He told us that there had been some wine coolers in the refrigerator and that he wanted to try some.

We were terribly upset and quite emotional. We so wanted to believe him, that it never really occurred to us to consider how many wine coolers he would have had to drink to get so terribly sick and pass out. Patty did not consume very much alcohol and I did not drink at all. We were just not attuned to what signs might have alerted us to Garrett using drugs or alcohol.

Several months passed and in mid June, we put Garrett on a plane for a trip to California to visit his biological father. While Garrett was gone, Patty's mother called and told Patty that Garrett had stolen money from his uncle Drew and had been associating with another young boy who had been using drugs. All of this occurred at the Connecticut shore when Garrett had spent a weekend with his grandmother just a few weeks before. When Patty told me of the call, it was as if blinders had been removed from my eyes. I had been in the habit of leaving my money on my bureau in the evenings. On several occasions, a ten or twenty dollar bill had been missing when I gathered up my cash the following day. At first, I attributed the shortfall to misplacing it or having spent more than I thought. Never did it enter my mind that my son would have taken anything from me! But now, I knew that he had been stealing from me all along. I was just too blind or too naive to realise what was happening.

Patty thought that if Garrett had taken money from me and money from his uncle, there was every reason to suspect that he would do the same thing to his father in California. We called Gary to warn him that Garrett might be drinking or using drugs and to be careful about money. Gary responded that he knew that Garrett had been taking money from him also. After talking with Gary, Patty and I decided that we would let Garrett finish his California visit because we were not sure what we were going to do about the problem. Since we wanted him to return home and not run away, we were afraid of accusing him at such a great distance.

While waiting for Garrett's return, Patty began rising before dawn each day to go out on the deck overlooking the Connecticut River, to pray for Garrett; to meditate on what had been happening and to contemplate a plan of action that would be constructive and help Garrett and our family. Finally, she arrived at that space where she left Garrett's recovery in God's hands and subject to His Divine Will. I would like to share with the reader Patty's own words about her meditations on Garrett during this emotional period:

> "I would come downstairs and go out onto the deck at dawn just as the sky began to lighten. I'd sit in a lawn chair overlooking the river. I'd send my petitions to God in the form of light, then just state: 'Thy will be done,' and I surrendered the result to God. I'd sit silently emptying my mind at that point and just meditate. It was during those quiet times that God spoke to me, not in words, but in ideas, visions of the next steps for me to take. My conscious mind was too overwhelmed to know what to do, plus I was guilt-ridden about somehow having failed as a parent for this to happen. My subconscious mind took over, being led by the voice within."

We had no idea of treatment sites and no knowledge of where to go, so she started with her insurance carrier who told her that Elmcrest Hospital was located within five miles of our home and that it was recognised as one of the better facilities in the area. Patty was very pleased. If Garrett were placed at Elmcrest, she would be able to visit him easily by just stopping in on him after she left work. The hospital was on her way home. But there was a problem. A psychiatrist was needed to recommend the placement of Garrett to the hospital. Since Garrett had not been treating with a psychiatrist, we didn't know if we could get a placement. Patty had a friend whose husband was a psychiatrist. He agreed that he would make the placement after having seen Garrett and making a judgment about whether placement might help him. We made our plans to get Garrett to the doctor as soon as he returned from California.

We picked Garrett up from the airport in the evening and drove home. We acted as if nothing were wrong as it was late and we saw no advantage to having him worry all night about what was about to happen. Further, we didn't know if he would bolt and run away because of the threat of placement. So, we told him nothing of our plan that night, but the next morning, at breakfast, we laid out all our information and confronted him with our evidence. He didn't deny anything. We took him to the psychiatrist immediately. After meeting with Garrett alone for about an hour, the doctor had enough information to make his decision. Garrett was certified in to the hospital for treatment of drug and alcohol abuse and possibly, addiction.

The treatment was very difficult for Garrett and for us. The hospital taught a "tough love" type programme where rules had to be observed and Patty and I had to be trained in standing firm when confronted with Garrett's rebellion. At first he was very defiant. On one occasion, he demanded that we bring him cigarettes. Well, cigarettes weren't allowed and we weren't about to help him **break** the rules. We didn't even know that he smoked. He was addicted to them also. He was almost disdainful of us, as he fought against allowing anybody to help him.

And, of course, since we had been so blind and hadn't seen any of this happening, we questioned ourselves as parents. It was a very difficult time, especially for Patty who blamed herself. **"If"** became a big word in our home. She would say: **"If** I weren't working, this would never have happened because I would have been home." Or she felt that she had been too selfish. **"If"** we hadn't socialised so much and paid more attention to the kids..."

But, as I said, Patty had prayed and meditated and consigned Garrett to the will of God. All the **"ifs"** in the world didn't matter, really. She had done all that she could do. The situation was now in the heart of God and she could only wait and hope. Garrett had only been at Elmcrest a short while, when we were asked to meet with the psychologist that was working with Garrett. When we saw his name on the door of his office, we knew instantly that Patty's prayers had been heard. That name was: "Abraham **Avasar**." Obviously, the "sign" or "symbol" that we recognised and which put our minds at ease, was the similarity between the word, *"Avatar"* and the name *"Avasar."* It was all we needed to immediately believe that Baba had taken over and that Garrett was in His hands. Some might feel that we were straining to find anything that would give us hope that Garrett would be all right and maybe that was part of our good feeling on seeing that name, but it wasn't the whole story. Both of us intuitively felt assured, deep down in our hearts, that Baba was telling us: "I am here. Do not fear. Garrett is mine!" Somehow, we knew that Baba was in control and we could release the fear to him.

The second part of Abraham Avasar's name was also a sign for us. In the Bible, the Patriarch, Abraham, was he who was willing to sacrifice his own son to the will of God. Baba seemed to be telling us to leave it to His Will and that He would take care of Garrett. Patty had reached that point through her meditations; I needed confirmation of Baba's protection of Garrett and I received it in the symbol, the name, "Abraham Avasar."

Garrett's road to recovery at Elmcrest was not easy. For a while, he fought the therapy and the staff and us, tooth and nail. Then, slowly, we began to see changes in his attitude. It became very clear that he had begun to love Abe Avasar, who, we realised, was genuinely interested in Garrett. When Garrett was ready for release into an out patient program, a group meeting with Abe, other patients, their parents, Garrett and Patty and me was held one evening. Everyone was asked to speak their mind and heart; the parents about their kids and their progress; the kids about their own growth and feelings. It was a very emotional evening as each one in turn spilled out their turmoil in a flood of emotion. When it was Garrett's turn, I really didn't expect him to say anything. Garrett's anger is often handled in a passive aggressive mode, where he fights back by not confronting or talking.

But, wow, did he surprise us! He looked squarely at Abe Avasar and told him that he **loved** him and explained how much Abe had come to mean to him. With his eyes filled with tears, Garrett told Abe that he had mixed emotions about leaving Elmcrest, because on the one hand, he wanted to end the confinement, but on the other hand, he didn't want to leave Abe. As Patty and I witnessed Garrett's emotions, hung out there for all to see, our own feelings flowed to the surface and we joined right in with alternating smiles and tears. By the end of the session, we were all pretty happy because the evening had been a wonderful, cleansing process where honest feelings were freely exchanged. We all felt hopeful for the future.

Garrett continued with a psychologist for a while, and participated in an out patient programme at Elmcrest with Patty and me. He began attending Narcotics Anonymous and Alcoholics Anonymous meetings in and around Middletown. He enjoyed them and stayed straight. But in his senior year of high school, Garrett and I argued and he decided to move out of our home. It was a horrible, wrenching time, especially for Patty and me, but the die had been cast and there was nothing to do but let him go. At eighteen years of age, one is considered legally an adult in Connecticut, and we had no way to keep him from moving away.

As much as we would have preferred that he not leave home, his going proved to be a pivotal action toward the good for Garrett. He finished high school while living on his own, remained active in the N.A. and A.A. programs, found an apartment, a job, began playing the bass guitar, formed a band and basically took care of himself. And all the while, he remained straight; no drugs, no alcohol. I know that he has been instrumental in helping many others remain drug and alcohol free. In many ways Garrett became my hero. He had a problem, he faced it and is beating it every day.

"Follow the Master, face the devil,
fight to the end and finish the game."

Sathya Sai Speaks
Volume X
Page 66

Garrett has been "clean" since the age of fourteen. He is now twenty-three. He doesn't drink alcohol, do drugs, or eat meat. He is very conscious of losing his place in life to addiction. He has taken a high path and Patty and I are very proud of his accomplishment. Also, the whole experience affirmed our belief that Sathya Sai Baba was there, active in our lives; aware of Garrett's challenge and responsive to Patty's cry for help. There is no doubt in Patty's mind or mine that all five of our children, not just Garrett, are being looked after and guided by Sathya Sai Baba. We are intensely aware that since we left the pictures of our family on the altar of the Shiva

Temple marking the spot of Baba's birth, they have been within His orbit of Grace, Love and Protection.

"The senses should not be allowed
to override man.
They must be instruments
within the control of man."

<u>Sathya Sai Speaks</u>
Volume V
Page 264

CHAPTER 18

THE SPIRALING JOURNEY INWARD

"When the sun is directly over your head
there will be no shadow.
So, too, when faith is steady in your mind
it will not cast shadows of doubt."

Teachings of Sri Satya Sai Baba
Chapter "Faith"
Page 99

Soon after Garrett had left home to live on his own, Leo Perrin, a bishop of a small congregation of a church blending Christianity and New Age concepts, asked Patty to speak to the members one Sunday. Patty had trouble selecting a topic to present. She was also unsure of the format that she would use in presenting whatever topic she finally chose. After much reflection, she decided to discuss the different milestones in her spiritual life; those events that defined her beliefs and guided her gently in new directions. Patty started her talk with prayer. She then walked around the small congregation sitting in a prayer circle and looked into the eyes of each person. She asked for their love and prayer that her talk would be meaningful to them. In order to evoke a clear image of the milestones, she diagrammed a spiral, writing each major spiritual event in her life, chronologically along the spiral. She spoke of yoga and pranayam, of meditation and ashram-hopping. She talked about astral projection, classes with Shirley McLaine and past life regressions. As she worked on the diagram, she realised that all of her spiritual high points were heading or pointing toward the central core of the spiral figure. In a flash of insight, she knew that the core, the center, was Baba! Patty says that on that day, with that realisation, she was reborn spiritually. She recognised that she was and had been a devotee of Bhagavan Sri Sathya Sai Baba.

Her intuitive cognition of her relationship with Baba had a positive meaning for me too. It meant that we could walk the Sai path **together.** My journey would not be a lonely one. For Patty, it meant the freedom to divinise her activity in Baba's name. She adopted Baba's concept of selfless service. She would henceforth offer her action and work to God.

At Leo's service that Sunday, after Patty had presented her talk using the spiral, an announcement was made that a five minute work stoppage to allow people throughout Connecticut to silently reflect on the evil of drug abuse was being encouraged for all businesses and State offices. Obviously, the subject of encouraging people to fight the cancer of illicit drugs and their debilitating effect on individuals and society was personal to Patty because of what she had lived through with our son, Garrett. So right after she had this experience that Baba was at the center of her spiritual life, a perfect opportunity for selfless service to others presented itself. She decided to participate fully in the symbolic work stoppage programme.

From her position as Deputy Director at Community Action for Greater Middletown, a social service agency dedicated to providing services to those in need, she organized not just a work stoppage, but a gathering on Main Street in Middletown, Connecticut, wherein about three hundred people including young school children, the homeless, shop owners, businessmen, professionals and, yes, our son Garrett, stood holding hands in a giant circle in the middle of the road, maintaining prayerful silence, while respectful police officers diverted traffic and protected the human mandala. An inner circle consisted of day care children and preschoolers from the Head Start programme. Photographers from the local newspapers took photos from the upper windows of the St. Vincent de Paul Soup Kitchen and homeless shelter. And there I stood, in my three piece-suit, holding hands with street people and gazing lovingly at my wife and son. Those were five minutes of total silence speaking profound volumes and for once, I was Sai-lent. With Garrett's hand in hers, Patty knew that Baba was in that circle, holding hands with us too!

"The lotus on the lake is far, far away from the sun;
but distance is no bar for the dawn of love;
the lotus blooms as soon as the sun peeps over the horizon."

Sai Baba Avatar
A New Journey into Power and Glory
Howard Murphet
Chapter 19
Page 149

CHAPTER 19

DEATH WHERE IS THY STING?[1]

"Everyone has to make his exit some day;
that movement should not be a moment of anguish;
one should depart gracefully,
with a smile and a bow."

Sathya Sai Speaks
Volume I
Chapter 3
Page 26

After Patty and I first heard of Sathya Sai Baba, Arthur and Edna Yuile helped us to learn more of Him by answering our questions and supplying us with books and tapes to help satisfy our eagerness to learn more. Art and Edna had been blessed to travel to India several times to see and hear Sai Baba. They had been granted several interviews, and experienced the joy of being in close proximity to Baba on several occasions. At the time that we became acquainted, the Windsor Sai Center met every Thursday in their home. Edna invited us to visit the Center and we did on several occasions. When Igor Sikorsy encouraged us to travel to Sai Baba to "see for ourselves" who and what He is, it was Edna who helped us prepare for the trip. She talked with us by phone and met with us to inform us what to do, what to bring and what to expect. When we returned from India, Patty and I didn't join a Center right away, but on occasion when we attended services, it was at the Sathya Sai Baba Center in Windsor with Art and Edna.

Art had always lived an active life, participating in such strenuous sports as downhill skiing and sailboat racing. He was a fighter pilot during the Second World War and flew in the Battle of Britain. But, over the years, and certainly since we knew him, Art became ill with diabetes which was diagnosed when he was only twenty four and serving with the Royal Canaadian Air Force in Alaska and emphysema, which he contracted later in life. At different times, while in his company, Art had told Patty that he felt that he had

---

1 Corinthians 15: 55-56

completed his time and purpose on earth and that he was not afraid to die. Actually, Art had already looked death squarely in the eye, having been shot down twice during the war and survived! Patty was struck with Art's apparent lack of anxiety or fear over the prospect of death and the matter of fact attitude that he had about it. Finally, Art's condition took a turn for the worse. In addition to his previous medical problems, he was diagnosed as having a melanoma tumor on his brain.

Art was given a maximum of six months to live. In fact, he lived only about three and a half months from the time of diagnosis. Edna told us that by Baba's Grace, Art didn't feel that he suffered during that time. Then, suddenly, he took a bad seizure and was confined to bed for eleven days before he died. During all that time he had a smile on his face in spite of the fact that he couldn't speak. Edna remembers the incredible feeling of love in the room where Art lay. She did not like to leave its aura. In the quiet of that room, Art appeared at peace.

When I was first informed of the gravity of Art's condition, I phoned Edna and asked if I could come for a visit. Edna agreed even though she was trying to keep visits to a minimum as Art was very weak. When I arrived, I waited for about fifteen minutes until Art was awake and prepared to receive visitors. Edna led me in. I was very nervous and concerned about how to act or what to say as I had never had the experience of talking with a man or woman, who I knew was about to die. Edna stood on one side of him and I stood on the other. She leaned down and told him that I was there. He opened his eyes for a moment, smiled and held my hand. I told him that I had wanted to tell him a joke or two, but I could only think of an off-coloured one and I knew that wasn't appropriate. He smiled broadly with his eyes closed as if to say: "It's okay Chuck, I understand that you are uncomfortable, but I am happy that you are here." That smile relaxed me and I was able to talk easily to him for a while. I say, "to him," because Art was not able to communicate with me verbally, but did communicate with his expressions. I can't remember most of what I said that day, except that I asked him to pray for me when he came into the presence of the Spirit of Baba, and Art smiled warmly at that. I leaned over and kissed him. I was surprised at myself for doing that, but I wanted to and it was good.

Edna told me that she had been with Art when he died on August 3, 1990, Patty's birthday. Patty always had a warm and loving feeling for Art and so that coincidence was meaningful to her. I guess it was a sign of the influence that Art and Edna have had on our journey to Sathya Sai Baba. Art died a conscious death and was aware that he was dying. Just before the end, he sat up and looking at Edna with eyes as big as saucers, he mouthed the words, though no sound came out: "Good-by, good-by, good-by!" Then he lay back on to the pillow and passed over. Edna told us that she felt the energy leaving his body and had a powerful sense of Art being one with Baba. She saw and felt two rays of light, peace and power pass from Art's eyes, entering her own body! She knew that the rays were sent by Baba and Art, **together.** Because of that realization, she never felt depressed that Art had left this plane.

Art's gentle passing showed me how death could be when the dying is a man or woman of faith and devotion. There was no fear in Art, only certainty, calm and conviction that there was no more to do in this world, and that it was okay to go.

"Think 'I am separate from the body.
This body is just a water bubble.
I am separate from the mind.
This mind is just a mad monkey.
I am the conscience.
I am the Atma.
I and God are one.'
Think like this.
Before this body formed, you were there.
You are omnipresent.
You are the unchanging Atma.
You are the all."

Bhagavan's Interview With
Foreign Devotees at Kodaikanal
April, 1985

It was true that Patty and Art got along very nicely. I remember that Patty, who now enjoys bhajan singing, told Art after we had returned from our first trip to India, that she didn't enjoy the Hindi and Sanskrit bhajans because she didn't understand what she was saying. A few weeks later, Edna, Art, Patty and I met for lunch at a small Italian restaurant. Art had brought along two English *bhajan* (devotional songs) audio tapes. Patty was very pleased with Art's thoughtfulness. She played those tapes all the time and thoroughly enjoyed them. On the very day that Art died, Patty was driving her car, listening to one of those English tapes. She knew that Art had passed on. The particular *bhajan* that was playing on the car stereo was "Love, Love, Love." There is one stanza in that song that made Patty think of Art and be aware of his presence:

> "Love, Love, Love,
> Love is God!
> Live, Live, Live,
> Live in Love!
> God is in you, With you,
> Above you, Around you,
> and Behind you!"

Driving alone in the car and listening to those words, Patty started crying. She said that she felt that Art was trying to tell her that he was merged in the All and was part of God!. Art was with her, in her, above her, around her and behind her!

Before he died, Art had specifically requested a memorial service. He told Edna that he wanted "no funeral." Edna arranged for the service which was centered in Sai Baba. It was simple and devotional with *bhajan* singing by devotees. Edna had the room filled with orange tiger lilies as a symbol of Baba. Patty mentioned to her that it was a wonderful coincidence that those lilies were in bloom around the date of Art's passing. "Baba completely looked after everything," Edna told us, referring to the details of Art's memorial service. She feels that He has taken care of her ever since. Edna remembers, as I do not, that I told Art on that last visit, that I would "look after Edna." The truth is, that she looks after me. We get together regularly for lunch just to talk and share our devotion to Sai Baba and she is the "source" for most of my awareness about new Baba books. Both Art and Edna have been important teachers for Patty and me. I know that Edna is one of the "angels" that Sai has sent me for my own spiritual uplift and growth, and Art has helped

Patty and me to understand that death is a necessary step on the path
to mergence with the Divine.

> *"Man is the child of Immortality*
> *swirling along helplessly towards Death!*
> *But the Immortal in him is awaiting discovery*
> *to confer bliss and liberation*
> *from birth and death.*
> *Cross the ocean of Death and Birth*
> *and be Children of Immortality."*

Baba The Breath of Sai
Page 119

CHAPTER 20

HIS ANGEL

"Everything that is born must die;
Everything that is constructed will disintegrate.
But you can escape death, by not being born again.
When you know that you are the limitless Self,
you are no longer subjected
to the limitation of birth.
That is the secret."

<u>Baba The Breath of Sai</u>
Page 148

Of all the people who have wound their way across my path, the one person who stands out most clearly in my memory is Aida Bellerose, the elderly psychic who I think of as my "third grandmother." From the time of my divorce, she was intricately a part of my life's pattern, encouraging me and urging me to carry on and to continue in spite of my perception that Fate had dealt me an unwanted and undeserved disruption of my family that I never anticipated. At first, in my despair, she was counselour; later she became a friend and finally she was family. I visited her regularly and Patty and I picked her up from time to time to visit with us at our home or to go on an excursion. I remember, once, helping to carry her in a chair from our car to a spot on the town green in Glastonbury, Connecticut, to watch the Drifters, a rock and roll singing group, famous in the 1950's and 1960's, reprise some of their hits from that era. She was in her eighties and had no appreciation of rock music at all, but was delighted to be with us and happy that we had brought her to a place filled with people and activity and life. Having to be carried in bothered her not at all. Of all that can be said of Aida, the most descriptive is that this lady loved people and loved life.

Aida claimed that when she was about five or six years old, an angel appeared to her and told her that she could choose, then and there, whether to grow old with a strong body or with a strong mind. She chose a strong mind. Her story seemed plausible because in her nineties, Aida was still sharp and aware, while many of those around her were mentally enfeebled, or senile or fighting Alzheimer's Disease. Shortly after the appearance of the angel, a tragic accident occurred during the harvest time at the family farm. Aida's leg was caught in a threshing machine driven by her father. She had pushed her younger sister out of the way of the oncoming thresher and did not have time to escape herself. From that early age, Aida was an amputee

At about the age of six years, she became aware that she had a multifaceted psychic ability to "read" the past and future of people by psychometry, automatic writing, and mediumship. Although her mother chastised her for her claims, her grandmother surreptitiously encouraged the young Aida to continue to develop her God-given talents. She claimed to converse with spirits and seemed at home both in the material world and in the world of spirit.

As she grew older, she developed a keen interest in the world around her, reading one or two newspapers a day, and listening to television newscasts regularly. She read books incessantly, especially the Bible and esoterica. She was always up to date on what was going on in the world, alert and intelligent and wonderfully able to converse on many subjects from the politics of the day to mysticism. It was delightful to talk with her. She could always teach you something that you didn't know before.

In her late eighties, Aida began to fail physically. With her wooden leg and constant, painful arthritis, she could no longer walk or go upstairs to her room. She had been living with her sixty-year old daughter who had taken care of her, moving her, helping her from bed, bathing her, changing her clothes and attaching her prosthesis. Then her daughter had a heart attack. Overnight, Aida's security was shattered with no one able to help her; no one to bathe her or lift her in and out of chairs or even cook for her.

Aida and her daughter's family had lived in a large two storey home in Glastonbury, Connecticut. It was more than sufficient for them especially after the grandchildren had moved out leaving Aida, her daughter and son-in-law. But now, the house was too big. The daughter was told that she should not be climbing stairs or cleaning such a large place. The decision to sell the house was made. Aida's daughter needed to move into a small, one-storey, ranch-style house. The problem was that she did not know how to tell her mother that she was no longer able to care for her. She was desperate! Her reaction was to avoid telling Aida anything, hoping that one of Aida's many friends would come to her rescue. But none of Aida's friends could take her in because her fragile condition required more attention than they were able to handle. Soon Aida realised the situation and became frightened that she would have no place to go to. The family made plans to move, but no one did anything about Aida because they simply didn't **know** what to do. Finally, in desperation, Aida called Patty.

When Patty was made aware of the problem, she decided to be honest with Aida. The only possible alternative was to place Aida in a rest home for the elderly and to fund her stay with help from the State of Connecticut under the Title 19 programme. The family was very relieved that someone had answers and even though Aida would rather have lived at home with her family, she realised the special needs that she had and she recognised that her family and friends could not meet those needs. In one sense, she felt betrayed and yet, she knew the inevitable had indeed happened.

Patty and I worried a great deal about Aida even after Patty arranged her acceptance as a resident in the rest home. We were afraid that no one would visit her and that her mind would eventually deteriorate. Yet, our fears were unfounded. The manager of the home told me that Aida received more visitors per day than any other resident living there. Her family visited her as did old friends. The Mormons sent visitors to share time with her because Aida had a daughter in Utah that was a member of the Mormon faith. Dozens of people still came to see her for psychic readings as her gift of knowing was undiminished. Many of these people for whom Aida "read," came back to see her not for psychic information but just because they considered this wonderful lady their friend.

Patty and I visited Aida weekly. We often took her to our home on holidays like Christmas Eve as part of our family. Our kids were in awe of her. They knew that she was a great psychic and they never knew if she knew what they were thinking. Of course, as long as I knew Aida, she never misused her gift, so I don't believe there was ever a time that she intruded on our thoughts or life without invitation.

I remember one characteristic of Aida that always impressed me. She was very tolerant of all religions and religious beliefs. For instance, she had been a Protestant minister when she was much younger. Later, she became involved with a spiritualist society, and in loving consideration for her daughter's beliefs, Aida allowed herself to be baptised into the Mormon faith. Some might judge her ungrounded, but , in reality, Aida just believed in God and the world around her and all of the paths that led up the mountain to divinity were okay with her.

> *"Religions are many but the road is the same;*
> *Flowers are many but worship is the same;*
> *Professions are many but living is the same.*
> *Therefore, you must all live in concord and brotherliness,*
> *helping each other and loving each other."*

Sathya Sai Speaks
Volume II
Page 42

She had a deep faith in Jesus and when she talked of Him, she called Him, "the Master." After knowing her for several years, Aida shared with me her belief that Jesus was reborn again and living on the earth. She didn't know where or in what form or how old He was, but her faith was strong that He was here again. I told her of Sathya Sai Baba and His claim to be an *Avatar*, or a vertical descent of the Godhead into manifestation. I explained to her Baba's explanation that Jesus never said: "I will return," but rather: "He who sent Me will come again." Baba stated that He was the Christ Consciousness that had sent Jesus into the world.

Peggy Mason and Ron Laing
Sai Baba, The Embodiment of Love
Book Two
Chapter 3
Page 152

Aida just looked at me, nodded her head and said: "Yes, maybe, you are right." Anyway, whatever her personal beliefs, she never discouraged mine or any one else's as far as I remember. I brought her books on Sai Baba and sometimes gave her *vibhuthi* when she wasn't feeling well. She always accepted the gift and in the case of the books, read them from cover to cover. There is an old saying : "Rejection of a gift is rejection of the giver." Aida never did that. She was always acceptance and unconditional love.

"No being is to be looked down upon
as secondary, inferior, unimportant or expendable.
Each has its allotted role
in the drama designed by the Almighty."

<u>Seva, A Flower At His Feet</u>
Page 188

Once, when Patty went to visit her, Aida told her that she had been having trouble sleeping at night because of the pain of arthritis. Patty led her in a guided meditation to take her out of her body so that she would not feel the pain but it did persist. One day she told Patty that Angel nuns with no faces and no feet had been coming to comfort her. She said they covered her with a gossamer blanket and the pain would go away allowing her to sleep peacefully. About the time that she told Patty of these angelic visitations, Aida began to tell us that she wanted to "go" and had been praying to die. She was over ninety-years old and in constant pain. Most of her waking hours, she was confined to a chair, unable even to walk down the hall. Once her eyesight failed and she could no longer read, she became bored and depressed. I would often find her dozing when I entered her room for a visit and noticed that she remained listless when awake. The woman who always was interested in life and in being with people, was worn out and giving up.

Because I was so worried about her, I asked a mutual friend, a psychiatrist, Richard Fahey to visit her. I remember how happy she was to see him. She always favoured men! But that was a temporary high for her, I believe, because she hadn't seen Dick for awhile. When I visited her a few days later, she was as tired and lifeless as before. I realised that she wanted to die.

One morning about three o'clock, I had a vivid dream. In the dream, I went up a flight of stairs to an upper landing and found Aida's chair empty. Since she had been unable to walk, I was surprised and tried to figure out how and where she could have gone. I concluded that she must be feeling stronger and may have taken her old walker and ambled down to the cafeteria. Suddenly, she appeared behind me in a wheel chair looking forty years younger. She smiled at me and said: "Yes, I am getting younger!" Her body began to pulsate with a bright, healthy, green light. I woke up, frightened, with my heart beating strongly.

Patty was asleep next to me. I shook her, all the while calling her to wake up. She opened her eyes and asked me what was wrong. I described my dream and said: "I think that she's dead! Both of us were rattled and couldn't sleep. The dream seemed real to Patty too. We didn't even want to get out of bed. Our feeling was fear.

At six a.m., I called the Rest Home. I told the nurse on duty why I was calling. "I know it sounds, weird, but I had a dream that Aida died and I've been worried sick all night." Much to my surprise, the nurse didn't think that I had gone off the deep end. Instead, she told me that Aida was alive but that the staff of the Home were greatly concerned about her. "She is very depressed," she explained. "It's as if she wants to die."

When I heard that Aida was alive, I was greatly relieved and resolved to get to her at the earliest possible time. The next morning I walked into her room. The scene that greeted me was unearthly. Aida was sitting in her chair, silhouetted against the large window at the back of her room. She was asleep. I walked closer to her and was startled by her appearance. Her head drooped down upon her breast; her tongue was hanging out of her mouth and she was breathing slowly, almost imperceptibly.

I tried to awaken her and couldn't. I rushed down the hall, calling for help. A nurse's aide came back with me to the room. She tried to rouse Aida, but to no avail. By that time, the head nurse came in and also failed to bring Aida around. Finally, there were two aides, the head nurse and myself trying everything to arouse her. For approximately 15 minutes Aida just sat there breathing quietly. I hit her arm thinking that she might be discomforted by her arthritis and jolted into coming back. I yelled her name into her ear; nothing worked! Then, when we had almost given up hope, she sat up abruptly and shouted: "I've got to catch my plane, I've got to catch my plane!" As she tried to stand, we had to hold her in place because she did not have her prosthesis on and would have fallen straight away if she could have risen at all.

I finally succeeded in calming her and bringing her back to reality, but when she came to her senses, she was inexplicably angry at all of us. At first, I couldn't figure it out. Why was she so upset with us? Then it dawned on me. Aida had been willing herself to die and would have, in fact, caught her "flight," left the body and gone on. I am sure that only my insistent badgering of her to wake up brought her spirit back to this plane. I had thwarted her plan, and she was livid with indignation. I believe that she came back because she sensed my love for her and my fear that she was dying, but it is not what she wanted. She wanted for it all to end.

Aida died four days later. When I heard the news, I left work and picked up Patty at her office and we went to a local restaurant where we could sit quietly alone. Patty listened to me compassionately, as I talked about my dear friend, my "third grandmother," Aida Bellerose. I started to cry. I couldn't stop! I was shocked by the depth of my feeling. She had been one of the most spiritually influential people in my life, teaching me that there was more to life than what the senses presented to me and teaching me with her gifts, a part of the perennial philosophy. Aida had been there for me through the pain of my divorce and she had predicted that Patty was coming into my life. She had instructed me about reincarnation and karma, about the gifts of the spirit, and psychic phenomena. For a period of my life, she was "guru," leading me higher from darkness toward light. Looking back on my relationship with her, there is no question in my mind that Aida Bellerose had been sent to me by a Higher Power. Today, I accept that Higher Power, as incarnated into this material plane in the form of Sathya Sai Baba. He sent Aida to me. She was His instrument, guiding me on the path toward Him. As the old saying goes, when the student is ready, the teacher will appear. Aida was my teacher for spirituality 101.

Aida's death taught me how powerful the will of a human being can be. With it, we can choose to survive when the facts around us demand that we collapse, and like Aida, we can employ it to leave when our mission is fulfilled. I realise now, that at a point in time, death, for all of us, is a blessing. When we have run the course, holding on is simply attachment and fear.

"The Atma does not die; only the body dies.
When man knows this,
death loses his sting,
death is not feared,
death is but a welcome voyage
into the known harbor."

<u>Sathya Sai Speaks</u>
Volume VI
Chapter 3
Page 157

CHAPTER 21

HE NEEDS NO PUBLICITY

*"In truth, you cannot understand the nature of My Reality
either today, or even after a thousand years
of steady austerity or ardent inquiry
even if all mankind joins in that effort."*

Baba
The Breath of Sai
Chapter 1
Page 4

*"Since I move about with you,
eat like you and talk with you,
you are deluded into the belief
that This is but an instance of common humanity.
Be warned against this mistake."*

Baba
The Breath of Sai
Chapter 1
Page 5

Patty and I were asked to serve as stockholders and directors for a New Age magazine by a lady who had conceived and founded the project. Several friends, psychics, astrologers, spiritual seekers, were participating. It sounded like a grand idea and Patty and I joined on happily. Although we had been interested in all of these disciplines, Sai Baba continued to call and like a haunting melody, we couldn't keep Him out of our minds. He continued to pursue us. On the Board of Directors, we were the "Sai Baba" people.

With a little money invested for printing costs, the magazine went to print and the first issues were published. It was a credit to the woman who had given birth to the idea and a lot of fun for those of us participating. In spite of the limited budget and the bootstrap operation, the published magazines were nicely done. They weren't as professionally produced as we would have liked them, but that was a function of dollars. It was hoped that as time went on and the readership expanded, our advertising base might grow also, allowing more dollars to be targeted for better paper, more colour and better quality covers.

After several issues, the publisher asked the board of directors for ideas and suggestions for future articles. Of course, I volunteered that any article on Sathya Sai Baba, His miracles, His teachings and His message would be perfect for our fledgling publication. The publisher objected vehemently! She believed that the "Age of Aquarius" that had just begun astrologically, precluded a full *Avatar* being born. In that age, the spiritual progress and growth of mankind was supposed to happen by people working in concert and harmony, not by being taught by a Higher Being. I pointed out that the two ideas were not incompatible. Humankind could function in harmony and by consensus, as the Age of Aquarius suggested, and still be taught and instructed by a God-Man incarnated on this earth for the purpose of guiding us and showing the Way.

But our publisher was insistent. She did not want an article on Sathya Sai Baba appearing on the pages of her magazine. I was put off, but not out. I explained to her how many groups had been formed in His Name for the express purpose of giving their time and concerted effort in selfless service for the betterment of others. "No," she said. "No, there will be no article on Sai Baba!" I backed off, but I realised that my path, that of following Sai Baba and His teachings, was not the path of this lady or her baby, the new magazine. I was drawn to Baba because of His teachings of inclusion and expansion, not exclusion and separation. Patty and I felt that we had no other choice but to resign from the Board of Directors; not because we couldn't get our way, but because walls were being built around the project. Doors were being closed, not opened. We left with an explanation, but with no hard feelings. We wished her well and hoped that the magazine might prosper.

The January 1987 issue of the publication arrived in the mail. Much to my shock, the publisher had written an editorial strongly attacking Sai Baba! From not wanting an article written on Baba at all, she elected to write a scathing assault **against** Him. Her language was in extremely poor taste, using sexual imagery to accentuate her argument. I was shocked by the article and told Patty that I wished I could write a rebuttal. Since we were no longer associated with the magazine, it didn't seem in the cards.

On the day of the much publicised Harmonic Convergence, an astrological alignment of certain   heavenly planets, we found ourselves at the farm of Emmi Mayr in Portland, Connecticut, to celebrate the event under the stars at a location on her farm, where Emmi believes there is a positive energy vortex. Don and Jocelyn Hayes, friends of ours and members of the Board of Directors of the magazine also attended.

Jocelyn approached me and explained that there had been a great hue and cry over the Sai Baba article, and that the Board of Directors had removed the writer from her positions as President and Operating Officer. Jocelyn had been chosen to take over the day to day operation of the magazine. She informed me that the Board of Directors and the other officers had no knowledge that the article was to be printed and that the views expressed therein were the views of the woman, herself, and not those of the magazine and its staff. She asked me if I would be willing to write an article on Baba from the positive side, not only to clear the record, but also to initiate a series of articles on *Avatars*, both modern and ancient.

I was elated! I was being given the opportunity to tell the readers of Sathya Sai Baba, not by attacking the venomous editorial, but rather, by concentrating on Baba and His teachings. The article could be a positive one, not a vindictive response to the attempted character assassination of Sai Baba. In my heart, I knew that it was Baba who had brought about my invitation to write an article and because of that, and in spite of my anger about the editorial, my writing had to be **about** Baba, not a **defense** of Him, nor an aggressive **assault** on the lady's vehement editorial. Sai Baba teaches, that we, as devotees, have no need to publicise Him, because we understand so little of Him:

"The Lord has no intention to publicise Himself.
I do not need publicity,
nor does any other Avatar of the Lord.
What are you daring to publicise?
Me?
What do you know about Me?"

A Recapitulation of Baba's
Divine Teachings
Page 6

Therefore, even an article **about** Sai Baba could be presumptuous if I felt that **I** was spreading His story or His teachings. And so, the article, for me, took a different path. On one hand, it was Baba's gift to allow me to write a positive article because I had been so upset by the editorial and on the other hand, it gave me an opportunity to study His life and His teachings in preparation for writing the article. I realised that the whole exercise would help me learn. I wouldn't attack the writer of the article and I couldn't publicise Baba, but I could learn more about Him and His Ways by writing for the magazine.

And yet, for all that logic, I have to admit, that to an extent, I did succumb to an ego trip, just thinking that an article of "mine" would be published in a magazine, albeit a minor one with a very small, limited readership. I was further inflated by a telephone call that I received from Jocelyn just prior to the publication of the issue containing the article. She said that she wanted me to know that she had read the article and had enjoyed it very much. So much in fact, that she took the opportunity to insert a quote about *Avatars* as a highlight to the article. I was puffed up like a water-logged sponge.

Well, Baba took care of all that. The magazine issue was mailed out on time and I eagerly awaited its arrival. Patty picked it up at the post office, ripped off the mailing jacket and flipped through the magazine until she found the article. There it was! She gasped! How was she supposed to tell me about what she saw? There was my name, in big black type, totally misspelled!

"I come only where sincerity and faith and surrender are valued.
Only inferior minds will revel in publicity and
self-aggrandisement.
These have no relevance in the case of Avatars.
They need no advertisement."

Sri Sathya Sai Baba's Discourse
to His devotees on His 43rd. birthday,
November 23rd., 1968,
as translated by Professor N. Kasturi

CHAPTER 22

GRACE AND THE PARACLETE

"Grace is showered on those who seek.
Knock, and the door shall be opened;
ask, and food will be served; search and treasure will be yours."

Sathya Sai Speaks
Volume VII
Page 124

It took several years after Patty and I had returned from our first pilgrimage to Sathya Sai Baba for us to join a Sai Center. Patty was not excited about a commitment to a spiritual group or community, especially since she had felt so torn when she realised that our divorces and then our remarriage had cut us off abruptly from being active communicants in the Catholic Church. She was a little gun-shy and didn't want to experience that feeling of not belonging again. But in spite of our growing awareness of Sai Baba, Patty experienced an emptiness, a void in her life instead of fulfillment. We both felt that knowing that an *Avatar* was alive in our world, should have brought us great joy, and in a sense it did, but for some reason, Patty felt that something was missing. One day, to her surprise as much as to mine, she blurted out: "Chuck, why don't we join a Sai Center? I think it's time for us to be with like-minded people." She was right, of course. We had very few people who would listen to us share our wonder of this extraordinary being, Sathya Sai Baba.

We had attended the Windsor Center at Edna Yuile's home from time to time, but that center met in the evenings over an hour away from our home. We felt that was too much travelling late at night. I remembered that Bernie and Marylou Shanley were Sai devotees who attended a center in the Manchester area. When we called the Shanleys to inquire, Bernie volunteered to take us to the Center the following Thursday as his guests. At that time, the Manchester Center met at the home of John and Elena Hartgering, about thirty minutes from our home. We decided to visit that Center and see if it met our needs. That was five years ago. From the day that Bernie so kindly invited us to be his guests, we have been members of the Manchester Center, participating in their Thursday devotions, their service projects and their study circles. The people that we have met there have become our friends, our spiritual family. The encouragement, reinforcement and love that we have felt from these people who are walking the Sai path, has stabilized us and helped us direct our spiritual energies. The void has been filled by friends who sing, meditate, pray and serve with us.

The Center, initially located at the home of the Hartgerings and later at the LoGrassos', has been the site of many Sai blessings. From evenings of worship, charged with the electricity of *bhajans* sung with devotion; of members returned from India sharing stories of Baba's miracles and love; of loving people reaching out in His name to touch one another with caring, the Presence of Sathya Sai Baba has often been felt in the hearts of the Center members. And from time to time, His Presence has also been evidenced by tangible manifestations that brought us to attention and made us acknowledge His involvement in the life of our Center.

Our current Center hosts, Tony and Maria LoGrasso, traveled to India in 1991 to be with Baba for the Festival of *MahaShivaratri*. While there, Maria bought a large amount of hard candy individually wrapped in paper. She wanted Baba to bless the candy and if He did, she intended to bring the candy back to the center to share with other Center members. Usually, when offered plates of candy, Baba takes a handful and throws them to the crowd as *prasad* (blessed food), representing His expansive Grace. On this occasion, He walked close to Maria and when she offered the candy to Him, He reached down into the bowl and taking several handfuls, sprayed it over those sitting near her. Maria was thrilled that Baba had acknowledged her in that fashion, but she was surprised that He had taken so much to throw to the crowd. She realised that the remaining blessed candy was just a smattering of what she had hoped to bring home with her.

Yet, whatever amount of candies were left, she did bring them to the Center. At the first Center meeting after her return, Maria told her story and passed the remaining candies around the room to those of us in attendance and asked each of us to take one piece until they ran out. If there were some who couldn't get a piece because there were not enough for all, so be it. But when the plate had travelled all around the room, it was discovered that there was just enough for each devotee present to get one piece. There was not one candy extra!

> *"...but, there is one Impartial Distributor*
> *of joy and sorrow, who gives you*
> *what you need, rather than what you desire."*
> <u>Sathya Sai Speaks</u>
> Volume VII
> Chapter 48
> Page 268

One Thursday night, Kathy Mathieu, then a member our Sai Center, was driving on Birch Mountain Road on her way to a Center meeting. At a point on her journey, she had to stop as there were two large birds standing in her path on the road. They were about two feet tall and she took them to be eagles. She didn't know at the time that the eagle is a symbol of Sai Baba and encountering one can be very auspicious.

At the Center that evening, the spiritual energy level was very high. There was a harmony and a group devotion that seemed to move everyone present. That aura was so pronounced for me, that during the silent meditation, I prayed earnestly to Baba to bless our Center and its members in some **tangible** way. I quietly hoped for *vibhuthi* to form on Baba's pictures in the room. Another devotee, Mary Beth Majesty, kept seeing a bird in her mind's eye during the meditation and try as she might, she couldn't clear her head of that image.

At the end of the service, Patty looked up to the picture window over the couch. The sun was still shining when we started our service but by the time that ther devotions had ended, darkness had fallen. An outside light shone on the window, clearly illuminating an imprint in the shape of a bird, wings spread like the Dove of Peace in Christian art depicting the Holy Spirit. "Look at the window!" Patty shouted. Everyone gathered around to gaze at the impression on the window. It was a bird, surely. It had form and a lot of detail and appeared to be white in colour. The material of the imprint resembled *vibhuthi*. Studying the image at close range, we could make out the body of the bird, its beak, the spread wings and even the outline of each tiny feather.

Somebody suggested that we go outside to see if a bird had crashed into the window and then fallen dead or injured. Upon inspection of the area under the window, not only was there no bird, conscious or unconscious, there was also no sign of a collision by a bird with the window. There were no feathers on the ground and no indication that a bird had fallen. We returned to the room and closely examined the imprint. The beak could be clearly seen in the middle of the bird's head. That was marvellous, because if a bird had flown into the window, there certainly would not be an oily impression of the beak! And, if a bird had hit the window and the oil of the wings made an impression, there surely would have been some smudging of the figure, so that each feather would not appear distinct. But in this case, each feather seemed clear and separate. It looked as if the bird had been etched carefully into the window. The image lasted for several weeks.

> *"Mama Maya My Maya;*
> *that is to say, this relative world*
> *is His Handiwork, His Leela, His Mahima,*
> *devised as a Training Ground, and Inspiration,*
> *for those who desire to see Him,*
> *the Source and Substance of all this."*
>
> <u>Sathya Sai Speaks</u>
> Volume III
> Page 195

What a night! Two eagles, a prayer for manifestation, an image of a bird in meditation and an imprint of a bird, beak, feathers and all, spread across a picture window like a Holy Dove. For us as devotees, there were only two explanations. The first was that there had been no bird that struck the window and that the image was Baba's creation. The second was that there had been a bird that smacked into that window leaving an amazing, detailed impression that spoke to our hearts and was all Baba's leela.

> *"There is no use if the fledgling stays in the nest;*
> *It should develop wings and fly into the sky.*
> *There is no use if man grovels in the dust;*
> *he should see the distant goal, clear and grand;*
> *he should take to his wings*
> *and fly."*
> <u>Chinna Katha</u>
> Page 119

CHAPTER 23

AMRITA

"The partaking of Amritha created by me
is only the first step in this process for you;
it does not mean much if you do not take the second step
and the third and march on towards self-realisation."

Sathya Sai Speaks
Volume II
Page 13

In May of 1991, Patty planned for us to go to the Sixteenth Annual Northeast Sai Baba Retreat and Conference at Camp Colang in Pennsylvania. I didn't want to go. First of all, I can't stand camping. Secondly, when mosquitoes smell me coming, they smell lasagna! For them, I'm a gourmet meal! Thirdly, having spent many weekends on retreat in the past, I felt that I would be bored. Fourthly, although the camp is found in a beautiful setting, a large cleared area nestled among the woods and hills of Northeast Pennsylvania, it is spartan in its amenities. There are cabins with no heat and approximately two showers for about sixteen to twenty people per cabin. The nights are cold and sleeping bags or a pile of blankets are needed if you hope to keep from becoming a human icicle.

So, I have to admit, I was looking for any excuse to "excuse" myself from going, but Patty was adamant. She really wanted to go. Also, our son, Garrett, told Patty that he would like to go with us and that settled the issue as far as Patty was concerned. Actually, we were both pleasantly surprised that Garrett showed an interest in attending. At the time, Garrett was living in an apartment in New Haven, Connecticut. He was only nineteen and we were not happy that he had chosen to leave home. He was working and taking care of his needs, but we were still concerned about him and how he was managing. So, when he jumped in the car with us for the ride to Pennsylvania, both Patty and I were elated. We weren't sure if he wanted to go camping or if he were interested in knowing more about Baba, but we figured that if he came along, Baba must have wanted him at that retreat.

When we arrived at about nine p.m., we were happy to find that Steve and Ruby, friends from Florida, had decided to drive up north to attend. (These names are not their real names. I have changed them to insure their privacy.) We had first met them when we visited the Sai Center of Jupiter, Florida. At the time of our visit, they had just returned from a pilgrimage to Baba in India and we were blessed to listen to them discuss their story.

Steve explained that within the year preceding their trip, he had encountered great financial stress in his life and needed to get away to recuperate and clear his muddled head. He called his father who lived out of state and asked him if he could come home for a while in order to try to empty his mind of the heavy weight of his financial problems. His father said that since these were financial problems, he would rather that Steve did not come home as Steve's financial problems might prove embarrassing to him and Steve's mother. Steve felt abandoned and in addition to his financial woes, thought that his father had rejected him when he was in need.

Steve and Ruby then laid out plans to go to India to see Sai Baba. Because Steve and Ruby weren't yet married, well-meaning yet judgmental devotees told them that their chances of getting the coveted interview with Baba would never happen. Yet, Baba called them for two interviews, the first one within hours of their arrival. We must understand that we can't make judgments or always know what He wants.

> *"There is a widely prevalent habit now*
> *of judging others*
> *and labelling them as*
> *Bhakthas (devout believers)*
> *or Nasthikas (unbelievers).*
> *What do you know, what can you know*
> *of the inner working of another's mind?"*
>
> <u>Sathya Sai Speaks</u>
> Volume I
> Page 18

He alone is able to fathom the depths of our hearts and comprehend our needs, and he alone knows what is the best remedy to heal our wounded psyches. Attempts at putting walls around Him or guessing what He will do in any given situation is like trying to imprison water in our hands by squeezing it.

During one of the interviews, Baba lovingly told Steve: *"I am your Father!"* Steve realised that Baba was letting him know that He knew of Steve's natural father's rejection of him. Already on his knees before Baba, he broke into sobs and dropped his head onto Baba's chest, holding Baba around the waist with both arms! Baba stroked Steve's head comforting and soothing him, showering divine, fatherly love on him, His wounded son.

Baba also materialised a ring for Steve which fit his finger perfectly. At a second interview, Baba had Ruby and Steve kneel at his feet. He placed His hands on their heads and said: *"We of the Universe bless you!"* Was this perhaps a symbolic marriage of their spirits by the Ultimate Authority?

After leaving the *ashram*, Steve and Ruby travelled to Mysore where they visited the orphanage founded by Halligappa, a former drug addict and burglar, whose heart was converted by Baba. When Baba had told Halligappa to give up his evil ways, he also commissioned him to begin an orphanage. Baba gave him a picture of Himself which began to produce *vibhuthi* in abundance and gave him two medallions about the size of small coins. These little medallions are constantly crying *amrita*, the "Nectar of the Gods!" This *amrita* is a honey-like liquid with a sweet ambrosial taste and a flowery aroma which Baba materialises as a sign of his Grace. It often has curative properties and can help reform the character of one who tastes it. "When we held the medallions in the palms of our hands, our palms filled up with *amrit*," Steve told us. I was mesmerized when Steve related this story to us as I had always wanted to taste *amrita*.

On the last day of the retreat at Camp Colang, Steve, who, over several days, had noticed our son, Garrett, came to me and asked: "Who is that kid that I see you talking to every day?" I explained that Garrett was my son. Steve told me that there was an intangible something about Garrett that intrigued him and he couldn't quite put his finger on it. I told Steve that Garrett was recovering from addiction and that we were quite proud of his ability to keep away from using any drugs or alcohol. Steve's voice rose: "That's it! I'm recovering too and so is Ruby. I must have just sensed that Garrett was fighting the same enemy as we are!"

Steve then asked me if he and Ruby could show Garrett something in their huge motor home. He didn't tell me what it was, but I figured it had something to do with addiction and the fight to keep clean, so I consented. I introduced Garrett to Steve and Ruby and the three of them went off to the camper. Soon thereafter, Patty and I were ready to leave the retreat and Garrett was still in the motor home. We became a little concerned, so we knocked on the door. Ruby opened the door and with a smile invited us in. Garrett was intently watching a television screen. A video tape of Steve and Ruby's visit to Baba and later to the orphanage was playing. Patty and I sat down and began to watch the tape ourselves. At the point on the tape where Steve was seen holding the miraculous medallions in his hands at Halligappa's orphanage and *amrita* was pouring forth from them into his palm, Ruby was bending over us with a teaspoon and a jar in hand. "Would you like to taste the *amrit*?" She asked. My eyes must have bulged out of their sockets! "Yes, yes, of course, I would!" I stammered. I couldn't believe it! I had wanted to taste *amrita* from the very first time that I had read about it. She handed me the teaspoon and poured a little of it from the jar. I raised the teaspoon to my lips and tasted its sweetness. It was lighter than honey and the aroma was like the scent of jasmine flowers. What a grace! What a grace to be able to experience and to taste a miraculous substance that had been written about for centuries, but experienced by so very few!

But tasting the holy, sweet and fragrant *amrita*, was not the only miracle we experienced on that last day of the retreat. Earlier, *vibhuthi* emanated from a small picture of Baba's Lotus Feet that had been placed in front of the altar. I lined up with everyone else to see the miracle. For some reason, I wasn't shocked. Seeing the *vibhuthi* forming on the glass just seemed natural to me. It was a gentle flow, not a lot of *vibuthi*. As I left the prayer hall, I saw Garrett running in my direction. "Have you seen the *vibuthi*?" I asked him. "What *vibhuthi*?" he wanted to know. I explained that *vibuthi* was issuing from the picture. "Not a lot though," I said. He ran off toward the hall.

Garrett waited for everyone else to examine the *vibhuthi* before he looked at it. I guess he wanted time to examine it and time to digest what he saw. After he spent some time in front of the picture, he came looking for me. "Are you crazy?" he shouted! "There is a lot of it forming on that picture, and there is a big pile of it that has fallen off the glass!" He had a look of wonder on his face! He realised that he had seen a miracle. Baba had controlled matter, time and space, creating *vibhuthi* nine thousand miles away from where His physical form resided in southern India!

After the retreat, the miracle of the *vibhuthi* and the sharing of the *amrita*, we drove Garrett back to his apartment in New Haven. He invited us up to his room in the third floor flat that he shared with several other young men. Garrett told us that there was something that he wanted to show us in the apartment, and so up we went. In the apartment, he opened a door and ducked under a low ceiling that was part of a stairway overhead. We lowered our heads and followed him into a small, ten by ten room. Patty and I blinked. We were flabbergasted! There, against the wall, was a *puja* table (altar) with candles, incense and Baba's pictures. We were so astounded that we couldn't speak right away. Garrett told us that this little hidden room was his "meditation room." In one instant, Patty and I realised that our son was okay and that Baba was very much a part of his life. Then and there we were peacefully assured of Garrett's spiritual path.

> *"Offer Me, Surrender to Me,*
> *Leave everything to Me.*
> *Whoever surrenders,*
> *Rama accepts*
> *on the spot, without reservations."*

Sai Avatar
Volume II
Page 237

I guess parents never really know what our beliefs mean to our children. We're never quite sure of what they are accepting from our example, as part of their reality. But, I guess, they do assimilate part of our opinions, good or bad, and make them their own. In this case, Garrett was taking on our belief in the *Avatar*, Sathya Sai Baba.

> *"If you do not honour the parents*
> *who are the creators in human form,*
> *how can you learn to honour the Creator in the Divine?*
> *Moreover, the parents reveal to you the glory of God*
> *and the means of worshipping Him;*
> *they are the first representatives of authority*
> *which you meet with, and you will learn*
> *through them, how to submit to the Lord.*
> *As the twig is bent, so the tree is inclined."*

Rita Bruce
Vision of Sai
Page 209

CHAPTER 24

IN HIS TIME

"Persist till the gift is granted."

Sathyam Sivam Sundaram
Part IV
Page 102

*"I insist on Dhyana (meditation) as an
indispensable item of Sadhana for
every member of this Organization."*

Sathya Sai Speaks
Volume VI
Page 221

The following May, in 1992, Patty and I went to the 17th Annual Mid-Atlantic and Northeast Region Sathya Sai Baba Conference and Retreat at Camp Colang in Pennsylvania. Once again, Garrett asked to join us and once again, I didn't want to go. My idea of camping is the Holiday Inn and Camp Colang was no Holiday Inn. But, Patty insisted and like all husbands who want to put our foot down, but don't, I simply changed my mind. This time we arrived at the beginning of the retreat because our Center was responsible for the food preparation.

I volunteered for kitchen duty baking the breads and rolls, consequently, I was unable to participate in all of the planned activities and programmes that were available. However, the word was out that the main speaker, Isaac Tigrett, had been chosen personally by Baba to speak at our retreat, so I really wanted to hear his presentation. Isaac is the founder of the Hard Rock Cafe restaurant chain and had been involved with rock music and the selling of liquor products. On the surface, his career seemed incongruous with the life of a Sai devotee. I thought that he would be worth hearing and so I arranged to leave the kitchen early in order to hear his talk.

The lecture was to be held in a big barn-like hall that was already filled to overflowing when I arrived. The barn itself was raised high on its foundation, so I had to walk up a few stairs to get to the large sliding door. The door opened into the hall of the barn near a large stage at one end. From the doorway, the stage was clearly visible. It had been decorated and prepared as an altar with candles, flowers, and large pictures of Shirdi Baba and Sathya Baba. I could see the altar and the podium and microphone in front of it, but I couldn't get into the hall. Devotees were sitting Indian style in tight formation and there seemed to be no extra space. I was able to sit on the edge of the door sill, with my back against one side of the doorway, but I was concerned that I might have trouble hearing Tigrett's talk. Then people in the barn started "schooching" (Patty's word for cramming close together in Sai Baba gatherings) and before I knew it, I had inched deeper and deeper into the hall until I was directly in front of the podium. Isaac was only about nine feet away from me when he began his talk.

After introductions, Isaac walked down the center aisle to the podium. He is an imposing man with a beard, chiselled features and long straight hair. He wore a white shirt with a Nehru type collar and a large black suit. Others have told me that he is well known for always wearing black. Like Johnnie Cash, the well known country singer, it is his trademark. His look and bearing and southern drawl instantly brought to mind an image of a Southern general of the Old Confederacy during the American Civil War.

As he began speaking, I found myself deeply engrossed in the story. Isaac had decided to share his life's march to Baba with the retreatants. The story was fascinating. During his early teen years, his younger brother died in his arms after an accident while they were playing together. He blamed himself for his brother's death. The tragedy affected the whole family and it wasn't very long before his father and mother were divorced. Once again, Isaac blamed himself for his parents dissolution. Isaac recalled that his father ran a lucrative business into the ground after that and then left Tennessee to live in England. He brought Isaac to live with him. In his late teens and early twenties, Isaac worked at factory jobs and after a while saved enough money to travel to America to see his mother. He bought her an old Rolls Royce in England for very little money. When he arrived in the United States with the Rolls, he was offered a large amount of money for the car. He sold it and earned a tidy profit. He realised that he had found a "window" in the used car market, and so began buying used luxury cars in Europe and selling them in the United States. Isaac accumulated a large sum of money in that business which he used as the seed money to start the first Hard Rock Cafe in

London. Working hard, he kept opening Hard Rock Cafes all over the world and met with much financial success. Isaac has said that he was very much into the rock music scene himself, including the use and abuse of alcohol and drugs.

Beginning about the age of thirteen years, Isaac began hearing voices or what he believed were spirit guides. One day, after he had become successful with the Hard Rock Cafes, he heard a voice say: "Buy the **Secret Life of Plants**." Over the years, he had realised that he could rely on these messages, but in this case, he had no idea what the "Secret Life of Plants" was. Later, while reading a news-magazine, he found a book being critiqued in the book review section whose title was the "Secret Life of Plants." The book was about paranormal events throughout the world. It was not well reviewed, but Isaac knew his messages had been reliable in the past, so he contacted the authors, Peter Tompkins and Christopher Bird, and told them that he wanted to buy the theatrical and film rights to the book. They told him that the book had not been very successful but if he wanted to buy the rights, they would be happy to sell them to him. Soon after the deal was consummated, the book shot up onto the New York Times Best Seller List and remained there for many weeks.

Isaac told us that he was soon able to make a film deal for the book and began to travel the world to research and film material for a documentary. He visited universities that were doing research and studies on paranormal phenomena, such as Duke University in North Carolina. Finally, he traveled to India with a list of gurus and holy men that he wanted to investigate. Sai Baba was not on that list. When he arrived in Aurrangabad, he checked into a hotel. Standing in the lobby he heard a voice in his head again. This time the voice said: *"At last you have come, I have been waiting for you."* He looked up and saw a picture of a man with a lot of hair. He asked the desk clerk who the man in the picture was. The clerk gently said: "That is our national treasure, Sathya Sai Baba."

Trusting his inner voice , Isaac went to see Baba. There, dressed in black and standing by the wall behind the hundreds of people sitting for *darshan*, Isaac waited for Baba to appear. Sai Baba worked His way through the crowd and approached Isaac. Baba waived His hand in the familiar circular motion, produced *vibhuthi* and placed it in Isaac's hand. *"Eat it, very good!"* Baba commanded. And Isaac did.

Well, Isaac was hooked. For fifteen years in a row, he travelled to India to wherever Baba was at the time and for fifteen straight years Baba never said another word to him nor did He invite him in for an interview. However, events occurred during that time that made Isaac realize that Baba was very aware of him and was looking after him. Once, he was driving a Porsche at very high speed while inebriated. He was on a twisting canyon road and sure enough, could not control that powerful machine around one hairpin turn. The Porsche sailed over a cliff, spinning in mid air as it fell about 400 feet! While spinning, Isaac saw Baba sitting beside him. Baba put his arm around Isaac and the next thing that Isaac remembered was waking up sitting near where the car had impacted the ground at the bottom of the cliff. The car was totally destroyed. There was nothing left, but Isaac did not have a scratch, not even a bruise. Recalling Baba being in the car with him, he believed that Baba had saved him, and so, he set off to India to thank Baba for rescuing him and preserving his life. Once again, Baba ostensibly ignored him.

"I am giving you interviews every day.
It is you who always avoid granting Me an interview,
an enter-in-view,
from viewing you as Me,
in Me."

Sathyam Sivam Sundaram
Part IV
Page 166

Isaac told us of a time, in a hotel room in Denver, Colorado, when he overdosed on drugs, and had an epileptic seizure. He had swallowed his tongue and was dying. Suddenly, he felt that he had left his body through the top of his head. From the ceiling, he realised that he was looking down on his inert body! He heard a voice talking to him: "Your time has not yet come, call your guru's name!" And so, he did. After calling the name, "Sai Baba", Isaac, from his vantage point up near the ceiling, saw Baba come into the room, pick up his dead body from the floor and place it on the bed. Then Sai cleared Isaac's throat and pushed on his chest. The next thing that Isaac recalled was being back in his body and alive. Once again, he flew to India to thank Baba for coming to his rescue, and once again, Baba outwardly paid him no attention.

Isaac said that he became the *ashram* joke. Everyone knew that he had visited time and time again and still the desired interview was withheld. Finally in his sixteenth year of being in the presence of the *Avatar*, Baba granted him an interview. When Baba motioned Isaac to go to the interview room, Isaac looked behind him as he thought Baba **must** be beckoning someone else, not him. In the interview room, Baba looked at Isaac and said, *"I saved this man's life two times, didn't I?"* Startled and amazed, Isaac stammered: "yes!" Baba leaned down and whispered: *"And many other times too."* In answer to how Isaac as a devotee could sell liquor and operate cafes and bars, Baba said that the Hard Rock Cafe, with its pictures of Baba on the wall and with Isaac's insistence that his employees approach their jobs righteously and lovingly, adhering to the *dharmic* path, was an *"Island of Light in an Ocean of Darkness."* And Sai Baba gave Isaac the motto for the Hard Rock Cafe, which Isaac had printed on thousands of packages of match sticks, tee shirts and other promotional items: *"Love All, Serve All."*

> *"All your activities should be suffused with Divinity.*
> *Whatever you see, see with a Divine feeling;*
> *whatever you hear, hear with a Divine feeling;*
> *whatever you do, do with a Divine feeling.*
> *Do everything for the pleasure of the Lord."*

> <u>Summer Showers in Brindavan 1993</u>
> Page 102

After running the Hard Rock Cafe Chain for several years and building it into a huge international operation, Isaac decided that it was taking a heavy toll on him, physically and mentally, so he agreed to sell his interest in the Hard Rock Organization. When negotiations for the sale were complete, the agreed upon price happened to be one hundred eight million dollars! Obviously, Baba was in control. When the numbers making up 108 are added together, they total 9, the number of the *Avatar*. Baba told Isaac that the "Hard Rock" belonged to Him.

When Isaac finished talking about the events that led him to Baba and some of his experiences with Baba, he spoke to us of meditation. I had been listening attentively to that point, not only because of the interesting stories but also because he was a successful businessman in the material world, who had become a devoted follower of Sai Baba and a focused spiritual aspirant. I was impressed that in spite of living in the world of power and greed, he had become successful financially and grown spiritually at the same time. Now, he began discussing meditation and its importance for him and, as it turned out, for me.

I had never been a meditator. Oh, I had tried to meditate but had never been very good at it. Whenever Patty would share her meditations or her insights gained in meditation, I marvelled that she could delve so deeply seeking the divine within her soul. Yet, as Isaac spoke, his words began to resonate within me and I found myself saying: "I can do that!" Isaac said that he meditated every day in the early morning hours before the sun rose, sitting quietly and focusing within. Baba often came to him in his meditations and led him deeper. Well, I didn't think Baba would necessarily come to me and lead my meditations but I knew that I could train myself to rise early and work on journeying inward. I felt that if Isaac could do it in the face of the temptations of liquor, drugs, money and sex that surrounded him in his business, I could learn to meditate too.

There were two meditation methods that Isaac shared with us that day. Baba had taught them to him and Phyllis Krystal, a counsellor from California, and Isaac taught them to us. They were quite simple and, I realised, methods that I as a beginner could do. Isaac called the first meditation, the **"Tree Meditation."** In that meditation, Isaac pictured himself leaning against a tree. Then, he would imagine becoming one with the tree and being the tree with leaves, branches and roots. After becoming the tree, he would pull female, creative or intuitive energy from mother earth into and through the roots, up the trunk or spine, passing through the *chakras* (energy centers of the body) until it rested at the top of the tree, or the crown *chakra* at the top of the head. Then, he would bring down the male, intellectual or logical energy from the leaves and branches of the tree, or the crown *chakra*, through the trunk of the tree and the other *chakras* into the roots of the tree. This meditation is an attempt to **balance** the male/female, intuitive/logical, creative/intellectual parts of our psyches and to harmonise the dualities that make up our being.

The second meditation that Isaac taught us that day was even easier. In that meditation, he addressed the God within himself and asked Him/Her to act through his mind and body. He would say: "Think through me, feel through me, speak through me, act through me and love through me." Repeating this mantra over and over again, he was affirming the act of surrender to Divine Will by asking that all his actions be governed by the Divine within. [God] think through me, [God] feel through me, [God] speak through me, [God] act through me, [God] love through me. Isaac told us that Baba told him to add: *"Breathe through me."* Baba's suggestion is obviously an affirmation that even the involuntary act of breathing is caused by and should be dedicated to God. Then Isaac sang the *bhajan*:

> "Make me like You Lord,
> Oh make me like You.
> You are a servant,
> make me one too!"

As Isaac sang, I was mesmerised. On the one hand, I knew that I was listening to a man who lives as a householder and a businessman, and in many ways was no different than myself or others except in the extent of his creative and financial success, and yet I recognised something more. I remember looking into his eyes which I perceived as gray and thinking: "This man is a master!" I found that I could not pull my eyes away from his because every word that he spoke etched itself into my soul. At that moment, in that hall, I decided to learn to meditate. I **wanted** to go within.

> "O Lord I am willing.
> Do what you must do
> to make me like You Lord.
> Make me like You!"

Ever since that May afternoon in 1992, I rise early each morning, between three a.m. and six a.m. and sit cross-legged in front of Sai Baba's picture and focus within. There is a little altar with *vibhuthi*, an oil lamp and the fragrance of incense fills the room. I meditate for about an hour or so doing some of the meditations that Isaac taught and others that I have learned along the way. I have missed doing meditation on some days due to illness, or oversleeping or some conflicting obligation, but really, very seldom. I love meditating; I love the quiet and the peace that it brings me. It prepares me for the day and strengthens me. I am not yet aware of how my life will change because of the meditating inspired by Isaac's talk, but I do know, that although I labour to get out of bed every morning, I do look forward to that hour of reaching for the Divine within me. Meditation has helped me focus on the Divine and helps to keep me in the Presence. I love being silent in front of my pictures of Baba and sometimes I **feel** transported and so peaceful. Where will meditation take me? I don't know, but I do know that thanks to Baba talking and teaching through Isaac that day in May, I have become quieter and closer to the God that is within me.

"Without meditation it is not possible
to control and master the mind.
Thus, meditation is essential
to immerse the mind
in Supreme Consciousness."

<u>Teachings of Sri Sathya Sai Baba</u>
Page 11

CHAPTER 25

FATHER'S DAY

"Let your Father be your God"

Sathya Sai Speaks
Volume VII
Chapter 12
Page 55

In June of 1992, Patty and I decided that we wanted to wish Baba a Happy Father's Day, by inviting devotees to participate in a *bhajan* and prayer service on Father's Day. Since Father's Day came on the Summer Solstice, the longest day of the year, we decided to do the service at daybreak, on our deck overlooking the Connecticut River. We were going to welcome the Light of the World with devotion and song. We invited all of the Sai Centers in the area, but because of the early hour, four thirty a.m., only about thirteen or fourteen people attended. Patty and I were up at four a.m., in the dark, to make sure that the altar was set and the deck prepared for the service.

Our home is deep in the woods and there are tall, deep green hemlock trees standing seventy-five feet high in some cases, on three sides. The back of the house faces the Connecticut River and the land drops precipitously toward the water. There is an upper deck at the living level and a lower deck at the bedroom level below. We held the service on the lower deck which looks out through a clearing in the trees overlooking the river. As the sun began to rise, the early morning fog floated lazily above the placid water. At that early hour, as we looked out on that lovely scene, our minds were calm and our hearts were at peace.

We had planned as part of the service that Pat Connors sing a song of love to our Father, Sai Baba, as a lead-in to a ten minute meditation. Now most people like to meditate with their eyes closed, but because of the beauty and tranquillity of the setting, I kept my eyes open during Pat's song and the following meditation. I wanted to meditate on the still, quiet beauty of nature that surrounded us.

I was looking at the river as Pat began singing, when a large orange-red ball, the colour of Baba's gown appeared from behind the trees on the right, floating in the middle of the river. It moved with the river's flow slowly in front of us and toward the sea thirty-five miles away. I followed it as Pat continued singing, and watched it disappear behind the trees lining the river to my left just as Pat finished the hymn. It was all so surreal! When the service was over, I asked, hesitatingly, whether anyone had seen "Baba's orange-red ball." Several of the others had also kept their eyes open during the song and the meditation and had seen what I saw. We all drew the same conclusion, that the orange ball was Baba's acknowledgement of our Father's Day greeting.

After inquiry, we found that the large orange-red ball was probably a mooring marker that had broken loose from an anchor line and then floated down the river. I took the event as a *leela* or sign from Baba that he blessed us all and was pleased with the devotion of our Father's Day Service. Then, while I was writing the outline for this book, Patty pointed out some of the words of a devotional song called "Let Me Fall," that we often sing at our center:

"Oh, be my father and be my mother,
be my sister and be my brother,
**BE THE ANCHOR OF MY LITTLE BOAT
UPON THE SEA.**
Be my lover, be my friend,
be my refuge till the end.
Let me fall, let me fall
in love with thee."

Coincidentally, "Let Me Fall" was the song that Pat sang that day. Symbolically, both the song and the orange mooring marker told us that Baba is our anchor in life. How appropriate that a symbol of **anchorage,** a mooring marker, would remind us to hold on to, trust in, rely on and surrender to the *Avatar*. The whole event, that early morning, was full of Divine symbolism and imagery. Even the journey of the orange ball toward the sea, brought to mind the journey of each soul floating down the river of life toward the Ocean of Divinity and merging therein.

"The disappearance of the wave form
and the wave name is called Moksha,
(Realisation)
that is the merging of the wave in the Ocean
from which it seemed to differ."
<u>Sathya Sai Speaks</u>
Volume I
Page 161

CHAPTER 26

THE INVITATION

"Learn lessons from every living being,
everything that you find around you."

Sathya Sai Speaks
Volume XI
Page 117

Two years ago, Patty and I attended a two-day Phyllis Krystal Seminar sponsored by the Shelton, Connecticut Sai Center. Phyllis Krystal is an ardent Sai devotee who Baba has blessed with magnificent teachings in psychology and in meditation. I had first learned of her through Isaac Tigrett's talk at the Sai Retreat in Pennsylvania in 1991. She has written several books, either about Sathya Sai Baba or inspired by him. Phyllis has a soft voice and even though it was amplified, I had trouble understanding her. In addition, the sound system in the room where the seminar was to be held wasn't very good, so she invited those who had trouble hearing to move forward to an open area in front of the stage. I took her cue and sat against the wall to the left of the stage.

A lady followed me to the front and sat beside me. At the first break, we struck up a conversation. She was a devotee from Chicago who had travelled to Connecticut just to participate in the programme. We began to share experiences related to Baba and for some reason, I felt compelled to tell her that I had prayed to Baba not to look at me when I was at the Ashram during my one and only visit there. I explained that I had been so aware of what I perceived as my own sins and shortcomings, that I was ashamed and afraid that I would melt before His gaze. I told her that when I returned to America from that visit and tried to think of Baba at the ashram, I always pictured Him in my mind's eye wearing a black cassock similar to those the Jesuits wear. I just could not image Him in the bright, orange-red robes that He really wears and I didn't know why I had that mental block. I knew Baba wore orange-red robes and not black, but try as I might, I could not see that colour in my mind.

This woman had a way of speaking without showing much emotion. She looked at me in a matter of fact way and said that the explanation for my seeing Baba only in black was easy to figure out. She said that Baba was trying to tell me that there was nothing for me to be afraid of, or ashamed of. I didn't have to avoid Him or His Eyes because of my imperfections and errors. The black cassock, she said, was a symbol that He had absorbed all of my transgressions unto Himself and forgiven me. She exhorted me to accept that forgiveness by mentally turning over all my shortcomings to Him.

> *"Bring to Me all the evil in you,*
> *and leaving it here*
> *take from Me*
> *what I have, viz.,*
> *Prema (Love)."*

Sathya Sai Speaks
Volume I
Page 173

I was amazed! Her interpretation touched me deeply and made sense to me. The black colour symbolised my errors. He had taken them! All I had to do was let them go. What a joyful revelation for me. In a moment, I was free of the disgrace and the ignominy; the burden carried for years lifted off my shoulders. From that day forward, I could imagine Baba at *darshan* wearing his lively and colourful orange-red robes.

That evening after the first day's programme, Patty and I went to dinner with fellow devotees. Over pizza, we talked of our hope that one day Baba might come to the United States. In a jocular mood, we decided that it was time for Him to travel here, so we began composing letters of invitation on our place mats. At first, we were joking and our invitations were comical and not serious. Tony LoGrasso owns his own business and is used to leading and commanding others, so his letter was demanding. It almost said: "Hey, Sai Baba, get over here!" Patty is an administrator and manager, and her invitation sounded as if she were writing to a state agency: "Dear Sai: Since you have not been here before, we felt that you might consider altering your schedule to accomodate...etc. etc." After a while, we became serious and jointly composed a respectful and warm letter of invitation to the *Avatar* to come in His physical form to our Northeast Regional Conference and Retreat in May of 1993. Our proposal took on real meaning to us and we decided that the invitation should be sent to Sai Baba.

Raj Kaushik went home to get his laptop computer and Teresa Mailonis typed the letter from our handwritten scrawl on the place mat at eleven o'clock in the evening. Raj took the lap top back to his home and made an original letter with several blank pages added so that devotees attending the Seminar could sign it. The next day, approximately two hundred devotees signed our loving letter asking Baba to come West and Grace us with His physical presence.

David Gries, the President of the Northeast Region of the Sathya Sai Organization at the time, was going to India in a few days, so we gave David the letter of invitation and asked him to deliver it to Baba if he got the chance. Well, David was blessed with an interview with Baba and did give Him the invitation. Baba opened the envelope, looked at the letter, held it to his temple like comedian Johnny Carson's stage character, Karnack the Magnificent, and said:

"Too many desires!"

When I heard that our letter really did get into Baba's Hands, I was thrilled! A part of me was in that letter and to think that it was received by the *Avatar* meant, for me, that I was received also. But I was disappointed by Baba's comment and took it personally. Most everyone else believed that since approximately two hundred people signed the letter, Baba's comments were a rebuke for all. Since Baba's words and actions usually have more than one meaning or are meant for more than one person, the general consensus was plausible. Baba was talking to all of us. But, for me, it wasn't quite that simple. I had written a large part of that letter and I couldn't help but feel that His words were meant directly for me. I have a lot of desires and I find it difficult to detach from any of them. I felt that I had to work on my attachments.

> *"Desire is the enemy number one of Liberation.*
> *Desire binds one to the wheel of birth and death;*
> *and brings about endless worry and tribulations."*

Sai Avatar
Volume II
Page 426

Baba told David that He would bless our upcoming Northeast Conference and Retreat. And that He did. There were no pictures oozing *vibuthi* or *amritha* at the conference, but the calm and peace that all felt at that retreat had to be due to His Grace. There were no mistakes, no glitches, no emergencies, no crises, no human error. It was a weekend of peace; a weekend of devotion that lifted everyone. So, in one sense, we received what we had asked for. Baba was in our midst that weekend. I should have known that He would be. After all, it was the 18th annual retreat for the Northeast Region. A sure sign of Sai!

> *"When you pray for the Vision of the Feet,*
> *you are rewarded with it.*
> *When you cry out in agony*
> *and call on Him to listen to your woe,*
> *His ears are there to respond.*
> *When you plead with Him sincerely to come,*
> *He comes,*
> *to give, He gives."*

Voice of the Avatar
Page 165

CHAPTER 27

THE CALL

"For youth is a stage of life
when self-control, self-examination and self-effort
are most needed and least exercised."

<u>Sathya Sai Speaks</u>
Volume X
Page 46

Our son, Garrett, has fought and continues to fight a valiant and successful battle against addiction and has remained straight, sober and clean from age fourteen. Today, at twenty-three he still exhibits *"self-control, self-examination and self-effort,"* when many of his peers are and have been indulging in easy to get drugs and alcohol. Patty and I are convinced that Sathya Sai Baba has listened to our constant prayers and meditations and has looked after our children. Once we realised that Garrett had his own *puja* (prayer room) and meditated regularly, while trying to follow Baba's teachings, we became aware that Baba was pursuing Garrett.

Patty had heard that Hal Honig was planning to bring a group of young men, "the boys," as Sai Baba called them, to India for the Summer Showers Course at Brindavan in May of 1993. Garrett had voiced a desire to go to India, so Patty wrote to Hal and asked him about his plans for the trip. Hal called her and told her that his preparations for the trip were well along and that he was being very selective about the boys because he was planning a play to be performed in Baba's presence. Some of the young men had been working on the play with Hal for some time and Hal wanted to make sure that the young men who came with him were of a serious mind set and not just making the trip for fun. He explained to Patty that he didn't know if everyone who had signed up would actually be going, so he didn't know at that time whether he had the full quota of twenty that Baba said he could bring.

Patty told Garrett about her correspondence with Hal, and Garrett called him. Hal invited Garrett to New York for an interview. Garrett left immediately for the visit. He stayed for a few days with Hal in order that they get to know each other. Finally Hal extended an invitation to Garrett to make the trip. For a long time, I didn't know why Hal chose Garrett. I thought perhaps Hal was impressed with

Garrett's fight against addiction; maybe he thought Garrett's musical abilities would be helpful in the performance to be presented before Baba; maybe it was Garrett's practice of meditation or maybe it was simply that Baba wanted Garrett to attend. However, recently, Hal told me that, at the time, he felt that Garrett was truly seeking a spiritual path and that is the reason that he chose to include Garrett in the group. In any event, Hal told Garrett that there would be room for him and that he could plan on joining the others.

When we got the news that Garrett was approved for the journey to Whitefield to attend the Summer Showers Programme with Hal, we were overjoyed. Patty, especially, felt that Garrett's acceptance was the result of Baba's intervention. She told Garrett that if he would save enough money to pay for half of his trip, she would match his funds and make the balance available for him. The wheels were in motion and the train was running down hill. Garrett was going to India.

As part of the preparation for the trip, Hal invited the boys closest to his home in New York City, to visit him and help in Seva projects such as making sandwiches for the homeless and distributing them. Garrett participated in these seva projects and Phyllis Krystal workshops with Hal. Hal also asked the young men to his apartment in the city to rehearse and write the play. Then, right after Christmas, Hal invited the group to his Palm Beach, Florida home for *satsang*, (meaningful gathering of spiritual aspirants for good and holy sharing and companionship) relaxation and rehearsals. Again, Garrett using his Christmas money and other savings, paid for his bus trip to Florida in order to participate. He was taking the responsibility of fully sharing in the preparation for the trip. He never asked us for the money necessary to go to Florida.

> *"So teach children not to receive*
> *anything for nothing.*
> *Let them earn by hard work*
> *the things they seek."*

Sathya Sai Speaks
Volume II
Page 192

Our friends from Florida, Bob and Addie Grauch, have a grandson, Chris, who was also selected as one of the boys to make the trip with Hal. They invited all the young men who were able to make the trip to Palm Beach to dinner at their home. Of course, Garrett had met them at the retreats in our Northeast Region and heard us talking lovingly about them, so he was pleased to attend. Soon after that gathering, Garrett developed a rash and began to itch one day after swimming in the ocean. Hal and Bob took him to a doctor who diagnosed: "sea lice," an aquatic bug that I had never heard of. The medication proscribed didn't seem to help and, in fact, aggravated the condition.

Garrett grew steadily worse. He didn't have enough money with him to fly home, but Hal called his travel agent who arranged for Garrett to fly to Newark where Patty picked him up. When Patty saw him, he looked terrible. He was very sick and very uncomfortable. That night, after Patty and Garrett had reached home, our son Marc and his fiancee, Terri, arrived from Washington, D.C. for a New Year's vacation with us. Marc and Terri are both pediatricians in the army and at that time they were assigned to Walter Reed Hospital. Patty explained to Marc that Garrett had been diagnosed as having sea lice. Of course, we had never heard of sea lice, and I wonder if Marc had either. He just looked closely at Garrett and exclaimed: "Garrett, you have chicken pox!" We couldn't believe it, but sure enough Marc was right on the money. Garrett, at age 21, had chicken pox! The poor kid was miserable.

Several days later, Hal called looking for Garrett. He was out. We asked Hal how he was and when he hesitated before answering, we sensed that something was wrong. We pressed him for an answer and he blurted out that **he** had chicken pox! We were shocked! Why did all this happen to Garrett and to Hal? We wondered whether Baba might be testing them by putting them through that very uncomfortable ailment. It so often happens when one decides to go to India to the Feet of the Avatar that obstacles and problems crop up, trying our resolve and our wills. Maybe Baba is burning off one's *karma*, when adversity strikes just prior to a pilgrimage to His Lotus Feet. With Hal and Garrett, Baba may have been cleansing them or strengthening them by placing some trial or tribulation in their path.

Patty reasoned that maybe the group had to learn to show concern and care for each other as they no doubt would have to do in India.

In May, 1993, both Garrett and our daughter, Leslie, joined Patty and me at the 18th. Annual Northeast Conference at the Sunrise Resort in Moodus, Connecticut. It was a great blessing that we could share our devotion to Sai Baba with our children, and it was a wonderful way for Garrett to prepare for his trip to the college at Whitefield. *Bhajans*, meditation, spiritual talks and *satsang* filled his mind and heart just days prior to his leaving for the Summer Showers Course and Sathya Sai Baba.

Around the time of the Conference, word came that Nicky LoGrasso, son of Tony and Maria LoGrasso, our dear friends and the hosts of our Sai Center, was approved by Hal Honig to join the boys going to India. We were delighted. Together with the LoGrassos, we took Garrett and Nicky to New York to meet Hal and the others for their flight to India. As they walked through the gate and out of our sight, I recalled Baba's teaching:

> *"It is on account of the store of merit in past births*
> *that we have attained the feet of Sai Baba"*

Shri Sai Satcharita
Chapter X
Page 62

Garrett had **earned** the right to be in the presence of the Avatar! What a shock for me. I had to try to think of our children **not** as the entities that we had raised in this life, but as timeless, ageless souls who had lived many lives prior to being our children. Who was Garrett in those unknown times? What did he do to merit being with the *Avatar* of the Age? Thinking about Garrett in this way boggled my mind.

Baba has also said:

> *"No one can come to Prasanthi Nilayam*
> *unless I call him."*

Sathyam Sivam Sundaram
Part IV
Page 83

The meaning of that statement, too, is awe-inspiring. Baba calls those that He **chooses** to call. He called Garrett. Somehow, Baba reached out through the billions of people that inhabit our planet, and tapped Garrett on the shoulder and beckoned him to His Side! Why? Why Garrett? Who is Garrett that he should be so honoured by the *Poorna Avatar*? The answer is locked in Baba's Heart. It is not for us to know. It is sufficient to rejoice that Garrett **earned** the invitation and that he answered "yes," when Baba **called.**

> *"You would not have come to me*
> *unless I called you;*
> *I know the past and the future of every one of you,*
> *What you are yearning for at present,*
> *And how and when your yearning will be fulfilled."*

N. Kasturi
Sathyam Sivam Sundaram
Part 3, Page 87

One last observation: Baba had told Hal that "twenty" boys could come when Hal asked Him how many he could bring with him to Summer Showers in May of 1993. There had been twenty boys signed up the previous year, 1992, but that trip did not materialise. When that trip was cancelled by Baba, some of those who had signed on that year, couldn't make it in 1993 so there was a change of members of Hal's team. The final group that made the trip in 1993 was made up of Hal, and **eighteen** young men! For Patty and me, that number was Baba's signature that the invitation was from Him and that He wanted those young men including our son, Garrett, at the Summer Showers Programme.

"I shall not give you up, even if you forsake Me;
for it is not in Me to forsake those who deny Me.
I have come for all.
Those who stray away will come back again to Me.
I bless you that you may earn the vision in this life itself,
with this body itself."

Sathya Sai Speaks
Volume II
Page 129

Baba manifests a ring for one of the American boys after the performance of their play. Notice the amazed expressions on their faces.

From left to right : Nicky LoGrasso, Garrett DiFazio, Patty DiFazio, Maria LoGrasso and Tony LoGrasso Bidding Bon Voyage to our boys as they prepare to fly to India and Baba at the Summer Showers Programme in Whitefield.

Sai Baba watches with rapt attention as the American Boys perform their play.

The boys at dinner with Swami.

Our son, Garret, is granted Padnamask

CHAPTER 28

THE DANCE

"The dance is a Divine Plan
to attract the material creation for all Divine Miracles
...are for drawing people to the Divine Presence
for the purpose of correcting or cleansing them,
or for confirming their faith
and then leading them on to the discipline of service
so that they may merge in ecstasy"

Sathya Sai Speaks
Volume X
Page 202

Several days after Garrett left for India, I picked up a new book about Sathya Sai Baba entitled: **"Vision of Sai."** I began reading it in the evenings. One early afternoon, thereafter, I received a call at my office from Craig Bruce, a devotee of Sai Baba from the St. Louis Center, who was in Connecticut on a work assignment. He had gotten my name from Ramesh Wadhwani of the Shelton, Connecticut Center. Craig liked to attend Sai centers while travelling on business and had called Ramesh to inquire about center meetings. Ramesh suggested that Craig could call us because he would be in our area on Thursday, when our Center met. I returned Craig's call, trying to reach him at his hotel, but he wasn't in. I didn't bother to call again.

That night, in bed, I was reading <u>Vision of Sai</u> ,when I realised that the author of the book was from St. Louis. I commented on that to Patty, asking rhetorically if the author might know Craig Bruce who had called me that day. Patty asked me who the author was. I checked the book's jacket and found, to my surprise, the author's name was Rita Bruce! I had taken Craig Bruce's hotel phone number home with me, so I rummaged through my wallet, located the number and called him immediately. It was late, about eleven o'clock. He was awake and after introducing myself, and before he could get a word in edgewise, I asked him who Rita Bruce was and he calmly answered: "My mother."

The synchronicity of the events was obvious to Patty and me. It was patent that Baba was choreographing something. I told Craig that I had been reading her book just a few minutes before I had called him. I just knew that the coincidence was Baba's *leela*. When I hung up the phone, after talking with Craig and arranging to get together with him at our Sai Center, I was so excited that I told Patty that I wished that I could call someone just to share my wonder at the coincidence. What were the odds that I would get a call from someone I didn't know just while I was reading a book written by his mother? I knew that it was Baba's play.

Suddenly, the phone rang. It was Bob and Addie Grauch calling from Florida. I was so happy to have someone to tell about our little coincidence, that I didn't give them a chance to tell us why they had called so late. It was so special to be able to share this little story knowing that they would understand our feelings and belief that it was Baba's doing. They had no clue as to **why** Baba would tease us with this little drama, but they felt that He was trying to get our attention.

Finally, I realised how late it was for Bob and Addie to be calling us. I guessed that their news was important. Bob told me that he had just received information from India about Hal and the boys. They had arrived safely and already had an interview and *padanamskara* (touching the feet of the saint, guru or *Avatar*)! We couldn't believe it! We hadn't been back to see Baba in the flesh for eight years, and here was Garrett talking with Baba and touching His feet! Once again, Bob and Addie were intricately intertwined in Baba's *leelas* and our life.

After our call from the Grauchs, we were so excited that we couldn't get back to bed. In spite of the hour, we called as many of the parents of the boys visiting Baba in India that we knew and relayed Bob and Addie's information. Then we called our daughter, Leslie, because of all our kids, she seemed the most interested in Garrett's pilgrimage. Also, she had been on retreat with us and Garrett just a few weeks earlier. We babbled on to Leslie about Garrett and Craig Bruce for a few minutes. For some reason, she asked us who were the chaperones that had accompanied the boys to India. I told her, Hal Honig was the chaperone and that we had word that Dr. and Mrs. Sandweiss were there and had spent some time with the group. She responded: "No way! Guess what book I am reading right this minute, The Holy Man and the Psychiatrist, by Sandweiss!"

The coincidence regarding Craig Bruce and his mother, Rita Bruce, highlighted Craig's entry into our lives. Craig travels to Connecticut quite regularly on business and his visits brought us a new friend and he found a home away from home. After meeting

Craig and enjoying his Sai stories, we feel he is part of our extended Sai family. Craig attends our Manchester Sai Center when he is in town and is considered an honorary member by all the devotees there. By sending Craig to us, Baba infused our Center with Craig's devotion and graced us with Craig's stories. What better way for Baba to signal that Craig was to be important in our lives, than Craig's mother's book?

The call from the Grauchs, too, might as well have been a direct call from Baba. In a sense, it was! The Grauchs were His communicators. He wanted Patty and me to know that Garrett was with Him and was fine. I think that He also wanted us to know that He had blessed Garrett by granting an interview, talking with him and touching him! We believed that He wanted us to know that Garrett was in His care.

My daughter, Leslie, has a natural belief that Baba is *Avatar*. The coincidence that Leslie was reading Sandweiss' book, "The Psychiatrist and the Holy Man," while Sandweiss was at Brindavan with Garrett and the rest of Hal's boys, I believe, was a signal from Baba to Leslie that Baba is aware of her, with her and drawing her closer to His Heart.

Now, you may feel that these coincidences were not earth-shattering and not positive proof of Baba's intervention . Yet, we are so comfortable with the belief that Baba was talking to us that night, that we **knew** and **felt** Him to be **present** in our lives, close by, loving us and concerned about us. We don't see those events simply as coincidences. We see them as meaningful. **He** was talking to **us**!

> *"You are as distant from the Lord as you think you are,*
> *as near Him as you feel you are.*
> *Well, let me tell you this.*
> *This distance from Me to you is the same*
> *as the distance from you to Me, is it not?*
> *But, you complain that I am far from you,*
> *though you are approaching nearer and nearer.*
> *How can that be?*
> *I am as near you as you are near Me."*

Thought For The Day
Page K140

CHAPTER 29

TOO SCATTERED

*"You should gradually get rid of the attachments
that lead you astray.
Then only can you stand erect,
without bending under the load.
But, nowadays, instead of the elimination of "Chiththavriththi"
or mental agitations, every effort is made to multiply them.
It is like giving a monkey a drink of toddy;
it will behave even more monkeyishly, that is all."*

Sathya Sai Speaks
Volume II
Page 169

Just before Garrett left for India in May, Patty asked him to ask Baba, if he got the chance, if we could come to India to see Him. We had only been to India once to see Baba and that had been eight years earlier. I pleaded with Him in prayer to make the funds available to us to pay for the trip. For all those years, He hadn't arranged it. Patty told Garret, that if Baba said we could come, to ask Him if we could **"shoot for August."** Well, Garrett had three interviews with Baba and had the opportunity to talk familiarly with Him. At one of the interviews, Garrett remembered to ask Him if Patty and I could come to visit Him. His answer: *"Yes, yes, anytime!"* Then Garrett tried to pin down "anytime." "Could they come in August," he asked? Baba looked to the side, then said: *"Don't shoot for August!"* He had used the exact words, in his response, as Patty had in her charge to Garrett! By way of explanation, Baba made the money sign by rubbing His first two fingers and thumb together indicating that He knew money was a problem for us.

Garrett also asked Baba if He had anything to say about his mother, and Baba answered: *"She is a good devotee, she has a good heart."* Garrett then asked about me and Baba replied: *"He is too scattered!"* Ouch! Once again, Baba showed that He knew what was happening in my life, and once again, like the time that He responded: *"Too many desires!"* to my letter inviting Him to the United States, I was crushed by His remark. The Destroyer, once more, made me come face to face with my own shortcomings, my own monkey mind.

"Do not move so fast with the world;
the cure for moving fast is to sit quiet.
Do not get entangled in the vain hubbub of the world;
the treatment for those who suffer from
the after-effects of that is silence and meditation."

Sathya Sai Speaks
Volume II
Page 30

CHAPTER 30

TESTING THE NAIL

*"This doubt is truly a component
of the Rakshasa (demonic) nature
for it eats into the vitals of Bhakthi (Faith)"*

Sathya Sai Speaks
Volume II
Page 17

Hal's boys were blessed with very close contact with Sai Baba during the Summer Showers programme. Baba gave them an interview almost immediately after their arrival at Brindavan. He asked them questions about themselves, established a warm, relaxed, loving atmosphere around them and even materialised rings and other items for some of them. Baba helped direct the play that Hal had planned to be staged for Him and He arranged for the necessary instruments and props. He sat in on rehearsal and made suggestions and changes. This group did not suffer the usual devotee uncertainties about whether Baba would talk to them, look at them, or grant interviews to them. In all, He granted the boys three interviews and all of them took *padanamaskar* (touching the feet of a holy person). In spite of this familiarity, or possibly because of it, several of the young men had questions or doubts about Baba . Baba seemed to cultivate an American style closeness with the boys rather than invoke the awe and respect traditionally granted to saints or philosophers by Eastern cultures like India. This closeness may have focused some of their minds on the **form** of Sai Baba rather than the vast power and the wonderful mystery behind that form. In any event, despite materialisation of rings and other objects and interviews where He spoke to the boys of leading lives of righteousness, Baba also did things, that to young American trained minds, were uncomfortable, disconcerting and confusing.

For instance, Baba materialised a bracelet for one boy in substitution for another, and when Baba left the room, the old bracelet was lying in the chair where Baba had been sitting. The young man thought that Baba must have used sleight of hand, producing one bracelet and hiding the other. He didn't know what to believe. He wanted Baba's divinity to be clear and unquestionable. What Baba gave him was something to think about. When one considers the manifestations of *vibhuthi* and *kumkum* in homes across the world, separated by thousands of miles from Baba's Puttaparthi, it is obvious that Baba is no mere magician. Yet, to that young man, at that time, there was no consideration of the many miracles across time and space. He was simply unnerved by his experience. But experts have tried to determine or prove that Baba was a magician, fooling the eye with deft hand movements, and not a Divine Incarnation capable of holding the created universe in the palm of His hands. To this date, no one has ever found the slightest hint of sorcery in any of Baba's miracles. In fact, they scratch their heads at reports from reliable, intelligent, educated and honest people who have testified to Baba being in two places at once; healing the sick from a distance and raising individuals from the dead. Why did Baba create such doubt in a young man who had travelled such a great distance to be with Him? No one really knows. At the very least, Baba has made the young man think and maybe that is all that He intended.

For another young man, Baba materialised a ring which He pronounced a "diamond." On the way back home, the fellow shopped for a ring for a girl friend. While doing so, he showed the ring that Baba had produced to the man behind the counter and asked him what it was. The man said that it wasn't a diamond. From all accounts, the jewellery counter clerk's response really upset the young man. Obviously, such an encounter would create the atmosphere for doubt. But again, the fact that Baba has materialised rings, pendants, bracelets and other material objects for thousands, many of which are huge diamonds or other gems of many shades, or gold or silver cannot be denied. Hal Honig, himself, wears a white diamond created by Baba and given to him several years ago. I have held or observed gifts that Baba has given to devotees, for whatever reason, that are made of material which most human cultures count as precious. Recently, I studied a ring made by Baba for a devotee now living in the Boston area. When that ring is moved slightly, the expression of the face of Baba changes from a solemn demeanour to a smile, and that ring is made of silver and gold!

Why did Baba set up circumstances to create doubts in the mind of this young man? I don't know, only Baba knows, but this boy, too, was left with questions that cry out for answers. Some of the questions that might be asked are: Was the jewellery counter man knowledgeable about gems? Did the ring hold a diamond for the boy, but an imitation for the counter man? Did the substance of the ring change because the boy asked to have it appraised? Or was Baba asking the boy, like He has of so many others, to work to control his mind: "Die Mind," His "play" on the word, "diamond," and have faith.

Even Garrett was confused by the interaction with Baba. Over the years, Garrett had known our psychic friend, Aida Bellerose, and had been aware of the reverence and love that she evoked in Patty and me. He knew that she had given us guidance in our lives and had helped us plan for the future with her insights and predictions. He had also seen some of those predictions become reality, so, it is not hard to understand what preconceptions Garrett had about Baba. He really expected that Baba would tell him what the future held; how to prepare for it and even how to handle it when it came about. I believe his ideas of Baba were greatly coloured by his knowledge of Aida. Like most young men of twenty-one, his concerns were about his future in this life, not necessarily about his knowledge of or the development of his unity with divinity!

Garrett wanted personal questions answered and if the other boys were like him in that respect, they too wanted to know what they could expect in their lives, not in philosophical terms, but in concrete, "this is how it will happen" terms. They expected God to give them the finished structures of their lives, and instead, Baba gave them blueprints for living their lives. Garrett asked Baba about his music and his band. He expected Baba to tell him what would happen with the band. Would it be successful? Where should he go with the band? What kind of reception would be given their music? Baba answered: "Study first!" Taken aback, Garrett asked what he should study, Baba answered: "Ask your parents!' Obviously, for a kid looking and hoping to find the path that would convert his dreams and aspirations into physical manifestation, Baba's answers were not what he wanted or expected.

He wanted help in knowing **what to do** to accomplish what he wanted to accomplish. His youthful dreams and aspirations did not include study or preparation. He wanted to make it happen **now**! Baba's answers meant work, discipline and listening to the very people that he was trying to break from, to win independence from. And so, Garrett, like some of the others came away from Baba confused and disillusioned.

As difficult as these challenges were to these young men, they paled next to their experiencing and living through the shocking event that enveloped Prasanthi Nilyam on their last day in India. The boys had followed Baba from Brindavan for a visit to the *ashram* before they returned home. When they awoke on that last day , they were stunned by the news that on the previous evening a serious attempt on the life of the *Avatar* had been made by four people alleged to have been students of Baba's College. That information was appalling, but was soon tempered by the reassuring report that Sai Baba was unharmed. The attackers had been unable to accomplish their evil intent. And then came the bombshell. The assailants had killed two of Sai Baba's aides. Police from Puttaparthi had rushed to the *ashram*, and stormed the room in the *mandir* (the temple housing Baba's small living quarters) where the assailants had barricaded themselves after their aborted attempt on Sai Baba's life. Each of the four perpetrators had themselves been killed by the police!

The American students were dumbfounded! How could that happen at Prasanthi Nilayam, the Abode of Peace? Why didn't Sai Baba prevent those deaths from occurring? Didn't He realize in advance that the whole event was going to happen? Obviously, the trauma of the incident added to the doubts about Baba that some of the boys had been experiencing. They never thought about other *Avatars* and their sufferings like Jesus on the cross or the over seventy-five recorded attempts on the life of Krishna. These young men were idealistic and wanted so much to believe that Sai Baba was above worldly affairs. They were dismayed to think that something so evil as an attempt on His life could even occur. In their dismay they could not recall Baba's explanation of why *Avatars* live as humans in our world:

*"The Avatar behaves in a human way
so that mankind can feel kinship,
but rises to superhuman heights
so that mankind can aspire
to those heights."*

Sathya Sai Speaks
Volume IV
Chapter 7
Page 41

But, in the heat of that ugly day, the boys can certainly be forgiven for not realising that an *Avatar* chooses to live in our every day world to show by His actions and teachings that Man can aspire higher. The time was not ripe for philosophical insight. They were simply overwhelmed with disbelief. Possibly no other occurrence could have confused them or caused them as much doubt as this one.

If I had **my** way, Garrett and all the other boys would have come back to the United States as fledgling saints. But Baba sent some of them back confused; some of them questioning; some of them seemingly unmoved in any way. Yet, He had told Hal before they went to Him: *"I will change them."* I assumed that meant sainthood. I was wrong. Baba made them questioners, thinkers, challengers. He was asking them to inquire and to be more aware. In the long run, whether their path is to Baba, Jesus, Allah or the unknown God, or whether their heart is set on His form or the Formless Absolute, these young men, blessed beyond their dreams, have been thrown out of the nest by the Divine Mother and asked to continue their quest for truth and spiritual understanding. Baba didn't make it easy for them by telling them what to expect and what to do. He made it exciting by making them inquire and think.

"When you hang a picture on the wall,
you shake the nail and find out
whether it is firm enough to bear
the weight of the picture.
So, too, in order to prevent the picture of God
(His image in your mind and heart)
from falling and being shattered to bits,
the nail...driven into the wall of the heart
has to be shaken to ascertain
whether it is firm and steady"

Sai Baba Avatar
Howard Murphet
Chapter 8
Page 58

CHAPTER 31

WHAT'S IN A NAME?

*"The Avatar comes as man
in order to demonstrate
that man is Divine,
in order to be within reach of man."*

Sathya Sai Speaks
Volulme VIII
Page 129

Two months after Garrett returned from India, he joined Patty and me for an automobile trip to Washington, D.C. to visit our sons, Marc and Andy. We planned to spend the July 4th. weekend with the boys and their friends and watch the fireworks at the Washington Monument. On the way, Garrett kept asking us to suggest names for a new rock band that he was forming. He drove us crazy! No matter what we were talking about, he brought the conversation back to names for that band. Finally, I shouted: "I have it! Avatar! Name the band, Avatar!" No, no way," said Garrett and then the game went on.

When we arrived in Washington, Garrett harassed Marc, Andy and all their friends to suggest names for his band. By the end of the weekend, Garrett had collected over a hundred names. One of the names on his list was "Avatar," written down just to appease me. I tried to make my case for that name simply because I felt that if the band was called "Avatar," and "advertised" as "Avatar," and introduced as "Avatar," Garrett would be reminded of the *Avatar* of the Age, Sathya Sai Baba, each time he heard the word.

When Garrett returned home, he called a meeting of the band and shared the names with them. They culled out about thirty names that were acceptable to one or more of the band members and put them in a hat. Lo and behold! One of the names that got into that hat was "Avatar." One of the members must have liked it. They all agreed that whatever name came out of the hat would be the name of the band. Sure enough, the hand went in to the hat and came out with the name, "Avatar!" Was it just coincidence, or was Baba telling Garrett that in spite of Garrett's doubts, He was with him?

"If Baba accepts a devotee,
He follows him and stands by him,
day and night, at his home or abroad.
Let the devotee go anywhere he likes,
Baba is there ahead of him
in some form,
in an inconceivable manner."

Sri Sai Satcharita
Chapter XLVI
Page 235

CHAPTER 32

GAYATHRI

*"Gayathri means
'that which saves when repeated'."*

Sathya Sai Speaks
Volume IV
Page 260

Our daughter, Andrea, seems bent on scaring us with emergencies and fear for her physical well-being. Soon after her daughter, Monica, was born, she was passing through a check out counter at a local supermarket when a heavy accounting book fell fifteen feet out of an office loft on to her head! Our three month old granddaughter, Monica, was in a little seat in the grocery cart and by God's Grace, the book missed hitting her and possibly killing her. Because of that accident, Andrea had serious physical problems to cope with, including fainting spells, migraine headaches, neck pain and sporadic paralysis in her leg which would cause her to fall. We were extremely concerned about her and her ability to care for the baby in that condition. For months she needed help with her daily routine tasks.

Early one evening several months later, while Craig Bruce was visiting us from Saint Louis, we received a telephone call from Patty's brother, Drew, who informed us that Andrea had been involved in a fatal car accident in Old Lyme. We were speechless! Drew had little information other than what he had been told by the police; that Andrea was involved, a fatality had occurred and Andrea had been taken by ambulance to Lawrence Memorial Hospital. We knew that Andrea was alive but we didn't know about her husband, Eric or our granddaughter, Monica. Andrea was six months pregnant with another baby. We didn't know if it was the baby in the womb who had died and we had no idea of Andrea's condition. Was she critically hurt; was she stable? We had a million questions and no answers.

Patty and I left immediately for the hospital in New London about an hour away. We left our overnight guest, Craig, in a state of confusion but we did think to ask him to pray for Andrea. Patty and I knew that if we rode in silence or in hysteria, we would crumble with fear, so we decided to repeat the *Gayathri Mantra* while picturing the form of Sathya Sai Baba for strength.

*"Never give up the Gayathri;
you may give up or ignore
any other mantra,
but you should recite it
at least a few times a day.
It will protect you from harm,
wherever you are..."*

Sathya Sai Speaks
Vol X
Page 153

The *Gayathri Mantra* is a special prayer that illuminates the intelligence and fosters **harmony and protection:**

"Om Bhur Bhuvaha Suvaha
Thath Savithur Varenyam
Bhargo Devasya Dheemahi
Dhiyo Yo Naha Prachodayath."

Translated, the *Gayathri* means:

"We contemplate the Glory of Light
illuminating the three worlds:
Gross, Subtle and Causal
I Am that Vivifying Power, Love,
Radiant Illumination, and
Divine Grace of Universal Intelligence.
We pray for the Divine Light
to illumine our minds."

An Index of Sathya Sai Speaks
Volumes I through XI
Page 70 and 71

While repeating the Divine *Gayathri* during our hour long jouney to New London, we tried to send Andrea our love and the protection of God in the form of the vibrations radiating from our repetition of the *Gayathri*. It is said that *Gayathri* is the divine power manifesting in a **sound body**. It is itself, God in sound form as much as Sai Baba is God in human form. In a sense, we tried to be one with Andrea through the *Gayathri*. Somehow, we remained calm and never broke down. When we arrived at the hospital, we found Andrea lying on a stretcher in the emergency room. She was bruised, whiplashed and mentally stressed, but she was alive, whole and in no danger of death. Splintered glass from the shattered windshield had caused little cuts over her face and chest. When we inquired about the baby that she was carrying, we were told that the foetus seemed to be fine and there were no contractions. Andrea was to stay at the hospital for two or three days to make sure that she was all right and to allow the hospital staff to monitor fetal activity.

Andrea, Eric and a state police officer filled us in on what had happened. Andrea had left home alone to pick up a video movie. Eric and Monica remained at home and were safe. Tragically, a man riding a motorcycle failed to negotiate a curve and struck Andrea's car head on! He died instantly. An autopsy, reported to us later, indicated that he had been drinking and was legally intoxicated. Although we were greatly saddened by his tragic death, we were also greatly relieved that our daughter was safe and sound.

Andrea gave birth to her second daughter, Felicia, several months later. Thank God the baby was beautiful and healthy and didn't seem to have any ill-effects from Andrea's accident. But Andrea's saga was to continue. One Friday afternoon, Andrea was preparing to entertain guests for dinner. She had put the babies to bed for their late afternoon nap and dinner was in the oven. She told Eric that she was going for a jog at Rocky Neck State Park opposite their street and that she would be back in about forty-five minutes, in time to greet their guests.

Meanwhile, Patty was driving home from work about the same time that Andrea was in the middle of her run. Patty was prayerfully thinking about our kids and reciting the *Gayathri Mantra* thirty five miles from where Andrea was jogging. As Andrea was running the last part of her loop around the park, she saw a man with close cropped hair wearing a green army jacket run out of the woods and begin running behind her. It made her nervous so she picked up speed. Suddenly, she was pulled backward as the man from the woods grabbed her by her pony tail and threw her into the trees. He assaulted her, punching her face until she lost consciousness!

No one knows, for sure, what happened next, but it seems that a jogger who had been running in front of Andrea by about sixty or seventy yards, finished his run in the direction that she had been going, turned around and began running back toward where Andrea was lying in the woods. He had a dog with him who ran ahead. The dog and the return of this jogger must have frightened the attacker because he ran off leaving Andrea unconscious. The jogger saw her lying there and when he realised that she was badly hurt, he ran to the park ranger who called for an ambulance. The jogger ran back to Andrea who was regaining consciousness. Once he was able to make her understand that he was trying to help her, Andrea tried to tell him who she was, but she could only remember her first name and the word, "Cherrystones", which is the name of Patty's family restaurant nearby. Andrea was whisked off by ambulance to Lawrence Memorial Hospital in New London where she regained full consciousness. Once notified, Eric flew to her side. By the grace of God, Andrea had not been raped and there was no major injury other than a badly battered face, which healed in a short time. At this time, the police have leads and hopefully Andrea's attacker will be arrested and brought to justice before any one else is harmed.

When Patty realised that the attack occurred at precisely the same time that she was chanting the *Gayathri Mantra* on her way home, she felt, once again, that Sai Baba had protected Andrea and saved her from rape or death. The *Gayathri* helped Patty keep a clear head, centered on Baba, when Andrea had been in her accident with the motorcyclist and Patty believes it was the Baba "radio" that sent its vibrations of love and protection to Andrea when she was attacked.

Sathya Sai Baba teaches us that we should not be swayed to and fro by our fears and even by our joys. He asks us to remain calm and clothed with equanimity no matter what life brings our way. In this world of duality, that is very difficult and in order to approach that objective, we must focus on the Divine. Reciting the *Gayathri* did not change the fact that the accident and the assault had occurred, but it allowed Patty to focus and approach each disturbing event with balance and peace.

"Your two eyes cannot reveal to you the magnificence
and the majesty of the realm of the spirit. They are
focused towards the objective world and its transient attractions.
So the Gayathri Mantra has been given to you as a third eye
to reveal to you that inner vision by which you may realise
Brahman.
Gayathri is a treasure you must guard throughout your lives.
If you have not caught the sounds of the mantra correctly now,
learn it from your parents or from your family priest.
Perhaps they may not know the Gayathri themselves,
or they might have forgotten it through culpable neglect.
Then I would ask them to learn it from you."

Sathya Sai Speaks
Volume X
Page 152

CHAPTER 33

MORRIS AND ESTHER

**"The question of not keeping his promises does not arise at all
but the time factor is always a big question with Baba.
He often promises something
but we do not know when the promise will be fulfilled.
In many cases it takes years."**

And the Greatest is Love
By: A.M.
Chapter 12
Page 77

Patty and I had not taken a special vacation in a while, when a friend and a client, who I will simply call the "Muffler Man," telephoned and said that he had tickets for a cruise out of Miami for four days in the Caribbean. He had won the tickets for attaining certain sales objectives in his company and wanted to know if we could join him and his wife. We were able to buy the tickets at a discount from him and a dream vacation became a reality.

We sailed on a beautiful, new luxury liner. The ship was clean, shiny and opulent. There was a five-storey atrium in the middle of the ship and everything seemed to be made of glass and brass. It was as luxurious as any grand hotel in any major city in the world. In the restaurant, there were eight seats at most tables and the tables were set up on several tiers. At each meal, we dined with the Muffler Man and his wife, Muffler Man II and his wife, and an older couple, Oscar and Muriel. Muffler Man told me that he knew Oscar's son and didn't get along with him very well, so he asked me if Patty and I would sit next to Oscar and his wife during the trip, as a buffer between the two couples. Muffler Man felt that it would be difficult for him to make small talk with Oscar and Muriel. We were happy to do so as Patty and I love to meet new people and we considered the arrangement an opportunity.

Now, it happened that everyone at our table, except Patty and me, were Jewish. Muriel was trying to figure out our nationality and more importantly to her, to what religion Patty and I belonged. After a while, she couldn't contain herself any longer and just came right out and asked us. I wasn't sure how to answer her, because although I was born, raised and educated a Catholic, I no longer felt myself a

Catholic. My divorce, the psychic, Aida Bellerose and many other people and experiences that I encountered on my life's journey, had dropped me squarely at the feet of Sathya Sai Baba. Of course, I just **knew** that Muriel would have no idea who or what Sai Baba is, so I hesitated before I replied, "Hindu, I am a Hindu!" I was shocked to hear myself say that, as I knew that I really wasn't a Hindu per se. I just couldn't think of any way to explain our devotion to Sai Baba as an Incarnation of God and I really didn't want to have to explain to people who I thought, would not understand.

But, surprisingly, Muriel was not put off by my claim of being a Hindu, and pressed us to more fully explain "what we do and what we believe." Finally, the circuitous route of my explanations became too unwieldy for me and I just blurted out that we were devotees of Sathya Sai Baba. To my utter amazement and delight, Oscar said, "My brother, Morris, who lives in Florida believes in Him." I was dumbfounded! I sat there with my mouth open. I would have bet a hundred bucks that there wasn't one person on that ship who had even heard of Sai Baba, and here I was sitting next to a guy whose brother was a devotee!

What had begun as curiosity on Muriel's part, turned into an animated conversation about Sai Baba! Oscar asked me if I really believed in the stories of miracles surrounding Baba and, of course, I said that I did. Patty and I shared stories of materialisation and cures and other inexplicable phenomena associated with Sai Baba. It was then that Oscar told us more about his brother, Morris, who, it seemed, was fighting a losing battle with cancer. It was clear that Oscar was wondering if Baba would or could cure his brother.

I asked Oscar to tell me a little about his brother. He replied that "Morris is a very good and wonderful man." He had been a bus driver in New York City and had been given an award as the best bus driver in the city. Oscar told us that on really bad weather days, Morris would often make an extra stop to drop off an elderly man or woman in front of their apartment so that they wouldn't have to fight the elements. Morris had a blind fellow that was a regular passenger on his route. If the blind man had not yet reached the bus stop when Morris' bus pulled up, Morris would stand up and do a song and soft shoe routine to the delight of the other passengers, just to give the tardy, handicapped man time to get to the bus. The bus company offered Morris a promotion to "work inside." He wouldn't take the job. "No way," he said, "I drive the bus because I love the people!"

> *"The easiest and the most fruitful expression*
> *of Dharma (righteous living)*
> *today consists in Seva, service*
> *as worship of the Divine around you.*
> *Dedicate all your skill, talents, wealth and scholarship*
> *to the living embodiments of Divinity*
> *that are around you."*

Sathya Sai Speaks
Volume VII
Page 529

We were planning to spend a week with Patty's parents in Highland Beach, Florida after the cruise, and since Morris and his wife, Esther, lived a short distance from Highland Beach, we took Morris' phone number and address from Oscar and promised him that we would give Morris a call and visit with him if he were up to it.

Shortly after we arrived at our family's condominium in Highland Beach, we called Morris. He didn't come to the phone, but we spoke with Esther who told us that Morris wasn't feeling too well. We informed her that we were aware that Morris belonged to a Sai Center and that we would like to go with them to their Center meeting that week while we were in the area. Esther said that she would call us back. About an hour later, we received a call from Bob and Addie Grauch, who confirmed that Morris was too ill to go out that week, but that they would be pleased to take us to the meeting.

We met Bob and Addie at a point half way between their home and my in-laws' condominium. Bob is in his seventies, tall and thin. His bright and ready smile made us feel like we had known each other forever. Addie is a delightful little lady with a soft, gentle voice and a beaming smile that matched her husband's sunny countenance. At their Center, we were asked to share our few experiences of Baba and we listened eagerly to Baba stories from different Center members. Patty and I shared with them, the story of the cruise, Oscar and Muriel, and how we happened to be with their Center that evening. We could sense Baba's hand setting up the chain of events leading to the wonderful *satsang* enjoyed by all of us that night.

At home several months later, we received a call from Bob and Addie who informed us that Oscar had decided to pay for Morris and his wife, Esther, to travel to Prasanthi Nilayam. They told us that although Oscar wasn't a devotee, our sharing of our belief in Sai Baba with him on the ship, convinced him that if Baba were a miracle worker, maybe He would heal his beloved brother, Morris. Anyway, cure or no cure, it was still Morris' wish to go to India to see Baba, and since Morris was dying, Oscar felt that his brother should at least have this, his last wish, fulfilled.

Soon thereafter, we again heard from Bob and Addie who informed us that they had brought Morris and Esther to the airport, the first step in their journey to the *Avatar*. It seemed almost impossible, but Morris was in India. Just prior to the trip, Morris was having fluid drained from his lungs regularly! Bob and Addie took him through the airport in a wheelchair. I inquired if Bob and Addie had heard how he was faring in India. Bob said yes, they had received a call from a friend in India, who informed them that Morris was doing fine. There had been no interview with Baba but Morris didn't seem to need the lung draining treatment that he required at home. Although Baba had not cured him, He was watching over him.

Patty and I decided to call Oscar to tell him that Morris was holding up, but we didn't have his telephone number. I called my friend, Muffler Man, who gave me Oscar's son's number. After a brief explanation, he furnished me with Oscar's home phone. When I had Oscar on the phone, I gave him as many of the details of Morris' condition as had been given to me by Bob and Addie. He was very pleased with the call, and relieved that his brother was not failing because of the arduous journey.

Then I told Oscar how pleased Patty and I were when we learned that he had paid for Morris' trip and what a wonderful act of love we felt it was. His response set me back. "What do you mean?" he asked, "I didn't pay for the trip." "Then, who did? I thought Morris couldn't afford it," I responded. "He couldn't," Oscar said, "and I couldn't either. I'm not a rich man, but I talked to my family and one by one, they all agreed to chip in something." He explained that his older sister gave one half of her life savings, which wasn't very much in amount but a great part of all that she had! Morris's brothers and sisters kicked in as did their children and even grandchildren. Morris's daughter contributed all of her savings into the pot.

When I hung up the phone after my call to Oscar, and shared with Patty how Oscar's family had come together in love so that Morris would have the chance to go to India and possibly be healed by Sathya Sai Baba, Patty and I were deeply moved. It was obvious that Baba had placed Patty and me on that cruise ship, when we shouldn't have had the opportunity for such a vacation, just to touch Oscar. Then Oscar was His instrument to move the whole extended family. The family was given the grace to respond to and grant a dying man, a good man, who had given so much to others, his dying wish. We could clearly see how Baba fit the pieces of this puzzle together over time until the whole picture was revealed.

> *"...for only when the cause,*
> *the time and the necessary actions*
> *are in fruitful combination*
> *will the event happen."*

> Baba's Birthday Discourse
> November 23, 1994
> Sathya Sai Newsletter, USA
> Volume 19, Number 3
> Page 2

Morris died several months later. In February of 1994, on a visit to Florida, Patty and I had the opportunity, thanks to Bob and Addie Grauch, to meet with Esther Colchamiro who filled us in on the Morris story as she lived it and saw it. Esther confirmed how good a man Morris had been. She told us that when Morris retired, he began driving young children from wealthy families to school. Some of the kids were spoiled, unruly and hard to control, so Morris made up stories about the fictional "Butter Brothers," and mesmerised those kids with his creative, funny, moving tales. The youngsters became so docile and well-behaved, that some of the parents began to question Morris' methods. On occasion, the parents would ride with Morris and the children to see if everything was all right. They too, were delighted with Morris and fascinated by his stories of the "Butter Brothers."

Esther told us that Morris had three wishes that he hoped would come true before he died: He wanted to see Sai Baba; he wanted to fly in a dirigible; and he wanted to travel under water in a submarine.

He accomplished all three. Esther believes that he was able to do so, due to the love and grace of the *Avatar*, Sathya Sai Baba.

When Morris's brother, Oscar, had told him of meeting Patty and me on the cruise ship, and asked Morris if he would like to see Sai Baba in India, Morris replied that he believed that Baba had miraculously arranged our meeting with Oscar and therefore, it must be Baba's wish that he travel to India to see Him. Morris accepted the loving gifts of money for the trip from his relatives, in spite of not being good at receiving, because, Esther said, Morris felt that Baba had designed, planned and ordered the whole scenario. By accepting the money and taking the trip, he was simply acceding to Baba's Divine Will.

After Oscar had contacted the family about raising the money to pay for the trip to India, checks began arriving at Morris' home one after another. Approximately six thousand dollars was received from his loving family. "It was just enough for the two of us to travel, stay in a hotel, eat and fly back," Esther reported. "We came back broke," she laughed. "We had just enough!" she repeated. "It was Baba's grace."

Morris and Esther had travelled first to Bangalore and then to Kodaikanal, India, to see Baba in April of 1993. Kodai is an old, British hill station which had been a resort for the British ruling class. Today, it is a cool mountain resort area visited during the hot days of the Indian summer by vacationing Indians. Baba usually spends April there, and so the Colchamiros had the good fortune of being able to stay at a good hotel while they were on pilgrimage to Sathya Sai Baba. The temperatures were in the seventies during their visit, quite comfortable for the terminally ill, Morris. It appeared that Sai Baba had lovingly ordered and planned their trip to give the least discomfort to Morris.

Patty and I had thought that Esther and Morris had journeyed just to Bangalore and Whitefield to visit Baba. When Esther told us that Kodai had been their destination because Baba had travelled there, we were pleasantly surprised. You see, we had been planning a trip to see Baba ourselves, two months later, in April of 1994 and we had heard that He would be at Kodai. We took the coincidence as a sign that Baba wanted Patty and me to make the trip. Having Esther confirm the date that Baba was likely to be at Kodai was like an invitation to us from the Lord to vacation with Him at Kodai-kanal!

When Morris and Esther arrived in Madurai, the major Indian city closest to the hill station, Kodai, they began a harrowing five-hour cab drive into the mountains around hairpin curves overlooking valleys thousands of feet below. Esther said that she was a nervous wreck. "But Morris didn't care. He was going away anyway, but I wasn't ready!" she joked.

Now at Kodai, just as it is in the *ashram*, Prasanthi Nilayam, the men and women have to sit separately to avoid distractions. At one of their early *darshans* after arriving at Kodai, Baba walked up to Esther and asked, *'Where are you from?"* Shocked that Baba would talk to her, Esther replied: "From Florida." Baba walked away saying, *"I know, I know."* After the *darshan*, Esther ran to Morris, all excited. "You'll never guess who spoke to me," she shouted. "Who?" Morris asked. "Baba!" she told him breathlessly. At that point, she wasn't sure why Baba would talk to her and not to Morris. "I'm only here for Morris," she thought, "why doesn't he go to Morris?"

Baba blessed Esther in many little ways while she was at Kodai. It seems that somehow, she was in the front row at every *darshan*. As anyone knows who has been to see Baba at Brindavan, Kodai or Puttaparthi, it is not easy to get in the front row, on any one day, let alone every *darshan*. Baba was obviously reaching out to Esther; perhaps to give her strength to cope with Morris' illness. It is said that Baba gives people just what they need. During one *darshan*, Esther had the opportunity for *Padnamaskar*, and touched Baba's feet. "His feet are so soft," she laughed. "And He's so cute!"

While Baba was letting Esther know that He knew she was there, Morris did not have any conversation with Baba nor did Baba approach him in the patients' section, but Morris did make direct eye contact with Him. Direct eye contact from the Avatar of the Age has been known to strike some devotees with such intensity, that their lives are forever changed. Often, a devotee will credit an intense stare from Baba's expressive eyes, with redirecting their goals in life, from the material to the spiritual. Morris' reaction to Baba looking at him and into him was: "It cured my mind!"

"Do not think that I do not care for you
or that I do not know you.

*I may not talk to you but
do not be under the impression
that I have no love."*

Sathya Sai Speaks
Volume IV
Chapter 19
page 113

Morris said that he became very "peaceful" and "that meant more to me than anything." That peaceful attitude radiated all over Morris. Bob Grauch said that when he and Addie went to pick up the Colchamiros, on their return from India, Morris was pushing his wheel chair with his baggage on it instead of his sitting in it and being pushed along by someone else. When Bob looked at Morris, Bob said that he felt a "warmth" throughout his entire body. Obviously, Morris' inner radiance deeply penetrated the heart of Bob Grauch.

But where Morris had an inner transformation of consciousness while at Kodai, Esther continued to have little Baba events occur which suggested to her that she was being guided by the *Avatar*. One day, she wandered into the wrong area, and found herself standing with a group of ladies. A woman asked her if she had an invitation, as that meeting was by invitation only. Realising that she had strayed into a private gathering, Esther was embarrassed and apologised for being in the wrong place. She volunteered to go. The woman looked at her and said, "No, you stay, your being here must be Baba's *leela*. you have His invitation." So Esther enjoyed an intimate *bhajan* session with the *Avatar*.

Esther had taken letters from American devotees to give to Baba. He took them from her, thereby indicating that He will, in some way, answer each writer. Morris, also, had brought letters from devotees but he was unable to hand them over to Baba. He was always seated too far away and was not being approached by Baba. So Morris gave Esther his letters too. Morris told her: "You take the letters." She did and Baba accepted them from her right away.

When Baba left His mountain retreat and headed toward Brindavan, Morris and Esther also left Kodai and travelled down the mountain on the first leg of their arduous trek home. Baba's car was in front of their taxi all the way down the mountain, granting the Colchamiros a final *darshan* of the *Avatar*. For Morris, who for years had been following the Lord, following Baba as He left Kodai was a grace and a fitting symbol.

Of course, we have no way of knowing Baba's intentions when He acts in our lives, but it seems that the pilgrimage of Morris and Esther to Baba's feet was as much for Esther's benefit as it was for Morris. Esther told us that she went to India for Morris, but when she saw Baba, she found herself "bubbling over" with joy. Her attitude was so positive, that Morris was "thrilled" to see her moved just by being in the presence of Swami. What a gift from Morris was Esther's trip to Baba; and what a gift from Baba to Morris was Esther's love and reverence for Sai Baba. Morris believed in Sai. He was so happy that his wife now shared his feelings.

It is interesting to note that the name, **Colchamiro**, a Greek-Jewish name, was adopted as the family name by Morris' grandfather when he immigrated to the United States. The name comes from the Yiddish word, "chumutz," which means "cleaning up for the holy days" I like to think Morris' last name to be symbolic of his having "cleaned up" his *karma* and become realized. Perhaps Morris was a soul who had completed his spiral back to the Lord and is now living his "holy days!" Esther told us that the reason that Morris wanted to go to see Baba, was to find out what his "next step in life" should be. But Baba didn't talk to Morris and gave him no directions, no new marching orders. Maybe that is because this good man, Morris Colchamiro, had accomplished all that he was supposed to in this life and there was simply no "next step." Only **He** knows.

Patty and I had been inexorably drawn into the saga of Esther and Morris, moved like pawns on a chess board by His Will. We were actors in His drama and He moved us and all the others across the stage of Morris' life, like the Director that He is. We never met Morris nor spoke to him, but Baba drew us into the circle of Morris' life and we somehow, became one with him; eager for him to travel to Baba; happy that he went; awed by the pieces that Baba put together to make Morris' trip a reality; and deeply moved by Esther's recitation of their time at Baba's feet in Kodai. By his example of living life fully by *dharma*; by his example of giving and receiving in love, Morris has touched our lives and helped us grow. Thank you, Morris. Thank you, Esther. Thank you, Baba.

> *"...above all, be an example to others*
> *by means of sweet speech, humility,*
> *reverence to elders, truthfulness,*
> *faith and steadfastness.*
> *That way, you will bring more*
> *into the fold of theism than by*
> *establishing societies, collecting donations*
> *and running mandirs."*

<u>Sathya Sai Speaks</u>
Volume IV
Page 92

CHAPTER 34

DEVOTEES

*"You become a devotee
when God has acknowledged your devotion.
The ego is the greatest obstacle in the way of such acceptance.
God has said, 'Yo mad bhakthah sa me priyah!'
He who is My devotee is My friend."*

Sathya Sai Speaks
Volume VIII
Page 21

Patty and I have been blessed to have met many devotees of Sai Baba whose interaction with Him has made us acutely aware of His Presence in the lives of His devotees and mindful of His profound spiritual teachings. One couple, Ramesh and Sunita Wadhwani of Shelton, Connecticut are such devotees. Over the years, they have received much grace from Bhagavan Sri Sathya Sai Baba. Their stories about Him have touched us deeply, and moved us to study Him and His message more intensely.

In August of 1982, the Wadhwani family experienced *vibhuthi* manifesting in their home. In a few days, the appearance of the holy ash grew into a storm of *vibhuthi* appearing almost everywhere. Pictures of Sai Baba, Krishna, Jesus and other saints were covered with *vibhuthi* and *amrita*, a clear, sweet, honey-like substance often referred to as the "Nectar of the Gods!" People came from as far away as Miami, Florida and St. Louis, Missouri to view the phenomenon and to place pictures of their own on a table. Soon *vibuthi* would appear on the photographs and paintings of the visitors also. Devotees came regularly to "Sai Nevas," the home of Sai, as the Wadhwanis called their home.

Patty and I visited the Wadhwani home for a celebration of Krishna's birthday one year, and a primary purpose of our visit was to examine the phenomena of *vibhuthi* and *amrita* forming on the pictures of saints and avatars. I remember looking from picture to picture hoping to understand what it all meant. Some of the pictures had vibhuthi between the picture and the glass while some had *amrita* flowing on the outside of the glass. I realized that there was no obvious pattern to the manifestation of the holy ash or the *amrita*. It did not appear that some human hand had purposefully applied the ash and honey to the pictures as the material produced seemed different in each picture. Although incomprehensible to my mind, it was obvious to my heart that Sai Baba had somehow materialized the *vibhuthi* and *amrita*. Surely these manifestations were a sign of His love and a call to wonderment, that from across nine thousand miles, time and space, Sathya Sai Baba could and would materialise the gray-white ash on the photographs of a devoted family.

Several years ago, Baba had materialised and given a gold ring with nine gems around the top to Ramesh. Over time, several of the stones came loose and were lost. Finally, the ring itself was broken in half horizontally. Ramesh brought it with him to India in March of 1994, and in an interview offered it to Baba. Baba took the top half of the ring, leaving the bottom half in Ramesh's hands. He showed it around to the others in the interview room. When it was returned to Him, Baba asked Ramesh, "what do you want, stones or Swami?" Of course, Ramesh asked for Baba. Holding the ring between His fingers, with a puff of His Divine breath, Baba changed the half ring into a beautiful gold ring with His image engraved on the surface. The ring did not fit at first, being too tight to pass over the last knuckle, but as the day wore on, it slipped softly over the resistant knuckle coming to a comfortable rest. Ramesh reports that it still gets "tight and at times is painful."

> *"The mind plays tricks with man,*
> *who believes that some things are good and some bad,*
> *some eternal and some transitory.*
> *There is no object without fault or failing;*
> *there is no pleasure that is unmixed with pain."*

Sathya Sai Speaks
Chapter 10
Page 14-15

Ramesh, all the while, had been holding the other half of the old ring in his palm. As Baba turned His attention to others, Ramesh thought, "Well, I'll just keep this too!" As he had the thought, the bottom half of that old ring vanished, in an instant, from his hand!

"I am aware of the past, present and future,
of your innermost thought
and carefully guarded secrets."

Sathya Sai Speaks
Volume VII
Chapter 59
Page 339

Just before our Eighteenth Annual Northeast Sai Conference and Retreat in May of 1993, Ramesh received word from India that his mother had a serious heart attack and was dying. He and his brothers and sisters living in other parts of the world rushed to India to be with her at the end. The family imported expensive prescriptions from abroad hoping to revive their mother's stricken heart, however, nothing seemed to work. The doctors told Ramesh that she would not last long, but yes, he had time to hasten to Baba at Whitefield for a day's visit to try to talk to Baba about his mother. When he arrived at Whitefield, Ramesh spent most of the day calling to Baba in his mind, bemoaning his mother's illness, and mulling over other personal worries. He continued to pray that Baba would grant him an interview.

Just before he was to leave, Baba called Ramesh in and said: *"why have you been talking to yourself 'whether Baba will see me or not.' You must have faith. Your faith is bumping and jumping like a monkey. This is not good."*

"So, have faith in the Assurance of the Lord;
When he says 'Why fear, I am here,
He means it;
when he says,
'I look to you, when you look to Me,'
He means it."

Chinna Katha
Stories and Parables
Bhagavan Sri Sathya Sai Baba
Page 226

Flabbergasted at Sai Baba's awareness of his prayers all day, Ramesh told Him of his mother. Baba answered: *"Yes, I know, she has a weak heart."* He told him not to worry. *"Leave it to God and do Seva to mother."* Baba told him that he would give prasad (consecrated food, blessed by God) for the mother and then changed the topic of conversation. Later, at the end of the interview, Swami gave *vibhuthi prasad* to Ramesh for his stricken mother.

Ramesh returned to his family and asked that the medicine treatment that was being administered to his mother be terminated. Intravenously, He gave her the *vibhuthi* sent by Baba three times a day. Ramesh then returned to his family in the United States. Within five days, Ramesh got a telephone call from his family that his mother had been moved from the Intensive Care Unit at the hospital to a regular room and was eating a normal diet. Within a month, she returned to her home. By Baba's Grace, her life was extended. All this, **after** the doctors had tried all procedures and imported special medications from the United States. Those procedures and medications had all failed to revive the ailing heart while the Grace of the *Avatar* strengthened and restored her.

Several months later, Ramesh arranged for his mother and his sister to meet him at the *ashram* to seek Baba's blessings and to thank Him for His granting her a second lease on life. Baba called them for an interview and conferred abundant blessings on the elderly woman. At that interview, the mother complained to Baba that the family would not grant her wish. She didn't say what that wish was. The mother had wanted to travel to a niece's wedding, but Ramesh and his siblings, would not let her go because they were concerned that the strenuous journey would be too much for her. Baba looked at Ramesh and said, *"Ramesh, let her go to the wedding!"* Astonished once again, Ramesh could only stammer something about her frail condition. Baba told him that He would take care of her and that He would be *"above her and around her"* and that the family *"should not worry!"* After all, if He could save her from death, it is surely true that He could and would watch over her on the journey to her niece's wedding.

Ramesh told us: "Again, He knows everything. Nothing is hidden from Him. This (Baba's Omniscience) He has demonstrated to many devotees again and again. But, we human devotees, fall prey to *Maya* (delusion) around us and tend to forget that someone up there is taking care of us."

> *"There will never be any dearth or scarcity,*
> *regarding food and clothes, in any **devotees'** homes.*
> *It is My special characteristic,*
> *that I always look to and provide,*
> *for the welfare of those devotees,*
> *who worship Me wholeheartedly*
> *with their minds ever fixed on Me."*

> <u>Shri Sai Satcharita</u>
> Chapter VI
> Page 32

In the past several years, Baba has granted many interviews to Ramesh and his family. But Ramesh had remained deprived of an interview for eleven consecutive years of travel to Puttaparthi. Some years, Ramesh would journey two or three times to the feet of the *Avatar*, and each time Baba would come to him and inquire: *"Where are you from?"* Each time, Ramesh would answer: "From St. Louis, Missouri" or "Virginia" or "Shelton, Connecticut," and always Baba would walk on. There would be no interview. Baba's question always bothered him. "He is God," reasoned Ramesh, "and He should know where I am living." Ramesh asked other devotees if they could explain why Baba asked him where he was from. They could not give Ramesh any satisfactory explanation.

Seven years after his first visit to Baba, Ramesh was sitting in *darshan*. Once again Baba asked the question and once again Ramesh answered by telling Swami the town and state that he was living in at the time. Baba walked on. Before the afternoon *darshan*, Ramesh was reading a spiritual book. The book explained that we are all a part of God. God is That from Which we came and That to Which we shall one day be reunited. With sudden insight, Ramesh realised that Baba was teaching him a spiritual lesson. He wanted Ramesh to realise his true identity. He wanted him to know that he came from God and was one with Him. Ramesh pledged to himself that he would remember to answer the question: *"Where are you from?"* correctly. He would answer: "From You, Baba!" But, in the afternoon, Baba never asked the question and He didn't ask the question again for a few years.

Then, on a visit to Puttaparthi, Ramesh was sitting in the Poornachandra Auditorium. Swami walked up to Ramesh and asked that question: *"Where are you from?"* Ramesh, swept up by the joy of talking with the *Avatar* of the Age said: "Baba, from Shelton." Aaarrgghh!" He had done it again! The closeness to Baba made him forget his resolve. Baba took the letters that Ramesh had in his hands and walked on. When Ramesh reflected on the incident, he realised that the repetition of the same mistake, in spite of resolve and in spite of thinking about the truth that we are all part of the Divine and one with God, was evidence that it takes a lot of **discipline** and **practice** in **addition** to our **resolve**, to **live** God's teachings!

In March of 1990, on Ramesh's birthday, Sai Baba came to Ramesh and asked him: *"Where are you from?"* Ramesh answered: "From you Swami." Baba gave him *vibhuthi prasad* (consecrated food) to eat, and called him in for an interview, his first of many with the Lord.

> *"The Bhaktha will not be perturbed,*
> *if another gets the interview first,*
> *if another is given greater consideration.*
> *He is humble and bides his time.*
> *He knows that there is a Higher Power*
> *that knows more and that It is just and impartial."*

Sathya Sai Speaks
Volume II
Page 15

CHAPTER 35

MAC

"Service to God, which is feeding the hungry with reverence and humility, is the selfless service that is urgent today."

Sathya Sai Speaks
Volume X
Page 300

One day, a man about sixty-years old walked into Patty's office at Community Action For Greater Middlesex County. He told her that he was looking for a sponsor for a food project called "SHARE," a programme that makes available $35.00 to $45.00 worth of quality food, once a month, in consideration for $13.00 and two hours of community service. This food co-op programme is international in scope and yet had only one site in Connecticut, a church in Norwich. "Mac," as the visitor was called, wanted the agency to host the programme in the Middletown area.

He explained that there were no barriers to participation. Any person, no matter what their sex, creed, race or economic status could participate. The goals of the programme were to make wholesome, nutritious food available for the people participating, for a minimum dollar payment, provided the participant put back something into the community by way of two hours of community service per month. Patty liked this idea of **inclusion** rather than **exclusion** and so she agreed to look at the programme. She was intrigued that there was no government funding involved, no surplus commodities distributed, no income eligibility; just people helping people obtain fresh fruits, vegetables, meats and staples.

One Saturday morning, she rose at six a.m. and rode with Mac to Norwich, Connecticut to learn about the SHARE programme by participating in what is known as SHARE Distribution Day. Patty fell in love with the programme immediately. She found that there were no administrative costs because the program operates solely with volunteers at the local level. On SHARE Distribution Day, the participants begin with a prayer to focus on why they are there and to ask God to help them treat each other with respect and dignity as they boxed up the hundreds of SHARE packages. There were no distinctions made between those on welfare and those who were more affluent. Everyone paid for their SHARE of food; everyone did their community service; and many helped with the distribution of the SHARES. She saw that everyone could do something on SHARE Distribution Day. All could contribute. Patty decided to host the programme and recruit participants. SHARE grew rapidly and helped to provide good food for over three hundred families in the Middletown area.

"The Gift of Food is the noblest of all gifts"

Sathya Sai Speaks
Volume IX
Page 196

Patty asked Mac if he would present the concept of SHARE to our Sai Center to see if the devotees wanted to host a SHARE programme in the Manchester area as our Sai Center's Seva (Service) project. Mac agreed willingly and with Patty's help, laid out the basic concepts of the programme for our Center members. After that, several of our members travelled to Middletown on SHARE Distribution Day to see, first hand, how the programme operates. After working out how we as devotees of a Sai Center could donate our time to work the project without being accountable for handling the money (Patty's agency took on that responsibility), our Sai Seva SHARE project now helps augment the food budget of over three hundred families and is providing, through participants, over six hundred hours of community service in the Greater Manchester-East Hartford area. Karin Carlson, a Sai devotee from our Sai Center was hired by another community action agency and is working to develop other host sites for the SHARE programme in Connecticut. The distribution of wholesome food at a fraction of its usual cost and the multiplication of community service hours being put back into the participating communities has grown considerably, thanks in part, to the determination and big heart of a guy named "Mac."

"And, the best type of Seva (Service)
is feeding the hungry"

Sathya Sai Speaks
Volume IX
Page 196

So, who was this guy named, "Mac?" Where did he get his education, training and community concern? Mostly on the streets. Mac had been an alcoholic and drug user until he was in his forties. In fact, he was a heroin addict. He served serious prison time for drug abuse and related criminal activities. When we met him, he was divorced from his wife who he said had been and was still using and abusing. But, at a point in time, Mac drifted into Narcotics Anonymous and within that programme, found his "Higher Power." Mac found God. He read voraciously, and found his truth in the ancient, Eastern philosophy of Vedanta. Mac worked hard at living by *dharma* (righteously). It wasn't easy for him; he was an addict and he had abused for a long time, but the goal of living in God's Presence meant everything to him. He worked very hard to stay clean and drug-free, and he did.

Mac had been straight for twelve years when Patty introduced him to me. He was a bald, arrogant, six-feet tall, toothless pain in the neck with tattoos of railroad tracks etched on his arms, signifying his drug use. Mac could infuriate me, because he thought that he knew everything. And, if there was something he didn't know, he had an opinion on it anyway. Yet, in spite of his abrasiveness, he became our friend. He would visit Patty at her office and both of us at our home, often spending several hours with us in an enjoyable satsang (sharing among good people).

Mac had the addict's penchant for wanting what he wanted, when he wanted it and how he wanted it and watch out if he couldn't get his way. Even at SHARE, he locked horns with others because of his insistence on the correctness of his ideas. But Mac had three qualities: Discipline, faith and compassion, that set him apart from most of us and when I think of it, probably above most of us.

Mac fought his addictions by strict adherence to the dictates of the twelve-step program of Narcotics Anonymous. This time-tested programme works if the addict keeps to the prescribed rules that it imposes. Mac bridged no short cuts in his own adherence to the twelve steps and he bridged no short cuts in the programmes of the men and women that he sponsored. He demanded that they follow the steps to the tee. If they stumbled, he placed them back on an earlier step and asked them to try again. But, he never gave up on anyone and he never demeaned anyone's halting attempts to get or stay clean.

His way was to help them by his example and his refusal to compromise. That dedication gave others the strength to work harder.

> *"The most effective discipline*
> *that man can adopt to attain*
> *this lofty goal,*
> (The unity of the self with the
> Paramatman),
> *is the control and conquest*
> *of the five senses."*

Sathya Sai Speaks
Volume X
Page 136

Mac practiced *Vedanta* (Metaphysical study of the Divine and the World culminating in realisation or liberation). He lived his life, after detoxing himself of drugs, by the code of *dharma* (righteous living) for himself and *prema* (Divine love) for others. He had very little need for material things. He worked as a night supervisor in a homeless shelter, so that he could afford to rent an apartment, eat, and maintain and fuel his old car. He travelled to Massachusetts to attend Vedic services and gaze upon his guru, an elderly and saintly Indian lady whom he revered and honoured. Her teachings and the Vedic teachings of India formed his spiritual life and direction and he strictly followed their mandates. He believed their message.

> *"Implicit faith*
> *is the road*
> *to spiritual success."*

Chinna Katha
Stories and Parables
Page 90

Mac genuinely loved people and tried to help and serve them. To other addicts, he was the father figure, guiding, teaching and loving by example and by severely demanding that they live truthfully by the twelve-step programme. He never compromised where drugs were concerned. But to anyone who needed help and reached to him, he would reach out no matter the distance, the cost or the hardship to

himself. There are many addicts who have pulled themselves up from
the abyss, due to Mac's light.

"I have come, Charles (Charles Penn), to bring the Light of Love
to the world.
That Love will reach the hearts of devotees
and they in turn will let its glow
surround them and reach outwards
to all they meet.
That Love is God;
It can drive away the darkness."

My Beloved
The Light of Love
Page 44
Charles Penn

Part of Mac's *Sadhana* (Spiritual Discipline) which was very near
and dear to him was meditation. Like everything else that he did in
his life of recovery, Mac was very disciplined about it. The time was
important and therefore he regularly meditated at the same hour every
day. The place was important so he maintained a puja (worship) altar
in his apartment and if he were not at home at the appointed hour, he
sought a calm, reflective place for his meditation. Often, he would
come to our home in the middle of the day, sometimes with other
recovering addicts, sit out on the deck overlooking the river and allow
himself to become immersed in the peace and quiet. The posture was
important, so he sat with his spine straight. The peace that he earned
and experienced during his meditations was his very life's blood.

"Real meditation is getting absorbed in God
as the only thought, the only goal.
God only, only God.
Think God,
breathe God,
love God."

Sai Baba and You:
Practical Spirituality
Chapter 1
Page 4

Well, it all caught up with Mac; all those years of using drugs and alcohol and abusing his body and psyche suddenly brought Mac down. He became very ill. Hepatitis had reoccurred and his liver was badly afflicted. He was failing and he was failing fast. His weakened condition was obvious to Patty, who responded with love and compassion, often visiting him and bringing him good food and *satsang*. And Mac talked. He told her that he was most upset that he couldn't meditate in his weakened condition. He was too sick to focus his mind. So Patty sent him a beautiful card and on it she wrote the suggestion that he simply repeat a name of God unceasingly and let that name be his meditation.

> *"For in this busy age of fear and anxiety*
> *the remembrance of God*
> *and the repetition of His Name*
> *is the one means of liberation*
> *that is accessible to all"*

<u>Sathya Sai Speaks</u>
Volume 10
Page 99

Every time Patty visited Mac, after sending him that card, she would find him lying down on his couch with his *japamala* beads (108 beads and similar to the rosary of Catholicism) hung around his neck. **Namasmarana**, the repetition of a name of God, had become his meditation. Mac died wearing his *japamala* beads and we pray with the Name of God on his lips.

> *"Hence man should wholeheartedly*
> *chant God's name*
> *for he may be saved*
> *in the hour of death."*

<u>Summer Showers in Brindavan 1993</u>
The Quest for Peace
Chapter 8
Page 64

Patty helped a few of Mac's N.A. friends organize a memorial service for him. Over one hundred people showed up, most of whom were recovering addicts of both genders and of all ages, shapes and sizes. Their loving, emotional tribute was an eloquent confirmation that Mac's last years were well-spent, filled with concern for others and overflowing with sharing and giving. The torrent of words that spoke of respect and admiration for Mac's fight against addiction in himself and in others, thrilled his daughter and her family, who had travelled from Ohio to attend the service. The testimony of those recovering addicts whose lives were brightened by Mac's light, spoke to a life that made a difference.

Patty and I led the singing of Amazing Grace and then sang a hymn that we had adapted for the Sai Center. Where we usually sang the name of Sai Baba, we substitued the word, "God," in order that those present, who were not Sai Baba devotees, would understand. The song, highlighted for Patty, her impression of Mac in his recovery years. One stanza of that song is:

"Where are you God?
Where is your Blissful Heart?
Where are you God?
When do You play Your Part?"

And then God Answers:

"WHEN YOU LOVE ALL MEN AS ONE
THAT'S WHEN MY GRACE
IN YOU DOES COME!"

And that was Mac! He reached out to the addicted, to the sick and to the hungry, and so, we trust that he died in God's Grace.

It is believed by some, that those souls who live this life with addictive bodies and personalities, are souls closest to liberation and mergence with God, because their fight is a concentrated battle against the most insidious kind of attachment: Attachment for substances directed by their genes and foisted on them by their environment. It is Patty's belief that Mac, who fought the battle so magnificently for the last twelve years of his life, had broken the chains of worldly attachments by his discipline, faith in God and compassion for his fellow human beings. It is her hope and prayer that he died with that *japamala* around his neck following Baba's advice, repeating the Name of his chosen God, over and over again as he journeyed into the heart of the All Compassionate God!

> *"...the Kali Age in which you are,*
> *requires only **Namasmarana***
> (constant repetition of a Name of God)
> *to win Liberation."*

Sathya Sai Speaks
Volume IV
Page 106

CHAPTER 36

EYE TO EYE

"Does thou know why you are given eyes?
To see whatever can be seen?
No! No!!
To fill the eye with Vision of God..."

Sathya Sai Speaks
Volume XI
Chapter 46
Page 262

When I was at the *ashram* for the first time in 1985, I had prayed that Baba would not look at me. I was so terribly aware of my shortcomings and what I perceived to be my sins, that I was ashamed in His Presence. Of course, Sai granted my wish and never looked my way. Toward the end of 1990, I was looking at all of the pictures of Sathya Sai Baba that we had in our home and suddenly, I realised, with a start, that Sai Baba did not look straight out at me from any picture that we had of Him. In each picture, His eyes looked to the left or to the right, but never, straight out at me. Clearly, Baba was still not looking at me! I worried about what that meant. Was Baba so offended by that prayer back in 1985 that He had chosen to ignore me, look away from me for years?

I spent much time trying to fathom why Baba would not even look at me from a photograph. Had I been cut off from Him all these years? Was He punishing me because I had been too fearful of His looking deeply into my soul with his Omniscient Eyes? I was perplexed and upset. But while sitting at my puja table meditating one evening, I turned my head to the left and gazed upon a large print of the face of Shirdi Sai Baba. The print was a gift from an Indian friend of mine, not a devotee, who had travelled to India and brought back this large picture of Shirdi Sai for me. The eyes of the *Shirdi Avatar* stared directly back at me! And then I knew! Sathya Sai Baba had granted my request and had not looked at me, but he had not abandoned me. He had averted His eyes, but He had not agreed to leave me alone. He had sent me Shirdi Sai Baba!

I tried to remember if there were times when I was aware of the presence of or influence of Shirdi Sai Baba in my life, other than when my friend gifted this picture of Him that now stares at me from the wall of my *puja* room. And yes, there were such times. I did remember! There was that large, old man who seemed to be cleaning the temple which marks Sathya Sai's birthplace. Who was that fellow that looked into the envelope containing the five photographs of our family members? Was that man Shirdi? Was it the first aspect of the *Sai Avatara* that responded to my prayers for a blessing on my relatives depicted in those photographs? Now, I am not sure. It is possible. It also may be that the old man looked enough like the descriptions of Shirdi that when I started asking myself about the influence of Shirdi in my life, the remembrance of that old man, was a sign that, yes, the Shirdi Energy and Grace had been **watching me and guiding me** over these last years, because the *Sathya Sai Avatar* was asked by myself, **in ignorance**, to look away from me. I turned from one form but the other form was sent to remind me that the all-knowing, formless God never is absent from our lives. We can turn our backs on God, but God never turns His back on us.

> *"Let me tell you one thing in the end;*
> *However you are,*
> *you are Mine.*
> *I will not give you up.*
> *Wherever you are,*
> *you are near Me;*
> *you cannot go beyond My Reach."*

> Sathya Sai Speaks
> Volume II
> Page 187

There was another incident, too, on that trip in 1985, where I had to ask myself whether Shirdi Baba was physically manifesting in my life. It was on the airplane between Bangalore and Bombay, after we had been to see Sathya Sai Baba at the Ashram. A tall man, seemingly in his fifties, dressed in an old gray white robe and wearing a turban on his head in the fashion of the Sikhs, boarded our plane. I first noticed him as he was placing a battered cloth bag in the overhead luggage compartment. I was sitting on the left side of the plane, on the aisle . The man in white sat on the right side of the plane also on the aisle, but two rows ahead of me. I don't know why I did, but I stared at the back of his head and asked myself, whether this man was a manifestation of Shirdi Baba. Slowly, he turned around and peered at me for several seconds. This scenario happened three or four times during the trip. I would stare at the back of his head and he would turn around and **look into my eyes**. It was very disconcerting!

But now that I knew that Sathya Sai Baba had granted my prayer and had not been looking at me, I decided that I had been wrong and that I had punished myself long enough. It was time to ask the present *Avatar* to reconsider His coolness toward me and to look my way. In order to attract his attention, I decided that I must change the *Karma* that I had incurred by my earlier prayer. I began by taking a symbolic first step to erase my fear of **His** gaze. A friend of mine, Bill Altman, was going to visit Baba in December of 1990. I asked Bill if he would find and purchase a picture of Swami that looked straight out at the viewer. When Bill returned from India, he brought with him several such large photographs and bade me pick one for myself. The picture that I selected was one that I had never before seen of Baba and in fact, I have never seen anywhere else since. It is a very stern looking Sai Baba that looks at you from that photograph. His hands are behind his back and He looks fierce. I chose that photograph, I think, because it made me feel that He was reprimanding me. After all, I had demanded that He look away from me; He had not initiated our separation.

> **"Blessed is the face of Sai.**
> **If we cast a glance at Him for a moment,**
> **He destroys the sorrow of many past births**
> **and confers great bliss on us;**
> **and if He looks at us with grace,**
> **our bondage of Karma is immediately snapped away**
> **and we are led to happiness."**

> Shri Sai Satcharita
> Chapter XLVII
> Page 239

For about a year, that photograph from Bill Altman remained the only picture of Baba looking at me. Then, Edna Yuile, who always seems to come up with a new book, or *vibhuthi* or just good *satsang* when I most need it, gave me a picture of Baba that she had purchased just for me. She knew my story about Baba not looking at me and she felt that this particular picture would be perfect for me. The picture is about twelve-inches high and is a close up photograph of Baba's face. His piercing eyes stare directly at you no matter where in the room you stand to return His gaze. That picture is now resting in the center of my *puja* table and when I sit to meditate, Baba's eyes look unwaveringly, unblinking at my soul! Sometimes, that image, that face changes as I meditate upon it. Often, it will remind me of different ages, and different races and beings, but always the eyes look at me.

From that time, I made up my mind that I wanted to see Baba in His physical form again, and I wanted Him to look at me. Although I still feared His Power and His Omniscience, I knew that I must run toward Him and not away from Him. He had given me abundant evidence through this experience, that He hears our prayers, positive and negative (as my prayer certainly was), and sometimes, you get exactly what you ask for. If negative, you will suffer loss. The severity of the look in the picture from Bill Altman and the intensity of the gaze in the picture from Edna Yuile, has made me reflect that rejection of Baba, in any way, is a grave error, especially when He tells us that He is here to teach men to love and expand, not to fear and contract!

> *"Sai will continue to love*
> *even those who revile Him.*
> *Sai will not forget anyone;*
> *even if he forgets Sai."*

Bhagavan's Discourse
At Poornachandra Auditorium
December 15,1984

CHAPTER 37

REMEMBER HIM ALWAYS

"Listen, O people! Revel in this Kali Yuga,
for there is none so propitious for liberation
that the mere remembrance of the Name of the Lord
and daring Him thus
are enough to win His Grace and set you free."

Sathya Sai Speaks
Volume 10
Page 83

One of the many thoughts that Isaac Tigrett shared with the retreatants at Camp Colang several years ago, was his goal of remembering the Lord every minute and of seeing Him in all people and in everything. Isaac was trying to live in the presence of Sai no matter what his activity. It is a Herculean task, but to begin to try constant remembrance is a step higher and therefore the effort alone brings us closer to Divinity. Because of Isaac I resolved to try to remember Lord Sai as much as possible. The question was: How to begin?

It was about this time, at our Sai Center, that Bill Altman gave a short talk and read excerpts from several writings of Sathya Sai Baba about the practice of **Namasmarana,** or the constant repetition of the Lord's Name, internally or outwardly. It is said that Sai Baba has promised that the constant repetition of a name of God, any name attributed to the Lord, be it Allah, Jehovah, Jesus, Buddha, Krishna, Rama or whatever, would not only change one's spiritual body and mental body, but even the atoms of one's physical body!

"Know that the name is the key to success
in your search for
consolation, confidence, courage
illumination and liberation."

Chinna Katha
Page 44

So, the first exercise or practice that I tried to help me accomplish this constant remembrance of Lord Sai was *Namasmarana.* I decided to use the name of Sai Baba in a *mantra*: "Om Sathya Sai Baba" as I didn't **know** Rama or Krishna nor did I want to use the name, "Jesus." All of these Godmen had gone before. I wanted to use the name of the *Avatar* physically alive in the world today, Bhagavan Sri Sathya Sai Baba. So, I selected His name to begin my practice of *Namasmarana*.

Since making that resolve, I have tried to repeat His name as much as possible, and in as many different circumstances as practical. For instance, instead of listening to a radio talk show while driving, I repeat the Name; when going to sleep, I hold my pillow, imagining that I am holding His Feet and I repeat the Name; often at work, while on the telephone, I will write the Name over and over; as I awake in the morning, I try to remember to repeat the Name as I shake the grogginess of sleep from my mind; and as I walk or jog through Hurd Park in the evenings, I picture His Form and repeat the Name.

Baba teaches us:

> *"In this Kali Yuga, due to the predominance*
> *of Rajasic (passionate) activity in Man,*
> *it is not possible to engage oneself*
> *in Dhyana (meditation), Yajna (sacrifice)*
> *and Worship. So Namasmarana is declared*
> *the best means to cross the ocean of delusion.*
> *Other Sadhanas (spiritual disciplines) like Dhyana,*
> *Yajna and Worship would be fruitful in this age*
> *only when the Divine Name and its Sweetness*
> *of love also merge in them."*

Namasmarana A Universal Sadhana
Compiled by Dr. Brahmanand
　　　　Mavinkurve
Page 7

Baba has said that dying with the Name of God on one's lips
ensures enlightenment:

> *"...it is quite enough if the Name of the Lord*
> *is remembered, however casually,*
> *at the very last moment of life!"*

Baba The Breath Of Sai
Page 172

But, he has also said:

> *"It is no mean achievement*
> *to get the Name of the Lord*
> *on one's tongue at the last moment.*
> *It needs the practice of many years,*
> *based on a deep-seated Faith."*
> *It needs a strong character,*
> *without hatred or malice;*
> *for the thought of God cannot survive*
> *in a climate of pride and greed."*

Baba The Breath of Sai
Page 173

What a promise! If we practice repeating the Name with Devotion and
Love, and can call His Name at the time of passing from this life, our
reward is nothing less than liberation, and mergence!

Another fun way of remembering Sri Sathya Sai Baba that I have
adopted is to look for the number 9 or any number that adds up to 9
like 27 or 36 or 108 or 261, for, as I pointed out earlier in this book,
9 is the number of the Avatar. It is Baba's number (See "Sathya Sai
Avatar," by R. Mohan Rai, Page 81). The number 9 is the only
number that multiplied by any other number equals a number, the
digits of which, when added, equal 9. For example;

$$9 \times 106 = 954$$
$$then \ 9 + 5 + 4 = 18 \ and$$
$$1 + 8 = 9.$$

In other words, nine never diminishes and therefore it stands for the infinite, perfect, omnipotent God.

> *"9 is the Brahman number, for it is always 9,*
> *however many times you multiply it.*
> *It is immutable, for 9 into any number*
> *adds up to 9 only."*
> <u>Sathya Sai Speaks</u>
> Volume VII
> Page 36

The number 9 is also the number of completion. For instance, in the Major Arcana of the Tarot Cards, the 9th card is the "Hermit" who stands at the top of a mountain, holding the lamp of God's Light represented by the Star of David, a symbol of God, and shining it downward as a beacon for others climbing the mountain of life toward God, Light and Liberation. The Hermit is the *Avatar*. He is at the apex. He is complete and has no need to strive for perfection which is already His. He is the peak that others seek to attain!

Baba has also related the meaning of the number 9 and 108 to man:

> *"Why is it that the strings of names of the gods are always 108?...*
> *All such mystic numbers have a deep meaning.*
> *Man breathes at the rate of 900 per hour,*
> *21,600 times per day, 10,800 during day time.*
> *With every breath, man is supposed to repeat Soham.*
> *"I am He,"*
> *and so, the figure 216 and its half, 108 has a deep significance.*

> <u>Sathya Sai Speaks</u>
> Volume IV
> Chapter 27
> Page 157

It is interesting to me that in the above quote, Baba is telling us that our own breath, *Prana,* is based on the number 9. Therefore, we too are the never-declining number 9! We are Divine! On the same page, in the same Volume IV of Sathya Sai Speaks, Baba also says that 9 is *"the number indicative of Brahmam."* Brahmam is the *"All*

Pervasive, Vast, Immanent, Divine, Nameless, Formless, Eternal Absolute, the Immanent Principle" (See Page 35 of "Translations by Baba," compiled by Homer S. Youngs). So the number 9 is, at once, a symbol of the *Avatar*, a symbol of the highest aspect of Man, and a symbol of Brahmam, the Formless God. **Sai and I and God are One!**

Now, when I observe the number 9 anywhere, I use it to remind me that Sai is in my life and that He is with me, around me and in me. More often than not, when I see it, for instance, on an automobile license plate whose digits add up to 9, it is when my mind is wandering from *Namasmarana* or flitting from one trivial thought to another. I am amazed at how often the number 9 will jump out at me when I am in need of confirmation that He is with me, loving me, and leading me.

If you will look above and find my citation of R. Mohan Rai's book, "Satya Sai Avatar," you will find that his discussion of the number 9 as being Baba's number is found on page **81**! I do not take that page number to be coincidence only, but rather confirmation that Baba uses the number 9 as a sign of His *Avatara*. Personally, it is a reminder to pay attention! He is all around us and wants us to be aware of His Presence.

Patty and I have lived in our home in Middle Haddam, Connecticut since 1979 on a rural road known to us only as Route 151. Our home, hidden away in the woods, is located more than a quarter of a mile from any other residence in the area. We never had a street number and mail comes to our post office box in a tiny one room post office that looks like it was lifted from Dodge City and dropped in our little village. When finances became difficult and we had trouble paying our mortgage, I offered our problems and our home to Baba, telling him in my offering that the house belonged to Him and that whatever happened would be okay with us. Within a week, we received sufficient dollars to bring our mortgage up to date, and the authorities of the town designated a street number for our home. The number was **207**! To us, this number which adds up to 9, was confirmation that Baba accepted our prayer and blessed our home.

Two of my sons, Marc and Andrew have lived together with other young men for the past three years in Washington, D.C. The number of their house is 9711, again a 9 number. Our daughter, Andrea, married a few years back and moved into a small home with her husband, Eric. The street number was 18, of course! For me, knowing those numbers are the numbers of the homes of my children, I take solace in believing that it is Baba's sign to me that He is protecting them and watching over them. The numbers themselves are not conferring a defense against anything or warding off anything, they are simply a **sign** of Baba's Presence and Divine Love in their lives.

I wait to rise each morning when the digital clock next to my bed projects hours and minutes that add up to 9. In that way, I am reminded to think about Baba when I am first rising to face the day, and sometimes that exercise helps me to offer my day and its ups and downs to Him.

Recently, Patty and I were visiting friends and fellow Sai aspirants, Jay and Meryl Borden at their home. They were showing us pictures of their trip to Puttaparthi in 1992. One of the pictures had Baba's car in it. I had heard that all of Baba's license plates on his cars have numbers that add up to 9, so I eagerly examined the photograph to see if that were true. To my delight, the plate number was visible. It read: "ADA 90!" It was true! Baba uses the number 9 on the plates as a sign that the cars belong to the *Avatar*.

But that particular license plate contained another meaning for me. If I sounded the letters, "ADA" on the license as one word with the first "A" a hard "A," then that word was pronounced the way we pronounced the first name of our deceased friend, Aida Bellerose. **For me**, Baba was not only identifying Himself with the number 9, but, at that time and in that space, He was also relating Himself to Aida, who I believe was sent to me by Baba to aid me in my journey towards Him. It is so comforting for me to believe that I was meant to read that license plate and recognise it as a symbol of Aida being with Baba, merged with Him and One with Him.

Baba says:
> *"Let no second pass without awareness of God;*
> *let no event lapse without reminding you*
> *that He is the artificer!"*

Chinna Katha
Page 162

That quotation highlights for me, the message of Sathya Sai Baba that all we do and say and think must be made holy, must be divinised. We as devotees have to figure out the **how**. Living in awareness of God just doesn't happen. The monkey mind intervenes and our awareness wanders, our concentration waivers. We have to practice the art of keeping Him in our mind and heart. Our effort must be focused and our resolve sustained. Anything that keeps Him in our **present moment** helps.

> *"To successfully perform your part,*
> *always remain centered upon Me."*

Spiritual Blueprints of My Journey
Chapter 3
Page 28

I am reminded of Sai Baba's story about the demonic enemy of Rama, Ravana, who was spiritually lifted because in his hatred of Rama, he constantly spit out Rama's name in his diatribes and harangues. If the demon, Ravana could be blessed by the caustic use of Rama's name in anger, hate and jealousy, how much more will we be blessed when, with good intention, we choose techniques, no matter how contrived, to help us keep the Lord in our awareness?

Since I am on the road a lot, driving to and from home or to appointments or court, I have a tendency to let my mind wander and dance as I become hypnotised by the drone of the motor and the monotony of the highway. So, I devise little games to help me pull back my mind to Sathya Sai Baba. For instance, if I see the road sign for the Town of **Cromwell**, Connecticut, I take a message from it: **"Om well,"** and begin to recite my *mantra*: "Om Sathya Sai Baba." The name of the hotel chain, **Ramada Inn**, reminds me of **Ada** or

"Aida," my deceased old friend, being one or merged or **"Inn" Rama,** or God. A passing **Saab 900** is an easy reminder of **Sai Baba** being the *Avatar* as symbolised by the number 9! Even a billboard sign advertising **Omega** watches brings to mind **"Om,"** the primeval Sound of Creation and of course, the **Alpha** and **Omega**, the **Beginning** and the **End**, the **First** and the **Last**: **God!**

Some of these exercises or games may sound silly for a man of fifty-six to do, but when you realise that Baba has said:

> *"All the twenty-four hours,*
> *you should be having*
> *remembrance of God."*

Sathya Sai Speaks
Volume XI
Page 105

You then begin to realize that any continuous practice which helps us to remember Baba, or to think of Him, or God or our own Spiritual Self is a **good habit** no matter how silly it might seem to anyone else. For instance, about the study of the symbolism of the number 9 and other numbers Baba has said:

> *"Every number has many such valuable inner meanings.*
> *It is an interesting subject.*
> *You must investigate and reason out,*
> *not laugh cynically and condemn.*
> *If you stand on the seashore*
> *and hesitate to dive into the waters,*
> *you cannot secure pearls."*

Sathya Sai Speaks
Volume 4
Chapter 27
Page 157

"Rise every day with the thought of God;
spend every day with the Name of God;
go back to bed with the thought
of His Glory as enshrined on His Name.
Dedicate your heart to God;
God will be one with you,
the heart of your heart."

<u>A Recapitulation</u>
<u>of Satya Sai Baba's Divine Teachings</u>
Page 58

CHAPTER 38

I AM THAT

"Dust and blade, drop and spot-
each is He,
He and He alone.
And, you are no exception,
you are also He.
The Realisation of this Truth,
this identity, the mergence,
this is Sakshatkara (self-realisation)."

Sathya Sai Speaks
Volume VII
Page 503

In March of 1994, Patty became ill and required heavy doses of antibiotics. Although she took the medication as prescribed, she was not responding and was feeling progressively worse. She ran a very high fever and broke out with a rash over her entire body. She was swelling so badly that she could hardly breathe. Because she wouldn't call the doctor, I decided to call my son, Marc, who was practising medicine in Washington D.C. When Marc heard what was happening, he insisted that I bring Patty into the emergency room immediately as Marc suspected an allergic reaction to the medication. Patty was just too sick to realize her condition.

The doctors at the hospital emergency room quickly sized up the situation and began the tests necessary to decide what must be done. Patty was asked to lie down in a small room and was kept under observation while the tests were run. She was sick, tired and frightened. As she often does when under stress, she began to recite the *Gayathri Mantra* and silently called to Baba to be with her. Through half-closed eyelids, she imagined an orange, horizontal beam which turned upright and moved toward her. She took a deep breath and what she believed was Baba, entered her heart *chakra*. She later told me that she immediately experienced a warm sensation which was pleasant and different from the hot flush of a temperature of 101 degrees. She felt a melting warmth around her heart that calmed her somewhat.

Moments later, she got off the examining table in order to remove the heart pendant that she always wears and which contained a picture of Sathya Sai Baba on one side and a picture of me on the other. Struggling with the clasp, she opened it up in order to concentrate on Baba and keep her mind off her discomfort. "Somehow, I hoped that He would send *vibhuthi* or something to calm me," she said. However, the picture of Baba had deteriorated and his face looked like a skull with deep set eyes and high cheek bones. Rather than calming down, she became very fearful and thought that she might be near death. She closed the locket and lay back on the table. "You did come into my heart tonight, Baba, I know that you did, but your face in my locket frightens me. Please give me a sign that it was really you and that you are here to comfort me."

Again in that little room, Baba seemed to appear in front of her. This time, she saw His form. He came toward her and entered her heart area. Breathing became easier. "Thank you, Swami," she said softly.

When she was released from the hospital, I brought her home and put her to bed, but she couldn't sleep. The emergency room medical team had given her a shot to combat the allergic reaction and she was really wired. The doctor told her the medication was the equivalent of "forty cups of coffee." As the swelling and redness subsided, the itching set in, tormenting her inside and out. It was almost too much for her to bear. She tossed and turned in bed. Finally, she went downstairs, sat on the couch in our family room and tried to read. Suddenly, she became aware of a flute playing a sweet melody. She got up and slowly walked around the house trying to ascertain where it was coming from. She opened the sliding door to the deck and couldn't find the source. She checked the stereo and tape player and nothing was on. "I must be imagining this," she told herself. All night long, the hidden flute continued to play. "It's in the air. I'm tuning into some frequency from somewhere, but how?" Patty never slept that night, and the hidden flute never stopped. It played all through the night.

The next morning, the gentle music continued to play. The melodies changed but that it was a flute was certain. The sound was unmistakable. It was outside as well as inside the house. Patty dressed and left for the pharmacy to fill one last prescription. About a half mile down the road, the flute began to play in the car and the soft sweet music was as clear as it might have been if it were being played on her tape deck. On her way home, Patty tried to rationalise what could be causing the phenomenon. Was it the wind in the trees? The hum of the motor? She could not find the source of that music and yet, she seemed to be lucid and aware of her surroundings.

She drove along, unable to locate where the beautiful music came from. It was just there. Suddenly, she said out loud: "My God! It's Krishna; Baba has sent me the cowherd boy!" She felt that He had been playing his *murali* (Indian flute) to take her attention away from her discomfort and pain. She wept with joy. Her mind had been distracted by the heavenly music. "Enough, at least, to keep my mind distracted from the itching and stinging," she recalls.

During the afternoon, Patty did a meditation in front of a picture of Krishna and His Consort, Radha and a small statue of Sathya Sai Baba. As she prepared herself, she chanted "Krishna and Baba are one. Together they burn the karma from me. I offer gladly this discomfort for the purification of my soul." During the meditation, Baba appeared in front of her closed eyes in His Form. He turned and walked toward her. He lifted his robe slightly as if to climb stairs and advanced toward her. He had letters in His hand and He held them up to her symbolically saying: "I have received your petitions and I answer them." Patty reached out to Him; did *pranayam* (controlled breathing) and He slowly approached her.

She continued the deep breathing and saw Him standing just outside her heart *chakra*. It was as if I was having *darshan*," she said, "but he appeared very little." Lines from *bhajans* came into her mind and she sang the words to Him. Again, He turned and walked toward her. Patty held out her hands to Him, asking mentally for *vibhuthi*. In her inner vision, she saw two other hands join with hers and together become an upturned lotus blossom; the fingers becoming the petals and then slowly unfolding. In the center of the lotus there appeared a packet of *vibhuthi*, which like the lotus, opened and unfolded. Patty accepted the imagined *vibhuthi* and symbolically wiped her swollen face with it. She believed that she was being shown to wash her face with actual *vibhuthi*.

Soon thereafter, she ended her meditation and fetched a silver and crystal bowl. She filled the bowl with water and sprinkled *vibhuthi* into the water. Ceremoniously, she carried it back to the picture of Krishna and statue of Sai Baba, sang the *vibhuthi* song and washed her swollen face with the *vibhuthi* water. Her relief was immediate! Her trembling, itching and stinging were temporarily relieved. That night, she used yoga techniques to focus on the itching, trying to observe it in a detached way, giving each itch a colour, size, and shape. From time to time, she bathed her face and scalp with the *vibhuthi* water. The itching was relieved and the red rash seemed to shrink on her scalp. Of course, she looked pretty funny as the muddied water dried on her hair, but, it was more soothing than the aloe or the calamine lotion that she had used the day before.

About six months later, we travelled to the Wappinger Falls, New York Sai Center to attend a celebration with the members there. Because of the large number of Sai devotees, the service was held in the Hindu temple. A special altar was set up with pictures of Sathya Sai and Shirdi Sai. During the ceremony, Patty fell into a deep meditative state. Her eyes were half-open as she gazed at the picture of Shirdi Sai. From that state of peace and calm, she was struck with a deep insight. The shape of Shirdi's face, His deep set eyes and high cheek bones suddenly reminded her of the skull-like image that she had seen in her locket when she was being treated at the emergency room months before. With clarity, she understood that Baba had never deserted her as she had feared when she imagined His face so like a skull. That night, in her fevered state, she had not been able to discern that Baba had appeared as Shirdi Sai in that locket.

> *"Like the coldness of the atmosphere*
> *which freezes the water,*
> *the compelling agony of the Bhaktha's heart*
> *solidifies the Niraakar (the One without Form)*
> *into the shape and the attribute*
> *that are yearned for.*
> *'Yad bhaavam, thad bhavathi'*
> *'as felt, so fashioned'*
> *He bows to your will, He carries your burden,*
> *provided you trust Him with it."*

Sathya Sai Speaks
Volume II
Page 10

Patty had encountered Shirdi Sai Baba, Krishna and Sathya Sai Baba during her illness. Through these three divine forms, the *Niraakar*, God without form, comforted her and helped her divert her attention from her suffering. Their instruments, the locket, the flute and the *vibhuthi* all attracted her attention and centered it, not on herself, but on the Divine. And Patty had taken the image of Baba into her heart. She made Him one with herself and in that act found the answer to her childhood question: "Who am I really?" She is one with Shirdi Sai who is one with Krishna and Sathya Sai, who are one with the Formless All. In her most essential being, Patty, like all the Universe, is divine. Patty with all the Universe is One.

> "I am God; I am God
> I am not different from God.
> I am the Infinite Supreme,
> The One Reality,
> I am Sat Chit Ananda Swaroopa.
> I am Om Tath Sath (That Which Is) Om

Verse of a Bhajan

CHAPTER 39

PILGRIMAGE TO KODAIKANAL

"...no invitation
has ever been printed and distributed on any
occasion, asking people to come. No one
has been specially requested to take part.
It is love, the invitations of the Heart to the heart,
that has brought you in tens of thousands
to this place."

Sathya Sai Speaks
Volume VII
Page 396

In late January of 1994, Patty visited Emmi Mayr, a Sai Baba devotee, at her horse farm in Portland, Connecticut. Around the time of Patty's visit, Emmi had begun a foot reflexology practice in a cabin on her farm. Reflexology is a discipline that teaches that by putting pressure on certain parts of the feet, healing energy is activated in particular organs or muscles of the body. It is similar, in some ways, to acupuncture. Emmi's therapy room has Baba pictures all around and she invariably plays bhajans as background music to "raise the healing energy," she says, and to relax her patients.

It was an appointment for a foot reflexology treatment, that brought Patty to Emmi's farm that January. During the session, Emmi told Patty that she had spoken with Hal Honig to see if he was going to be leading a group to India that year, as she had some candidates who were interested in going. Hal told her that he had planned a trip for August and was also thinking of spending the month of April with Baba in Kodaikanal. The name, Kodaikanal struck a resonant chord with Emmi. She strongly felt that she should go there to see Baba. When Patty heard that Emmi was thinking of travelling to India, she became excited and told Emmi that we would go too! The "group" had begun to take shape.

That evening, Patty, with her big cheshire cat grin, happily told me: "We're going to Baba!" I looked at her blankly. Since finances had not been going very well at the time, I told her that I couldn't afford it. She responded that she had been saving money for over a year for this purpose, and that she had sufficient dollars put away for our hotel, air travel and food. I was shocked! On the one hand I was thrilled and elated to think that after **nine** years, Baba might be allowing our return to see Him once more, but on the other hand, I felt badly that I did not have the resources myself to pay for the trip.

> *"For one who is blinded by his ego*
> *and is unable to see anything around him,*
> *is life going to give him any sweetness at all?"*

Summer Roses on the Blue Mountains
Chapter 12
Page 92

But, of course, I wanted to go and so we began making our plans. I had to renew my passport and we gathered information on travel arrangements from our friend, Ram Kumar, who had helped us while we were in India **nine** years ago. Ram had left India several years ago and had settled in Connecticut and was operating a travel agency. Emmi Mayr is a real dynamo. She began spreading the word among the members of the Windsor Sai Baba Center that we were going to India and soon other people contacted Ram and signed up to go to Kodai. I told Patty that I felt, somehow, that **nine** would be the number of people that would travel to see Baba on this trip. However, when everyone had signed in, the total number had increased to **eighteen**! We would be travelling on four separate planes and had decided to get together as one American group while in India.

Our journey took us approximately **thirty-six** hours from door to door. We foolishly had decided to travel directly to Kodai without stopping anywhere to rest and re-energise our bodies. We travelled by car to the Limousine Service (a tourist bus), by bus to Kennedy International Airport in New York, and by Air India to London, Delhi and Bombay. A bus ride took us to the airport for Indian Airlines where we boarded another jet to Madauri. Finally an unairconditioned bus brought us five hours across the hot plains and up the mountain to Kodaikanal and Baba.

On the **747,** headed toward our first stop at Heathrow Airport in London, I made a list of my "desires" that I wanted Baba to grant. Baba teaches that we should have a "Ceiling on Desires," but as I wrote, I talked to Him in prayer and told Him that since we were flying "above the clouds," there was no ceiling and therefore I had this opportunity to lay all my "I wants" out for Him to see. I promised

Him that once we landed in India, my desires would be put on the back burner and I would try not to ask Him for anything. And so, the desires filled the pages of my little notebook.

"Reduce your wants; minimise your desires.
All these material knick-knacks are short-lived."

<u>Sathya Sai Speaks</u>
Volume II
Page 112

I told Him that I wanted Him to materialise a gold bracelet for me with a central chain strung through letters that continuously and repetitively spelled: "Om Sathya Sai Baba," which is my personal *mantra*. I prayed for a cure for my nephew's autism. I begged Him for a safe and successful delivery for my son, Marc, and his wife, Terri, who were expecting their first child in July of 1994. Of course, I badgered him, again, for relief from my financial problems. I asked Him for a blessing on the outline for this book, which I was bringing with me to India. And lastly, I asked Him not to appear to me as Shiva, the Destroyer aspect of God, when I saw Him on this trip. I had been so depressed and worried over the last two years, that I honestly felt that the image of Vishnu, the Preserver aspect, was all I could handle. In fact, I told Him that I wanted to feel and experience His loving radiance as Mother.

At the Indian Airlines terminal in Bombay, we sat through a two and a half hour delay before we could complete the next leg of our journey to Madauri, a city in southeast India, famous for its Shiva Temple. From Madauri we began a harrowing five-hour drive in a bus with no air conditioning, over the hot plain and then up the mountain to Kodaikanal. As we drove through the rural villages, we were pleased to see how friendly the people were. We would smile and wave frantically from our windows to little old men sitting on shop verandahs and women cooking over open fires. They would smile, sometimes with broad toothless grins and wave back at us. Each village was crowded with throngs of humanity and the smells of burning cow dung, exhaust fumes from ancient vehicles and food cooking in the open air permeated the atmosphere and accosted us at every turn.

Soon we began our ascent up the mountain toward Kodaikanal. The road was a winding, twisting snake that clung to the side of the mountain. Driving on the left hand side of the road, we were always close to the edge of the mountain, looking down thousands of feet into the valley below. It was a frightening ride, with cars and buses careening down the road from the top of the mountain. I marvelled at our driver's ability to dodge them without sending us into the deep abyss! Sometimes, it was better not to look. The windows of our bus were open and we gradually became aware of the change in temperature from the onerous heat of Madauri to the more moderate temperatures of the mountain and Kodaikanal. The cooler temperature was a welcome relief for our band of weary travellers. Most of the time, while at Kodai, we experienced temperatures in the seventies and low eighties.

We made pit stops along the way, buying lemon Limca soda, a sugary, lemon-lime concoction that never seemed cold enough. Driving slowly around the twisting curves, we could see bananas hanging from trees, and monkeys playing and jumping madly from limb to limb or simply staring at us as we stared at them. On top of our bus, tied down with thick hemp rope, was bag upon bag of our luggage. About fifteen minutes from Kodai, it started to rain gently. Our driver pulled the bus over and he and George Condon climbed to the roof, untied our luggage, covered it with a water proof tarp and then tied it down again just in the nick of time! The skies opened and sheets of water poured down upon us as we manoeuvered the last few miles up to where Baba would be giving *darshan* in just a few minutes.

As we approached Kodai, it stopped raining, so most of us decided to attempt to make Baba's four p.m. *darshan*. George Condon agreed to go on with the bus to our hotel to oversee the luggage for all of us. We arrived in front of Baba's Residence at three forty-five p.m. and ran through the gate and up the hill as fast as we could. All of us were grubby and dishevelled; the men unshaven. We had been travelling for thirty-six hours straight and were thoroughly exhausted. The ladies were herded by the female Seva Dal leaders to a point on the ground looking up at the bhajan hall and the verandah which ran the complete length of the buildings from Baba's residence to the far end of the *bhajan* hall. Patty was placed in the front row! All of the men were waved up a flight of stone stairs to a concrete patio to the right of the *bhajan* hall and at the end of the verandah. This area was to become my home away from home during afternoon *darshan* and *bhajans*.

From inside the hall, *bhajans* were piped outside, so that the devotees sitting outdoors could hear and follow along. Suddenly, a hush fell over the several thousand people who had been waiting patiently for Baba to appear. From where I was sitting, on the patio, around the corner of the hall, I could not see Sai Baba walking along the verandah, but I knew that He was coming and I knew approximately where He was on that verandah, because I could see the ladies looking at Him. Their eyes were riveted on Him. As He advanced closer to where I sat, their heads moved from left to right watching His every step. He appeared abruptly from behind the corner of the building and stood at the end of the verandah, looking over the men sitting on the patio. I was so tired that I wasn't at all consciously excited. Here I had just travelled nine thousand miles to see Him, and I wasn't excited. My first thought was of the brightness of his orange-red robe. He seemed very natural, very warm and very loving. I was viewing the Mother aspect of Sai Baba. I suddenly realised that I was not afraid! In an instant, I knew that this trip would have a different "feel," a different "aura," for me than the feeling of fear that I experienced on my first trip to Baba at Puttaparthi, nine years before.

Quietly, Martin Kenny, one of our group, leaned over toward me and said: "He looks so old and tired, like He has the weight of the world on His shoulders." I was surprised at the comment because I had been thinking the same thing. Later, however, the ladies reported that at that time, He looked light and beautiful to them. Knowing that Baba can appear different to different people, even to the colour of His skin, I realised that to those of us, who were so, so tired, Baba was mirroring our own fatigue and carrying the weight of our exhaustion. I felt that He was letting us know that He understood and appreciated our journey and its tiresome tediousness. He knew that we had arrived.

*"Life is a pilgrimage towards God, where man drags his feet
along the rough and thorny road of his years.
But, with the Name of God on his lips, he will have no thirst;
with the Form of God in his heart, he will feel no exhaustion;*

*the company of the holy will inspire him to travel
in Hope and Faith.
The assurance that God is within call, that He is ever near,
will lend strength to his limbs and courage to his eye.
Remember that with every step, you are nearing God,
and, God too, when you take one step
towards Him, takes ten towards you.
There is no stopping place in this pilgrimage;
it is one continuous journey,
through day and night; through valley and desert;
through tears and smiles, through death and birth
through tomb and womb.
When the goal is gained, man finds that he has travelled
only from himself to himself,
that though the way was long and lonesome,
the God that drew him, was, all the while,
with him and beside him!"*

Sathya Sai Speaks
Volume VII
Page 3

This beautiful morning Darshan started with Baba giving us a double blessing as He came out of His residence at Kodai.

Here is Patty, a little glassy eyed after an afternoon meditation on our patio at the Carlton Hotel on our first day at Kodai.

Here I am, joyous, an hour after Baba blessed the outline.

CHAPTER 40

LEELAS AND INSIGHTS AT KODAI

"I am determined to correct you only after
informing you of My credentials.
That is why I am now and then announcing
My nature by means of miracles;
that is, acts which are beyond human capacity
and human understanding.
Not that I am anxious to show off My powers.
The object is to draw you closer to Me,
to cement your hearts
to Me."

Sathya Sai Speaks
Volume II
Page 118

Kodaikanal

Kodaikanal was established around the end of the last century by the British when two small lakes were discovered two miles above sea level in a mountainous tropical forest. Originally, because of its cool climate, it was a hill station where officers of the British Raj would take summer holiday to escape the searing heat of the valleys. Today, it is considered one of the beautiful places of India, and in so many ways it is. There are waterfalls cascading over mountain rocks into the valley below and lush tropical rain forests. Patty and I took a taxi to an area overlooking a place called Green Valley. Clouds were both above us and below us and the view was breathtaking. From a mountain cliff, we looked upon the rich green of the trees and vegetation on the surrounding mountains and the valley below. Hills were terraced for the planting of crops, and the green lakes of Kodai reflected the fauna around them. Patty, thinking that we were alone, sat at the edge of the cliff and spontaneously started chanting the *Gayathri Mantra.* As she chanted, several people emerged from quiet meditation spots in the woods, sat on the cliff and chanted along with her. The *Gayathri* echoed through the mountains and out over the valley below and reverberated within our souls!

And yet, as quiet and serene as that mountain is, the City of Kodai is similar to most of the cities and towns of the subcontinent. The streets teem with people dressed in saris and dhotis, walking barefooted along badly maintained streets, and seemingly oblivious to the noise and chaotic activity all around them. Horns blare their warning while drivers manoeuvre their automobiles through and around and over places that seem too bumpy, too narrow, too crowded with pedestrians and too dangerous for driving. Cows, sacred to Hinduism, walk the streets and lanes unfettered and unafraid of the bustling humanity around them. Dogs bark, bicycles bump over gravel stones, while oxen drawn carts carry dung and hay and stone. The air is thick with pollution from burning dung and petrol fumes released directly into the air from automobiles with no catalytic converters to filter the discharge. The pollution aggravates throats causing soreness and coughing. But amid all that confusion, and all that hustle and bustle, there is an aura of timelessness and a feeling of eternity that pervades everything around you and is quite appropriate for the land of *Avatars*.

The lakes at Kodai have moods of their own. In the early morning hours, we would watch the fog roll silently across the water as we stood groggy eyed in *darshan* line waiting to enter the grounds of Baba's residence. By afternoon, the lakes were alive as a playground for families, fishermen and boaters. In the haunting light of early evening, they exuded an aura of peace and tranquillity as clouds reflected pink and purple skies into their depths.

Our reservations were at the Carlton Hotel, which is also a vestige of the British, having been a lodge for officers of the Raj. Today, it is a beautiful five-star hotel, sitting atop a hill overlooking the upper lake. Its manicured lawns and gardens, stone walls and tiled roof set it apart from the shoddy, tired buildings that line the streets of Kodai. It is comfortable, neat and clean and the service is excellent. For a Westerner, it probably has the best food in Kodai. I was "attached" to the western breakfast served daily and eagerly ventured into the restaurant after *darshan* each morning to taste a little bit of home. The Carlton was a far cry from the shed at Puttaparthi nine years earlier when Patty and I lived within our cloth enclosure under mosquito nets. Baba, we thought, was pampering us. And it was at the Carlton, that Baba began giving us signs of His Presence by His *leelas* (Divine Play).

522

The bellhop and the desk clerk, both told us that our fifth floor, corner room was the "most beautiful in the house," and they were probably right. Our king-size bed faced a huge bay window overlooking the large lake and a set of French doors on a side wall opened on to a patio overlooking rolling lawns, flower gardens and the smaller lake. The room had a television, which we never watched, a chair and couch set around a coffee table, a large well-equipped bath with shower and plenty of built-in bureau and closet space. Patty noticed on our first day there that our room number was **522,** which, of course, adds up to **nine,** Baba's number! We took that as a sign that Baba was letting us know that He was in charge of our trip and our stay! Our Divine Hotelier!

The Puddle

One afternoon just before sunset there had been a short shower. Patty was meditating on our patio overlooking the hotel gardens below. She called me outside. "Chuck, Baba is here!" She said. I joined her on the patio. She pointed toward the garden five storeys below. I saw it immediately. There, in a puddle that had formed over a metal door set in the garden, covering an area about six feet by three feet, was a **clear** image of Sathya Sai Baba's hair, head and shoulders! It was like a **photograph**, not a vague outline or a fuzzy image. Linda Green, who was on her patio next to us, but hidden from our view by a wall, overheard us talking. "Where is Baba?" She asked. I told her to look at the puddle on top of the metal door below. There was a pause as she looked for it and then she cried out:, "Oh, my God!" She saw Him too.

"You are the reflections, the images
I am the Bimba, the Object so reflected.
Can there be any question of difference
between the Object and its images?
You are all I.
I am all you."

Sathya Sai Speaks
Volume VIII
Page 35

Slow Motion

On the first day following our arrival, I was sitting under the green sun shield for morning *darshan*. I was facing toward Baba's residence. He came out of the building through a door directly in front of me, and walked down the stairs to the ground on my left. He meandered among the students, Seva Dal workers and devotees, and then started walking along the carpeted path from my left to right. There were about four rows of devotees in front of me. When Baba was about twenty feet away from me, he stopped and was facing towards us with his back to His residence. There were people offering Him plates or bowls of hard candy wrapped in paper. Usually, He would take some and throw it to the crowd as prasad (food offered to God, usually blessed by a saint, guru or *Avatar* and shared among the people). This time, while facing in my direction, He reached **behind** Himself to someone who was on the other side of His carpeted pathway through the crowd. Suddenly, he flipped up a handful of candy into the air in my direction. He had an impish look on His Face, as if He were saying: "Oh look, what a surprise I have for you!"

Then the strangest thing happened. As the pieces of candy were in the air, I realised that I was watching them flying in **slow motion**! So slow, in fact, that I had time to think calmly and say to myself: "Don't move or struggle for the candy *prasad*; a piece will fall into my lap." Then, immediately, one piece zoomed in and landed squarely in my lap! I say "zoomed" because the speed of the pieces of candy seemed to quicken as soon as I had that thought. It landed with a forceful "whack," as I sat there quietly.

*"If Bhagavan desires, He can turn time about
as He likes.
What would involve a number of days
in human terms,
I have compressed in a moment.
Similarly it can also be expanded
by Divine Will."*

Baba: Satya Sai
Part I
Chapter 39
Page 411

I was a little timid about telling this story to anyone, because I was the only one who experienced it, as far as I could tell, but I believe that I really did see those candies sailing in the air in slow motion. When I described this event at our Center one evening, Tony LoGrasso said, "Chuck, I know what you mean. The same thing happened to me. I actually counted the pieces in flight because I had the time. I counted over thirty-nine pieces of candy! They were moving so slowly."

Tom Mortimer, a member of our Sai Center, and a good friend, recently travelled with his thirteen-year old son, Justin, to Brindavan to see Baba. While there Baba threw sprays of candy three times in a row. Tom said that he thought that each toss was not indiscriminate, but rather, each candy was projected on a selected course like a guided missile, with one devotee being its particular target.

Phoenix

Tony and Maria LoGrasso had a son, Nicholas, who traveled with Hal Honig, our son, Garrett, and sixteen other young men to Brindavan for the Summer Showers Programme in 1993. Several months after returning to the United States, Nicky moved to San Francisco, California, where he died unexpectedly at age twenty. His death was understandably difficult for all who knew him and devastating to our dear friends, Tony and Maria. Their only consolation was that Nicky left this world on *MahaShivaratri*, an auspicious, holy day. On this day, Hindus, in general, and Baba devotees, in particular, pray and sing *bhajans* around the clock, honouring Nataraja, the Dancing Shiva, whose many-armed dance attracts the minds of men to focus on the Divine. Tony and Maria had spent the month of March with Baba for the previous few years and had celebrated *MahaShivaratri* in His Divine Presence. For some inexplicable reason, they did not go to Prasanthi Nilayam for this celebration in 1994. They spent the night singing *bhajans* with our center members while millions of devotees around the country and around the world sang and chanted *bhajans* to the glory of God. And, in that aura of intense spiritual energy, Nicky LoGrasso's soul left this physical plane.

About three weeks after Nicky's death, Tony talked to his son in prayer before retiring one evening: "Nicky, if you can hear me, please come to your mother in a dream and let her know that you are all right." That night, Maria had a dream of Nicky and he was smiling at her. "Where are you?" she asked. "Phoenix!" was Nicky's reply. "Phoenix, what are you doing there?"

When Maria awoke, she told Tony the details of her dream. She did not know of Tony's prayer for her the evening before. Tony was very pleased. Besides recognising that his petition had been answered, it seemed that he had contacted his son. Tony was also aware of the esoteric meaning of "Phoenix." The Phoenix is a mythical bird, which after death and a long lapse of time, rises from the ashes to live again. The Phoenix symbolises rebirth, reincarnation or the "passing to a better place." Tony believes that Nicky was trying to tell him that where he was, was good and that he was all right.

A few days later, the LoGrassos received a phone call from a friend in California who did not know that Nicky had died. She told them that four nights earlier (on the same night that Maria had her dream), she had seen Nicky at the foot of her bed smiling at her. And, at the time, she was in...Phoenix, Arizona!

Now, how does this story tie into our trip to Kodai? Well, one of my "desires" that I had asked Baba to fulfill for me, while I was writing my list of petitions to Baba during our Air India flight "above the clouds," was to have some little thing happen about Nicky while in Kodai; some *leela* or sign that Baba was aware of Nicky's death and the grief and pain of separation being experienced by Tony and Maria; some symbol that we could take back to them to help ease their hurt and grant them some comfort. That symbol or sign was not long in coming. On the first full day after our arrival at Kodai, I was standing in *darshan* line. I struck up a conversation with a man from California who was standing behind me. He pointed out Dr. Sam Sandweiss, author of **The Holy Man and the Psychiatrist,** who was also from California. I commented that I would like to meet Dr. Sandweiss, as he had been at Brindavan with the boys who had gone to Summer Showers in 1993 with Hal Honig. My new acquaintance said, "hhhmmm, Summer Showers, I just met a kid who went on that trip; He was from...Phoenix, I believe."

Well, as you can imagine, I almost jumped out of my skin. I was really startled. It was all too synchronistic. The fellow was from **California** where Nicky died. **Dr. Sandweiss**, also from California, who had been with the boys was in line with us. And this guy said he met a young man from the 1993 trip who was from **Phoenix**! I felt that Baba had just given me the sign for Tony and Maria that I had asked for. After *darshan*, I went looking for Patty to tell her of the coincidence. She stopped me in mid-sentence. "Wait, don't tell me anything yet. I have something to tell you, that you won't believe!" Well, like all good husbands, I let my wife speak first! She told me that one of the youthful vendors of trinkets that had set up sales stands along the road, had come up to her to sell her something. She tried to ignore him and kept on walking. He fell along side of her and struck up a conversation. "Where are you from?" He inquired. "From the United States," Patty responded. "From U.S.A.?" he asked again. "Yes," she replied. "Do you know Tony and Maria?" He asked. Patty was dumbfounded! Tony and Maria! She stood in the middle of the road-with a shocked look on her face. "How could you know our friends? They have never been to Kodai!" She said. "I met them in Puttaparthi," said the boy. "They were there for *Shivaratri*. I go where Baba goes." There are thousands of people in the streets of Kodai and hundreds of westerners when Baba is in town. Patty was amazed that of all those people, this boy who knew Tony and Maria, approached her and asked her if she knew them. When I heard the story I was overwhelmed! There was no question in my mind that these two incidents were Baba's *leelas*. Both Patty and I had been given parts of the story to bring back to Tony and Maria. Baba knew about Nicky; He knew the hurt of Tony and Maria. He was aware!

A few days later, I was sitting under the green canopy shielding the devotees from the sun's rays, waiting for Baba's *darshan*. A young man from Russia, who spoke perfect English, was sitting next to me. I was holding a picture of Nicky doing *Padanamaskar* at Baba's feet. The photograph was taken the prior year during Summer Showers. The young Russian asked me who the boy in the picture was. I told him and explained that I wanted to hand the picture to Baba on behalf of the parents. The young man gently took the picture from my hands and looked at it for a long time in deep silence. As he handed it back to me, he said: "Tell the parents that he is in a better place."

Finally, as if to underline and underscore our impression that all the events were Baba's *leela* and His way of telling us that Nicky was all right, Baba took all of the letters that we had brought to Him from family and friends. Included in that handful of letters was one envelope from Maria, containing her heartfelt letter to Baba and the U.S.A. scarf that Nicky had worn at Summer Showers.

Smokestacks

Baba has a great sense of humour. I have often said that someone should write a book just on His jokes and teasing and funny responses. There was one comical event that highlighted His humour for us while we were at Kodai. There were two smokers in our group, Linda Green and Lynne Bouchey. Their need to smoke added difficulties for both of them throughout the trip. While flying to India, they had to sit in the smoking section of the plane, separate from the rest of us. Since Baba discourages smoking and doesn't allow it within the gates of the residence grounds at Kodai, the two women had to wait until after *darshan* to have a cigarette. One day, Linda and Lynne walked down along the lake and bought cigarettes from a vendor about one half mile from the residence. They were standing by the road, smoking happily and talking. Suddenly, the "Baba Wireless" went into operation as the word passed swiftly, from person to person, all the way to Lynne and Linda: "Baba is coming, Baba is coming!" Like young schoolgirls, afraid of being caught smoking by a teacher, they quickly dropped their cigarettes on the ground and waited expectantly with all the others for Baba's car to appear around the bend.

About a minute later, a bus, carrying Baba's students and a red Jaguar automobile, with Baba as its passenger appeared. As the

Jaguar was slowly driven past Linda and Lynne, Baba leaned forward toward them and putting His forefinger and middle finger up to His mouth, made puffing gestures with His lips as if He were smoking a cigarette, and smiled impishly at them. Needless to say they were greatly surprised by Baba's actions. It seemed He knew that they had been smoking.

> *"Now the one who strives hard to rid himself of impurities*
> *by pouring 'clean' water into his vessel (body)*
> *will begin to 'feel' differently--uplifted.*
> *He feels released from the draw of earthly things and desires.*
> *By continually practising walking along the Pure Path*
> *he will enjoy Shanti and in time, his rounds of*
> *births and deaths will cease victoriously."*

Charles Penn
My Beloved
Page 37

Halo

Our group was blessed to be at Kodaikanal for Rama's Birthday Celebration on April 20, 1994. For that occasion, Baba was going to give a discourse in the morning. A large chair was placed on the verandah in front of the *bhajan* hall and a table was placed in front of the chair. Microphones were set on the table. There were gaily decorated umbrellas all along the verandah, garlands of orange and white jasmine flowers and banners of yellow, green and pink. When Baba got up to speak, I was aware of receiving a second special blessing, that of **hearing** the Avatar. At Puttaparthi in 1985, I had *darshan*, seeing the Avatar but I had never heard Him speak. So, I thanked Him in my heart for this *sambhashan*, the hearing of the *Avatar*.

One aspect of His talk that impressed me was that He never read anything, never paused or stammered or hesitated in any way. Then with a start, I became aware of a large, white halo around His Head! I knew that others like Hislop had seen a **golden** halo and so I thought that I might only be imagining a white one and not really seeing anything at all. So, I closed one eye and then the other; I shifted from left to right on the ground; I closed both eyes and opened them again, only to see that halo in every instance. It was apparent to me for several minutes and then it vanished.

After His discourse, Baba led a *Rama bhajan*. After each line, we all responded. Then Baba sang two or three lines so fast that it seemed to me to be humanly impossible. Some of us in our area laughed because there was no way we could respond and sing along as fast!

"Besides, in a congregation,
the bhajan must not evoke
a sad, sagging mentality.
There should be no slackness or sloth
in the melody and rhythm.
Vibrant speed is a must,
to hold the attention of the rest."

Ra. Ganapati
Baba: Satya Sai
Part I
Chapter 7
Page 55

Sai-lence!

Patty is an organized person and as the one who contacted the travel agency for most of us, felt a responsibility toward all of us and so, became the spokesperson for our group. But Patty soon realised that Baba did not intend that these eighteen people become one unit. The trip toward God is a solitary journey and our separateness reflected that idea. Initially, Patty felt frustrated by the lack of organization but very soon she realised that Baba did not want her taking charge. On our first day at Kodai, He helped her remove her ego by giving her a bad case of laryngitis. She was forced to let go because He made her Sai-lent. But Patty doesn't quit easily. She still tried to be the mother hen by organizing in sign language! Finally, she surrendered to His Will and went within for her journey from God to God.

We were an American "group," in many ways, but in others we were not. We had gathered at our home prior to the trip to organize ourselves and to educate each other on the pitfalls of such a pilgrimage half way around the world. We were all staying at the same hotel and we all wore the same green scarf with USA emblazoned on it. We encouraged each other and prayed for each other and helped each other. But we also acted independently and marched to different drums. We never ate all together; we didn't set up a time every day for *bhajans* and *satsang* to recount our experiences of the day. We didn't leave the hotel and go to *darshan* as a team at the same time and we didn't all sit together when we arrived inside the residence grounds. Each of us seemed to have a different agenda for ourselves. Some spent time absorbing the culture of India; some joined a singing group made up of Americans from North, South and Central American countries to sing *bhajans* every day; some walked off alone for deep reflection and meditation; others were very social; and some were silent or as I like to say: Sai-lent.

Mary Adamoski chose a vow of silence for the entire stay at Kodai. She spoke only in sign language or wrote out her messages. She spent much time alone deep in meditation and prayer. Lynne Bouchey would go off alone along the lake shore and listen to the Baba voice inside her own head and heart. Soon, we became aware, that one of the reasons for our group not coming together as a unit, was this sense of Sai-lence that we all felt in some way. I had a feeling that Baba wanted us to spend our time projecting inward rather than outward.

> *"Stillness and Silence mean the nature*
> *of Pure Consciousness.*
> *He who has reached it will be*
> *in the highest peace*
> *and highest bliss."*

Teachings of Sri Satya Sai Baba
Page 25
Paragraph 43

One quiet evening in our hotel room, Patty was writing in her journal and I was strumming my guitar idly while deep in thought. As

I played, the words and tune to a prayerful song came to me. The melody flowed effortlessly as I asked Patty to listen to these words:

> "Baba work on me
> Baba work on me
> You know what is good for me
> Baba work on me
>
> Help me
> Quiet me
> O Baba
> Sai-lence me!"

Obviously, Baba wanted me to reflect on Sai-lence too! Of all the little *leelas* and messages and lessons learned on our trip, if I had to identify a theme that was common to all of us, it was that Baba wanted us to quiet ourselves; to stop talking and to listen in Sai-lence to His words deep within our hearts.

> *"It is only in the depth of that silence*
> *that the voice of God can be heard.*
> *Speak as low as possible;*
> *as little as possible,*
> *as sweet as possible."*

<u>Sathya Sai Speaks</u>
Volume VI
Page 277

Patty's last *darshan* was her ultimate experience at Kodai. Debbie Bussman, Mamata Kalle and she went through the *darshan* waiting game. When they got to the top of the hill in front of the gate to the residence area, Roni, the captain of the women Seva Dal workers asked them if they were leaving on the following day. Patty responded, "yes, we are." Roni escorted them into the *bhajan* hall, down the side aisle and placed them in the front row. Patty was seated at the foot of the altar on the opposite side from where Baba's chair is placed. Once settled in His chair and after *bhajan*s had begun, Baba looked over to Patty and stared at her. She was so happy that she responded by giving Him a big cheshire cat grin. "All teeth!"

was her description. She told us later that she probably looked like an idiot but she didn't care. She felt warm, loving energy from the *bhajans* and from Baba's intense look. She felt filled up with emotion and love. Baba looked over at her twice more during the *bhajan* session. She was so high from His piercing gaze that she couldn't talk when the *bhajans* came to a close.

> *"Silence is not a matter of resolve!*
> *It is always there*
> *Silence is the endless flow of Pure God*
> *into you, into the world."*

Sathyam Sivam Sundaram
Part III
Page 105
N. Kasturi

After Baba left the hall, Patty put her head down on the altar step and stayed there for a minute or two. Then she placed the picture of Nicky LoGrasso doing *Padnamaskar* at Baba's feet during the Summer Showers programme, on the altar and took a picture of it there for Nicky's parents, Tony and Maria. Then Patty, Debbie and Mamata walked back to the hotel in silence. The honking of horns, ringing of bells and the noise of people rushing to and fro in Kodai seemed laughable. They maintained that silence even after Hemu Kalle, Mamata's husband and I caught up with them. They indicated that they wanted to remain quiet a little longer so Hemu and I got in step behind them and let them walk along in meditation.

Patty went out into the garden of the hotel and wrote her feelings of Baba's gaze into her journal and stayed in a state of Sai-lence a little while longer. She went in and out of crying spells as her emotions were very high. The tears were tears of joy. She felt in love with the whole world! As she reflected on the *darshan*, she felt a fluttering filling her chest in the area of her heart. She said later that she knew that her heart *chakra* was wide open and vibrating about a foot in front of her! She was light headed and feeling a slight buzz in the very top of her head and the tears just kept coming. She had seen Krishna in Baba. "Pure Love, Divine Love!"

Charles Gregory read Baba's words about maintaining silence to Patty. Baba had encouraged people to remain silent after *darshan*, because chattering and talking turns away the Divine Energy that He has given during *darshan* and returns to Him unused. Realizing that Baba had filled her with His Loving Divine Energy, she wanted to savour it forever. She was really zapped!

> *"You feel the Presence of God when silence reigns.*
> *In the excitement and confusion of the market-place,*
> *you cannot hear His footfall.*
> *He is Sabdabrahma (sound of God),*
> *resounding when all is filled with silence.*
> *That is why I insist on silence, the practice*
> *of low speech and minimum sound.*
> *Talk low, talk little, talk in whispers,*
> *sweet and true."*

<u>Sathya Sai Speaks</u>
Volume V
Page 234

CHAPTER 41

FROM WHERE DID YOU COME?

"You are Niraakaaram (Formless God) come in Naraakaaram
(human form), the Infinite come in the role of the Finite,
the Formless Infinite appearing as the Formful Infinitesimal,
the Absolute pretending to be the Relative,
the Atma behaving as the Body,
the Metaphysical masquerading as the merely Physical.
The Universal Atma
is the basis
of all being."

Voice of the Avatar
Page 16

Sometime in 1993, I decided that I would like to write a book of Patty's and my spiritual journey toward the Feet of the *Avatar*. In fifteen minutes, I wrote an outline with little thought or effort and put it on my *puja* table at home. Then I wrote out two paper chits, one of which said: "No, don't write the book," while the other read: "Yes, write the book!" I placed the two chits with their messages into a small metal container and prayed over them. Then, I closed my eyes, shook the vessel and reaching into it, pulled out the "No, don't write the book" chit! Since I have used this chit method to teach myself the "habit" of doing what I believe is the Will of God, I tore up the outline and for a time, put the thought of a book out of my mind.

Several months later, I was talking with a Sai devotee at our Center about what I had done with the chits and the outline. He told me that there were `several other possible answers that could have been placed on chits in addition to the "write-don't write" alternatives that I had used. He suggested: "Don't write **now!**" or "Don't write from **this** outline!" and "Write, but **modify** this outline!" Therefore, he encouraged me to think about writing a new outline and then doing the chits again with the expanded possible answers. "After all," he said, "if Baba really doesn't want you to write a book, you'll get the same 'No!'" that you did before.

His suggestion and encouragement also made me think of the casual, unthinking, almost flippant way I had dashed off that first outline. There was certainly no work involved.

> *"Have always some work to do
> and do it so well
> that you get joy"*

Sathya Sai Speaks
Volume I
Page 90

I realised that the "Don't write" answer may have been given because I hadn't **earned** the right to begin writing.

So I began writing a new outline. This time I thought about what I wanted to include. I worked on it for several months. In December, 1993 and January, 1994, I transcribed the outline from a penned document to type on an old word processor. A rough draft of the outline began to take shape. Then Patty's dad asked us if we were coming down to visit him in Florida. "No Dad," she responded, "if we travel anywhere this year, it will be to see Baba in India. "I'm Baba!" He stated emphatically. In an enlightened moment, Patty realised that he was right. Her father really wanted us to visit. She knew that Baba would want her to respect her dad's wishes and to honour her parents. So, in February, 1994, Patty and I flew to Florida to visit her mom and dad.

> *"Let your mother be your God;
> Let your father be your God-
> that is the teaching.
> Yes; how else can you thank them?
> What else can you give, in return,
> than your Love and Service?
> Think of all the care, all the love, all the pain,
> all the hunger and sleeplessness they underwent
> and undergo for your sake.
> Be kind, be soft and sweet to make them happy;
> obey them, for they know much more than you do
> of the world and its dangers.
> That is the way to worship them."*

Sathya Sai Speaks
Volume VII
Page 54

I brought the outline for the book to Florida with me. I soon realised that Patty's decision to visit her parents before we travelled to India afforded me the time to rewrite and expand parts of the outline. During that vacation, I spent many hours at a table out on the deck with a scissors and a stapler, doing a cut and paste job and penning in additions, connectors and Patty's suggestions. If we hadn't gone to Florida I don't think that I would have had the time to pull that outline together. By the time we returned home, we knew that we would be going to Kodaikanal in April of 1994. Instead of doing the chits to help know His Will about working on a book, I decided to take the final outline to Baba in Kodai and pray that He would bless the project.

Once that decision was made, I felt that the outline had to be done in good form as I was hoping to hand it to Sai Baba. So, I sent chapters from that outline about specific people, directly to those people for their corrections and amendments. I researched Baba's words to find quotes that would highlight the story content of each chapter and I put all of that into the word processor and printed it. To my utter astonishment, the printout of that outline totaled exactly 108 pages! It appeared that Baba was sending me little signs to encourage me to keep at it.

When I examined the finished product, it didn't look good enough to take to the *Avatar*. I had an old computer with an obsolete word processing programme. My inexpensive printer didn't work well either and the final copy just wasn't sharp enough. Actually, now that I think about it, it **looked** like I had typed it. So I asked a Sai devotee and friend, John Hartgering, to put my product into his computer word processing programme which was far advanced over what I had. John did a magical job. With his computer, his skill and his loving effort, the outline took on a shine and a luster. It looked wonderful and I felt that it was a more fitting presentation for Bhagavan Sai Baba. And so, I was prepared to set off for Kodaikanal; the outline, in a three ring binder, ready for Baba and hopefully, for His Blessing.

At Kodai, I dutifully brought the binder with me to every morning *darshan* and every afternoon *darshan* and *bhajan* hour, hoping to be able to present it to Him. As each day went by without my getting any closer than the fourth row, I began to despair of having the opportunity to offer Him the fruit of those many months of work. One afternoon, during *bhajans*, it began to rain gently. Once again, I was sitting in my favourite spot, the patio next to the *bhajan* hall. Having no umbrella or raincoat with me, I prayed to Baba to protect the outline. Suddenly, a plastic tarp was thrown on to my head! A Seva Dal worker had appeared tossing several of them to some of us who were sitting there unprotected. I found myself, outline tucked under my shirt and against my chest, sitting beneath a tent made of the plastic, my head being the center pole holding everything up. And the rain came, gently at first, then deluge! I felt uncomfortable as my legs and feet got wet, not from the falling rain but from the water that collected around me on the concrete patio. Then it struck me! I had prayed for protection for the outline and I was thrown a plastic covering that preserved it from water damage. In joy and relief, I began to laugh, all by myself, under my little tent. I thanked Baba for His speedy and loving response to my call for help.

Yet, day after day, I continued to be seated by the Seva Dal workers too far from Him to be able to offer Him the outline. One morning after *darshan*, I thought: "If He wants the outline, He is going to have to arrange to take it Himself because I simply can't get close enough to hand it to Him."

That afternoon, I decided to walk the two miles from the hotel to Baba's residence for *bhajans* rather than to take our usual taxi ride. Knowing then that it seemed to rain every afternoon precisely at three o'clock, I went prepared. I wore a plastic raincoat (whose armpits were ripped because it was too small for me), and I carried an umbrella. In order to be comfortable about the outline, I wrapped it in a plastic bag that Patty had brought from home. Sure enough, as I began to walk, it began to rain, and it rained steadily until I reached the residence. When I arrived, most of the men had already been seated in their usual places under the green plastic sun roof, or on the bare ground in front of Baba's House or for the lucky ones, in the *bhajan* hall. A Seva Dal worker directed me to walk toward the green sun roof area, but I asked him if I could please sit up on the patio once more. With that peculiar, side to side, rocking movement of his head, so common among Indians, he gave me permission and gestured toward the stairway. When I reached the top of the stair, another Seva Dal worker motioned that I should go left along the verandah in front of the *bhajan* hall. As I did, I became aware that there was another man walking slightly behind me. He quickly sat down next to Baba's carpet that traversed the verandah. Another Seva Dal leader ran up to him and asked him to get up and move. The man refused. Obviously, this seat was very advantageous and would give the man a chance to be very close to Sai Baba as He walked along the carpet. I thought, "What is this guy doing? Why is this man breaking Baba's rules? I'll go wherever the Seva Dal sends me."

At that moment, the same Seva Dal leader turned to me and motioned me inside the *bhajan* hall! I entered quickly but just as quickly, I was intercepted inside the door by another Seva Dal worker who asked me to leave. So, I did. But the Seva Dal who had waved me inside, again came to my aid and commanded the worker inside the hall: "Let this man pass!" The hall was already quite full, but I was directed down the center aisle between the men and the women to the front row on the gents' side. As soon as I had seated myself on the spot designated as my area by the Seva Dal, I looked up and couldn't believe what I saw. There was nothing between me and Baba's chair just a few feet away. I was wonder struck! How had it happened? How was I placed in such a great seat? How did I wind up in the hall in the first place? The whole episode seemed like a fast moving blur.

We were always trying to figure out ways to get selected to be seated in the bhajan hall for the forty-five minute *darshan* during *bhajans*, but since only about two hundred people out of the three thousand or so devotees present could be accommodated in the hall, the chances of even getting into the hall were slim. And yet, there I was, not even having tried to get in, sitting just a short distance from where Baba would be sitting! I had an urge to pray, and pray I did! I prayed for Patty, my mother and father, my brother, my kids, the center members back home, the people in the hall with me, the people traveling in our group and anyone else that came to mind. I just prayed up a storm.

The college boys who were to lead the singing came in and sat between me and Baba's chair. I was greatly relieved. At least, there would be a buffer between Him and me. I still retained some of that fear and awe of Him that so weighed me down on the previous trip at Puttaparthi. Waiting for Baba to appear, I felt myself getting higher and higher emotionally as the energy in that room grew stronger. I still couldn't believe that I would be so close to Baba and for so long a period. Baba came in to the room from the door behind us. He walked slowly down the center aisle, talking to some, taking letters from others. He stepped up onto the dais where his chair was set and sat down. Then a strange thing happened, I became aware that my fear had vanished. I thought of Baba as Mother, as love, and I was free of my trepidation of being in the Presence of the *Avatar*.

Although Baba seemed relaxed and calm, I felt great power in His bearing. It seemed to me that Baba was in charge of the singing, the beat, the thoughts in our heads, the universe, everything! I didn't know most of the *bhajans* and I really couldn't understand the words that were being sung in Hindi and Sanskrit. So, instead of singing, I just let the vibration of the music and the physical vision of the *Avatar* lift my spirits. When Baba sits in the chair, He makes eye movements and hand movements that seem timed to the beat of the music. Watching these movements was thrilling because they created a spiritual aura that filled the room and filled my heart. Baba, himself, has said that nothing that He does is meaningless, and He has explained that those hand and eye gestures are indications of His Cosmic Self working in other places and in other realms at the same time.

As the time for the *bhajans* was drawing to a close, I was aware, fully aware, that Baba's carpeted path from His chair to the exit from the room, was right in front of me. I knew that when He left his chair, He would walk down the middle aisle for a short distance, then take a right turn toward the door, walking right by where I was seated. I had done nothing, controlled nothing, to bring me to that spot. As I had mused earlier in the day, I could not get close enough to Baba to offer Him the outline unless He took steps to arrange it. It was apparent to me that He had! I shook my head in wonder. I knew that I was to have the opportunity to offer the outline to the *Avatar*. He had arranged it so. Whether he would accept it was the next question.

At the end of the *bhajans*, Baba lit the *aarti* flame while joyous singing of "Narayana Narayana" rose from all throats. He slowly walked down the center aisle, took a right turn and followed the carpet in the direction of the door. He advanced a few steps then stopped and began talking with a man, kneeling in front of Him. As their conversation dragged on, my anxiety increased. I thought that if Baba wanted to ignore me, He could do so by looking to His right as I sat on His left.

But, when He ceased speaking with the man on his knees, He walked in my direction. I held up the binder containing the outline to Him and said, "Baba, your book." He raised His eyebrows in mock surprise, bent over and opened the cover of the binder. He was staring at His Name, "Sathya Sai Baba," written across the page. While I held my hands under the binder cover which I was offering to Him, He put His hand on the page for several seconds. I had not named the book, hoping that He would name it and, by doing so, give me more direction when I actually sat down to write the book itself. So, I asked Him if He would name the book. He shook His head, *"no,"* and in my mind, I heard the words, as clearly as if spoken vocally: *"Not now!"* Then I thought I heard Him say aloud, *"I will talk to you later."* Turning quickly, He walked away. I didn't follow Him with my gaze and so He was gone from the building before I realized that I had been looking down at my lap and not after Him. I can't describe what I felt or what the impact was on me from this short encounter with Baba's energy and love. I was somewhat dazed, and felt slightly out of sync. I wasn't joyous, but I did feel very good.

When I got up and walked outside, I was thinking that maybe He didn't really talk to me. Maybe I so wanted to believe that He talked to me, that I had convinced myself that He had. Then Martin Kenny, one of our group, ran up to me and said, "Baba talked to you! What did He say?" Martin had been outside of the *bhajan* hall on the verandah so I couldn't figure out how He knew what went on in the hall. "I was looking through the window and I saw Him talking to you," Martin shouted. It was then that I knew that I had not been hallucinating. Martin had seen! "He blessed you!" Martin told me. He had seen Baba raise His hand in blessing as He talked with me! I hadn't been aware of that and I was so happy that Martin had seen it happen and reported it to me.

Two days later at the afternoon *bhajan darshan*, I was sitting in my usual area on the concrete patio next to the *bhajan* hall. If Baba walked along the verandah in front of the *bhajan* hall, He would be walking right toward me. There was an open expanse of concrete between me and the end of the verandah and no one was sitting in front of me. Usually, Baba would come to the end of the carpet, turn left into a vestibule that led to the door of the hall, but as I sat on that patio, awaiting His appearance, I **knew** that Baba would walk to the edge of the carpet on the verandah and then walk straight across the concrete to me. Sure enough, when He did reach the carpet's edge, instead of turning left toward the vestibule, He looked at me, raised his eyebrows as if in recognition, and walked across the concrete patio in bare feet. When He was right in front of me He asked:

"From where did you come?"

There it was: The same question that He had asked of Ramesh Wadwani so many times! I argued with myself, not knowing how I should answer. I wanted to say: "From You, Baba!" as Ramesh had learned to do, but I felt that I wasn't sure exactly what that answer meant and I questioned myself whether that answer, coming from me at that particular time, was sincere. Scrupulously, I shrunk back and hesitated. Then I thought that I might answer, "From Connecticut in the United States, Baba." That answer might have prompted Him to ask me:

"How many?"

Then I could tell Him there were eighteen in our group and He might ask us in for an interview.

Now, I know that it is difficult to believe that I was able to have that much thought about possible answers to Baba's question. After all, His movements demand that one responds immediately, but I really did consider the different answers and bounced them around in my head for what felt like a very long time. Looking back now, I believe that He must have suspended time again just as He had when I saw the candy floating in slow motion, because it seemed to me that I had all day to think about my answer.

Finally, Ramesh's experience tipped the scale and I blurted out my response: "From You, Baba!" He did a double take as if my answer surprised Him, and then He bent down and lightly touched my cheek! He said something to me, over his shoulder, as He walked away from me, but I had no conscious idea of what it was that he said. Hopefully, He had spoken to my subconscious and what was said was for my Inner Being.

"What is Man's journey? Where is he going?
Why is he continuously reborn?
In order to seek the right path and the knowledge of truth.
What road should one seek?
You should return whence you have come.
That is seeking.
You have come from the Divine Essence, from God,
and you must return to Him."

Don Mario Mazzoleni
A Catholic Priest Meets Sai Baba
Chapter 13
Page 174

Once again, I was dazed by Baba's energy. He walked away from me and once again, my eyes never followed Him as He walked toward and then into the bhajan hall some thirty or forty feet away. I sat there happy and mellow. After bhajans, I turned to the men who had been sitting behind me and inquired whether anyone had heard what Baba had said to me. None of them spoke English. I don't know why that surprised me, after all, there were people at Kodai from all over the world. None of them had an inkling as to what I was asking them, so no one could tell me if they had heard Baba's comment. When my daughter, Andrea, heard that I couldn't make out what Baba had said, she jokingly teased me: "See, I told you that you needed Miracle Ear (a brand of hearing aid)! He probably gave you the name for your book. You just didn't hear it!"

Later, I wondered whether I had been wrong to answer: "From You, Baba." and whether the light touch on my cheek was really a mild rebuke for an unfeeling reply. But a conversation with Charles Gregory allayed my fears. Charles told me not to worry. Whether Baba was being loving or was chastising me, it comes to the same thing. Whether taking the time to bless me or to correct me, Baba was advancing my spirit.

Also, I realised that Baba had done what He had promised me He would do two days earlier when He said: *"I will talk to you later."* This was the "later." Nothing that Baba says or does is wasted. All that He says and does has meaning and all is fulfilled in His time. But most importantly, Baba had touched me. In so doing, He had granted me another special grace, *Sparsan*, the touch of the *Avatar*. So on that trip to Kodai, I had seen Him, heard Him, and been touched by Him. How wonderful!

> *"Cultivate nearness with Me in the heart*
> *and you will be rewarded.*
> *Then you too will acquire a fraction of the supreme Prema.*
> *This is the great chance.*
> *This chance will not come your way again, beware of that.*
> *If you cannot, if you do not,*
> *cross the sea of grief now,*
> *taking hold of this chance,*
> *when again can you get such a chance"*
> *Really, you are the fortunate few;*
> *out of the millions of the millions of people you have come,*
> *though no one specially invited you to be present here.*
> *That is what I call the mark of destiny."*

Indulal Shah
Spiritual Blueprints of My Journey
Introductory quotation from
Sri Sathya Sai

Baba accepting letters from the ladies at Darshan in Kodaikanal.

Charles Gregory "zapped" by Baba's loving energy.
This picture was taken about fifteen minutes after.
Baba blessed Charles book, "Lightwing and the Dreamwalker."

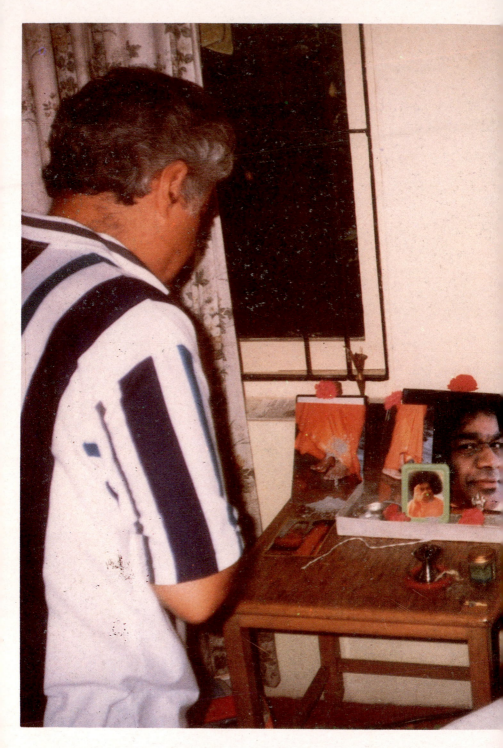

We witnessed the appearance of Vibhuti forming on the pictures of Baba in the hotel room of Dr. and Mrs. Sundarajan while Baba was three miles away.

Baba walking away from me (green scarf) after asking me : "From where did you come ?"

CHAPTER 42

DO UNTO OTHERS
AS YOU WOULD HAVE THEM DO UNTO YOU

"Do not judge others, to decide whether
they deserve your service. Find out only
whether they are distressed; that is
enough credential. Do not examine
how they behave towards others.;
they can be transformed by love.
Seva or Service, is for you as
sacred as a vow, a sadhana, a spiritual
path. It is the very breath; it can end only
when breath takes leave of you."

Voice of the Avatar
Page 218

Charles and Edith Gregory of Lyme, New Hampshire, were two of the eighteen people in our group at Kodaikanal. Charles is a slender, handsome, distinguished looking man, seventy years young, with graying hair combed back at the temples. Edith, always well groomed and neat, is like Charles, slender, partially a result of proper and modest eating habits. She has gray blonde hair, is quite pretty and is always prepared to beam a loving and pleasant smile which seems to pour out from an inner light to those around her. Both Edith and Charles have adopted a service or seva orientation in their lives. Their *sadhana* (spiritual excercise, surrendering and offering all thoughts, words and deeds to God), although including meditation and *bhakthi* (devotional practices), is pointed toward the path of loving service.

At Kodai, Patty and I found ourselves drawn to the Gregorys, enjoying the *satsang* of their company. They believe that we all should be conscious of not wasting anything, including our words and they make it a practice not to engage in idle chatter or talk for the sake of talking. And yet, each time we were together with them during the trip to Kodai, the conversation, for me, was stimulating and uplifting. We enjoyed some quiet meals with them at the Carlton and I had a long talk with them in the garden of the hotel.

On or about the third day that we were at Kodai, I became aware that wherever Charles sat during morning and afternoon *darshan*, I had an uninterrupted view of him. Whether he sat to the left or to the right of me, in front or behind me, if I simply looked in his direction, no person or thing blocked my view of Charles Gregory. And so, I became a Charles watcher. I noticed that whenever Baba came out, Charles would well up with emotion and become all teary eyed. His face radiated love and affection for the *Avatar*. I felt warm and peaceful just watching Charles looking at Baba.

Charles has written a book entitled: "Lightwing and the Dreamwalker." It is different from other Sathya Sai Baba inspired books that I have read in that it is a novel, an allegory to be precise, about a red bird with a black head, being the Baba figure, and a young boy in a wheel chair, representing Charles' and maybe all of our wounded psyches. The bird, Lightwing by name, encourages the boy to get out of the wheel chair and walk, by expounding teachings based on Baba's discourses, pronouncements, and exhortations.

Although Baba had blessed the book several months before, on an earlier visit, Charles hoped to have Baba place His signature on the book as a final blessing. Yet, by the seventh full day of our stay at Kodai, Charles had not gotten close enough to Baba for Baba to acknowledge him or the book in any way. Patty and I were hopeful that He would do so as Charles and Edith loved Him so. Now, on the twenty fourth of April, most of the men in our group were up on the concrete patio at the end of the verandah. We were facing in the direction of the ladies sitting under the green sun shade, who were looking up toward us. Charles was sitting against the railing of the patio with his back to the ladies and looking straight at me. Once again, nothing impeded my view of Charles.

I was excited because Charles was seated right at the foot of Baba's carpet at the end of the verandah. If Baba walked to the end of that carpet during the *bhajan darshan*, Charles would have the opportunity to present his book to Him. Baba came along at the start of *bhajans* and went directly into the hall through another door and didn't walk down the carpet to its end where Charles was waiting. During the *bhajans*, Charles was straining to see Baba through the window of the hall while tears of happiness filled his eyes. Later that night I wrote of Charles in my journal: "Baba so touches his heart!"

After *bhajans*, Baba came from the hall and walked down the carpet in the direction of the patio and Charles. When He reached Charles, He stopped and then looked around at the rest of us crowded on the concrete. Charles held up his book to Baba, but Baba didn't acknowledge the book or Charles for several seconds. He just kept looking from side to side at us and at the ladies sitting below. I was getting so intense! I wanted Baba to satisfy all of our hopes and sign Charles' book. I talked to Baba in my mind and not reverently either: "C'mon! Touch the man! Sign his book!" I demanded. Abruptly, Baba looked down at Charles, smiled at him and touched him on the face. Then He took the book and the proffered pen from Charles and wrote:

"With Love, Baba"

I was so elated that I almost applauded! Luckily, I stopped myself just as my palms faced each other, eager to slam together and create a sound that in those circumstances and at that place would have been solitary and so disrespectful. Baba asked Charles:

"Where are you from?"

Charles answered, "New Hampshire, America." Baba smiled. Charles later said that he "...couldn't believe that anybody could smile like that!" Then Baba tapped the top of Charles' head three times. Charles said that "there was enormous resonance" in his head. Slowly, Baba turned and walked away, heading back toward His residence.

I jumped up as soon as Baba disappeared into the house. I walked over to Charles who sat holding his head in his hands. I stood there, patiently waiting for Charles to recover and get up, but after several minutes, he was still sitting, obviously zapped by Baba's loving energy. Finally, I decided to move on and leave Charles undisturbed in his meditative state, but before I did, I took a photograph of him sitting there. I have included that picture in this book. It clearly shows Charles drained of conscious action and deeply affected by Baba's love.

All of our group, the women from the area below, and the men on the verandah saw Baba's loving attention to Charles when He signed that book. We were all so happy, that after *darshan*, we were hugging each other and smiling as if Baba had blessed us...and maybe that is just what He did. Charles' gift was our gift too. We are all One! His joy was shared by us all.

> *"...behind everything,*
> *the same divinity is existing*
> *and out of this comes*
> *the basis of morality."*

John Hislop
Letter to John Hislop
From Sathya Sai Baba
My Baba and I
Letters
Page 242

Selva

In December of 1992, Selva got out of a cab in Madras, India. Some evil-minded person, walked up to him and threw sulphuric acid at him, melting the right side of his face! During the police investigation, Selva could not shed any light on why anyone would do such a horrific thing to him. He had no idea who did it or who would want to do it. The despicable and cowardly act left one side of his face handsome, the other side, tragically disfigured. Selva went into a deep depression, thinking, feeling and believing that his life was over. He didn't believe that he could face the world with this terrible injury. How could anyone know the beauty of the soul that was dwelling in his body? Who would take the time to see beyond the form? He could only think of himself as that badly maimed body that he felt no one could love.

> *"God is not attracted by your appearance*
> *but that God Will look at the cleanliness*
> *of the inner self."*

Sai Avatar
Volume II
Section 127
Page 68

Selva's mother was a Sai devotee. He was not. The mother travelled to Puttaparthi soon after Selva was attacked to ask for Sai Baba's help and she was granted an interview. She prayed that Baba take care of Selva, her son. Baba answered her by repeating three times:

> *"I'm looking into it; I'm looking into it;*
> *I'm looking into it!"*

The family tried to find help for Selva, but there was no one in India to take on such major reconstructive surgery and the costs associated with the surgery needed was prohibitive both abroad and in India.

In March of 1993, Charles and Edith travelled to see Baba in Whitefield near Bangalore. While there, Charles met Selva in *darshan* line. Selva wore a rubber mask to protect and hold his face in place, and given the deep state of his depression, probably to hide his embarrassment and hurt. Yet, in spite of Selva's melancholy, he and the Gregorys managed to become fast friends. Charles and Edith saw beyond the mask deep into the soul of the tormented Selva, and they loved him. After returning home to New Hampshire in the United States, they kept in touch with Selva and his family by telephone and by mail.

"Do not serve for the sake of reward,
attracting attention, or earning gratitude,
or from a sense of pride
at your own superiority in skill, wealth,
status or authority.
Serve because you are urged by love."

<u>Yoga of Action</u>
Page 52

Toward the end of our stay at Kodaikanal the following year, Selva arrived with his mother and sought out Charles and Edith. He was not wearing a mask. Once again, I was in the vicinity of Charles when he and Selva found each other and I witnessed them embracing in joy as friends. I was struck at how Charles didn't seem to see the disfigured face, but rather looked past it to a deeper place.

"Serving anyone is serving Me,
for I am in all.
The relief and joy that you give
to the sick and the sad
reach Me,
for I am in their hearts,
and I am the One they call out for."

<u>Yoga of Action</u>
Page 60

Dr. Sundararajan, an Indian born plastic surgeon, had recently returned to his native land and was residing at Madras. He is a Sai devotee. Doctor Sundararajan met Selva and took the case. In just one year, Selva underwent fourteen operations and many more were planned. When we met Selva in Kodaikanal, he was much improved. Baba was "looking into it" all right! Dr. Sundararajan and his wife had travelled to Kodai with Selva and Selva's family. On the day of their arrival, Patty and I were introduced to them all. We spoke to the doctor about Selva and his chances for recovery. Dr. Sundararajan told Patty that when he operates on Selva, he feels that Sai Baba takes over his hands! "My dream is that I will be able, with

Baba's Grace, to return him to ninety percent of his former self," he told us affirmatively.

Both the doctor and Selva's family are very aware of the love that the Gregorys feel for Selva and are cognisant of their concern for him. In warm appreciation for their being such loving friends, Selva and his mother presented Charles and Edith with silver and gold *padukas* (sandals symbolic of the feet of the Guru, Saint or Avatar) which they had made especially for the Gregorys. Charles and Edith were overwhelmed! They never expected anything for simply being themselves.

> *"The fulfillment of human life*
> *consists in the service that man renders*
> *without any thought of return,*
> *in an attitude of selflessness"*
>
> <u>Voice of the Avatar</u>
> Page 2

Selva, his mother and the doctor encouraged the Gregorys to try to offer the *padukas* to Baba to be blessed and showed them how to prepare the beautiful sandals for the presentation. They were placed on Edith's new silk sari and carried on a silver tray. Orange and white jasmine flowers from Dr. Sundararajan were attractively placed around the gold and silver padukas. The next day, waiting for Baba's morning *darshan*, the doctor, Selva and Charles were seated in the front row at the bottom of the stairs of Baba's residence with the padukas set out in the lovingly adorned silver tray.

Baba usually walked down the stairs and approached a group of students or Seva Dal workers before meandering among the crowd. On this day, he walked right down the stairs directly to Charles. Once again, I had a clear line of sight right to Charles' face but I didn't know that he had the *padukas* with him. When Baba reached Charles, He immediately stepped into the *padukas* that were lying there before Him. I saw Him smiling at Charles, and tousling his hair. The image was of the playful parent enjoying a child. Of course, Charles was radiant with joy!

Being able only to see Charles from the shoulders up, I had no idea what Baba was doing, but it was told to me later, that after stepping into the *padukas*, Baba purposefully stepped upon the unworn sari that Edith had placed on the silver tray under the blessed sandals. Graciously, Baba was blessing Edith too!

After Baba walked away from Charles, several Indian men lurched forward, jumping all over themselves, diving, it appeared, at Charles' feet. I thought they were trying to touch Charles because of something Baba may have said to him. It appeared that they were giving Charles a sign of respect because of the grace that Baba had showered on him. Little did I know that they were falling over Charles to reach the *padukas* because Baba had stepped into them. They believed that the *padukas* would impart Baba's Grace and Energy into all who touched them.

After *darshan*, Charles stood smiling as we surrounded him and said to us: "Today I must be the luckiest man in the world!" Dr. Sundararajan looked at him and said meaningfully: "Yes, today you **are** the luckiest man in the world."

Dr. Sundararajan invited Charles and Edith and Patty and me to his hotel for lunch the following afternoon with Selva and his family. For some reason, which I still don't understand, I didn't want to go, but I felt compelled as the invitation had been warm and genuine. Maybe the doctor felt that since Charles had introduced me as his friend, it would be comfortable for Charles and Edith to have us along. Then, as the visit progressed, I became convinced that the invitation was really part of Baba's plan. You see, Baba had kept me very involved in the unfolding drama around Charles by allowing me to be able to see Charles at every opportune moment. I was there when his book was blessed; I was there when the *padukas* were blessed. I was able to share in the joy of Charles and Edith as Baba showered His love upon them. I feel that Baba wanted Patty and me to observe His motherly love for devotees such as Charles, Edith and the Sundararajans who respond to his call and carry out His teaching by serving others with no thought of reward. He was teaching us through them.

The doctor's hotel was a collection of time share apartments set on a hillside with green gardens highlighted by multicoloured flowers and green plants. When we arrived, instead of proceeding to the restaurant, the doctor met us outside and invited us to his condominium. "I have something to show you," he said. I was a little self-conscious as he herded us all into his bedroom. I really didn't know what was going on or what to expect. Then he gestured toward

his *puja* table which was a little night stand with three Baba pictures
on it. At first, we were bewildered as the scene looked ordinary
enough. Either Charles or I made a comment about "making do,"
when one is travelling. We were thinking of the modest size of the
night stand serving as an altar. Then Dr. Sudararajan pointed to the
gray area in two of the three pictures. *Vibhuthi!!* It was forming right
on the glass! The doctor and his wife explained to us that the
vibhuthi that was appearing on the pictures at that time had formed
there only since the morning. They had already collected the *vibhuthi*
from the day before in a small container.

Patty noticed a pile of *vibhuthi* in front of the pictures. Dr.
Sundararajan explained that in that heap was a tiny *lingam* that had
materialized (one of four for each of the four months prior to April,
1994) on their center's puja table in their home in Madras. A *lingam*
is a stone, gem or crystal having an oval shape, somewhat like an egg.
There is no beginning or ending to an oval, so a *lingam* is a symbol
of the formless God. Mrs. Sundararajan opened the small container
of *vibhuthi* and offered some to us. Patty was overcome with the
wonder of Baba's gift. Filled with emotion and reverence, she fell to
her knees before the *puja* table. Edith, Charles and I did likewise.

It appeared that Baba was showering His grace on the doctor and
his family. Why they had earned Baba's approval, I can't say for
sure, but I believe that part of the reason was the fact that the doctor
was working with Selva, in Baba's Name. And for Patty and me, it
was wonderful to witness Baba's love and grace. Awed, we, too, felt
blessed.

When we left Kodai, Charles and Edith followed Baba to
Whitefield. I knew in my heart that Baba would grant them an
interview soon after we had departed for the United States and He
did. But that is their personal story that Charles may commit to
writing some day, and so nothing of that here. I have reflected on why
Patty and I became so intertwined with the Gregorys, Selva and the
Sundararajans on this trip, and why we were allowed to see the Divine
Mother pour forth Her blessing on these gentle people. Charles,
Edith, and Doctor and Mrs. Sundararajan epitomise devotees
committed to doing selfless service, Seva, in His name and with no
thought of gain. Patty observed that Selva's name is the Sanskrit
word for service: "Seva," with an "L" for "love" added to it. The gift
to Patty and me from this whole experience was that we saw, first

hand, God's love for those who toil in His pastures and live His teachings. We witnessed Baba showering affection and parental love on His children for work done lovingly for others in His name. I believe He was telling Patty and me to go and do likewise.

"...so, earn the compassion of Swami and earn His love through service activities and fill your lives with meaning."

Yoga of Action
Page 68

CHAPTER 43

LIVING IN HIS PRESENCE

"This very moment is the moment!
The minute that has elapsed
is beyond your grasp;
so, too, the minute that is approaching,
is not yours!
It is only the individual which has engraved
this understanding on its heart
that can merge in Siva"

Baba The Breath of Sai
Page 166

One day, while I was standing in *darshan* line awaiting the opening of the gate to the residence grounds, an Indian gentleman struck up an ardent conversation with me about Baba. As I remember our discussion, he had some thought provoking dreams or meditations on Baba and had come to Kodai eager for *darshan* of the *Avatar*. I was struck with the man's intensity. He spoke rapidly and continuously. I am known as a talker, but I could not keep up with Mr. Sanwal. His rapid fire outpouring of words and ideas stunned me so that I could only interject a word or two every few minutes. During the next two days, I ran into him at least twice. Each time, he suggested that Patty and I have dinner with him at his hotel one evening. I was surprised by the invitation because I couldn't figure out why he felt so friendly toward me. He acted as if we were old friends. Finally, I suggested that he join Patty and me at our hotel, as we were travelling with others who might like to join us. He readily agreed and we arranged to meet in the restaurant of the Carlton Hotel on the following evening.

Mr. Sanwal arrived promptly and after introductions, we sat down for dinner with three others from our group. He began talking immediately about Baba and spiritual ideas. He talked so much that he barely touched his food. Excitedly, he regaled us with little stories that had a moral and taught a lesson. As I listened to him, I asked myself: "What is going on here? Why is this man in my life at this moment? Who is he? Did Baba arrange our meeting?" I wondered why he had taken such a shine to us and why he felt so driven to tell us his little stories.

It was only when I began writing in my journal that night, recapping the events of the day and noting some of the stories that Mr. Sanwal shared with us, that I became aware of why I had to meet him. I understood that he brought me a message in his parables and I suddenly realised that this message was from Baba. Mr. Sanwal was an instrument for Sai Baba, carrying a profound idea, a spiritual teaching meant for my uplift. I want to share, in paraphrase, one of the wonderful stories that he told that night, which spoke directly to my soul:

> In Ancient India, there lived a wealthy seth (a businessman). Through diligence, hard work, and good character, he had amassed a great fortune. A friend told him that if he worked hard enough and remained righteous, he could insure that his wealth and his good virtues and values would be passed on to a future generation and he might also win redemption for the soul of a loved one, now dead.
>
> The man began, with almost miserly attention, to save his money for it became his intention to assure that each member of his family, deceased for seven generations, would be redeemed and that his wealth and good values would be passed on to his descendants for seven generations to come. When he calculated the amount needed by mathematical formulae to accomplish his goals, he realised that his life span could not be long enough to accumulate the sum necessary to guarantee salvation for seven generations into the past and prosperity for seven generations into the future.
>
> And so, he despaired. His depression increased. His wife, unaware of the reason for her husband's anxiety, but conscious of his deterioration, became fearful for his mental health. She called on his *guru*, who

was fortunately just arrived from the Himalayas. The good woman asked the saint to visit her husband in order to encourage him to shake his doldrums and regain his former vitality. The *guru* did what he was asked, but the unhappy man could only recount his misery and the *guru* could only listen attentively for he knew of no way to solve his friend's problem.

Putting his hand on the despondent man's shoulder, the *guru* suggested that he pray to God for an answer to his problem and to observe a fast on certain auspicious days. He further advised the seth to give a bag of rice as *dakshina* (offerings made in gratitude for services rendered) to a brahmin asking him to pray for a resolution of his problem.

The businessman followed his *guru's* instructions with all dedication, but there was no improvement in his health nor any answer to his dilemma. He and his wife decided to journey to his native village in order to rest and regain his strength.

When they arrived at their destination, and in spite of his ill health, he went in search of an old brahmin priest who the seth knew from his childhood. The ancient priest still performed the services and holy rites in a small temple near the river side just a little way from the village. The simple priest was not a learned brahmin, but he was a dedicated man with high values. Now the seth, being very important, could have chosen a larger and wealthier temple and sought out a more educated brahmin. Instead, on that auspicious day, he returned to the familiar, old temple that he and his family had frequented when he was a lad. The aged priest at the temple was overjoyed to see him and welcomed him warmly.

After the businessman told the priest the reason for his visit, he offered the *dakshina* of rice to him. The venerable priest said that he would pray for the seth's intentions but the rice should be offered to his wife who was in the temple kitchen as all offerings of rice were within her domain.

The dejected man went into the kitchen which was nothing more than a small thatched hut attached to the dilapidated, old temple. There, in that simple kitchen, the ancient lady welcomed him with affection. Although the seth had not been in his native village for a long time, the old woman recognised him and with genuine affection, immediately served him a cup of tea.

While sipping his tea and after exchanging courteous pleasantries with the brahmin's wife, the seth explained his reason for bringing the bag of rice as *dakshina* to the temple and offered it to her. Although the aged lady wore an old and tattered sari, she appeared dignified and properly attentive as she listened to his story. Nodding her head, she held up her hand indicating that he should wait. She went to the cupboard and inspected her supply of rice. Turning to the anguished seth, she smiled, and said: "I am sorry, good sir, but I can not take your rice. I have examined my cupboard and I find that I have just enough rice for this evening's dinner."

At first, the wealthy man could not quite understand the meaning of her words, but as he gazed into her smiling eyes, a broad grin stole across his face. "What need have I to worry about relatives dead and eaten by worms or generations to come whom I will never see! My wealth and good fortune shall be used, today, for the living!" He had learned a great and valuable lesson and his burden was lifted.

"The past is past;
do not lose time looking back
on the road you have traversed.
Look forward, deciding to march on
with confidence and courage.
Take the first step now.
Tomorrow may be too late."

Sathya Sai Speaks
Volume X
Page 53

When I had completed my notes on Mr. Sanwal's story, I recognised its application in my life. How many hours had I spent daydreaming about the future or reliving the past and ignored the present moment and the color and texture of my life in the **now**? How many subtle smiles had gone unnoticed; how many little joys were unappreciated? How many times had I failed to recognise the happiness or fear of my children, my wife and my friends? I remembered the days that I so despaired about being able to meet obligations, that I became immobile and withdrawn, unable to see, let alone enjoy, the fabric of life being woven around me.

"...the most blessed time is the 'present',
this very second..."

Sathya Sai Speaks
Volume V
Page 223

Mr. Sanwal's story encourages us to live in the present, for there is no longer reality in the past and the future is not yet here. However, this lesson, to live in the present, is only a stepping stone. It is not the final destination. After all, we can live **badly** in the moment. We can do evil in the present. Our focus can be to live in negativity and blackness. In what manner then, does Sathya Sai Baba expect us to live in the present?

"Know that I am always with you,
prompting you and guiding you.
Live always in that
CONSTANT PRESENCE."

Indulal Shah
Spiritual Blueprints of My Journey
Page 158

It is not enough to live in **the present**, we must attempt to live in **His Presence!** We must be aware of Divinity in all things and in all people. We must divinize the now. The question then, for us, is: How do we do that? How can we comply with Baba's teaching:

"Your whole life should be lived
in the CONSTANT PRESENCE
of the Lord."

Sathya Sai Speaks
Volume I
Page 115

I remember Charles and Edith Gregory telling me that they are consciously trying to live in the Presence of the Lord. In their case, they have chosen to live in a rural area of New Hampshire and to live a semi monastic life, venturing out from home daily to share themselves in loving service to others and then returning to their quiet, secluded home nestled deep in the woods. But that is not all they do to live in His Presence. SAI-lence is not their only tool to help them live in God. There are other practices that remind them of Him. When eating, they bless the food and offer it to Him. They have pictures of Baba in every room, to keep Him in their mind's eye. Charles has a large picture of Baba behind his desk, so that when he is writing and doing his work, he is conscious of Baba watching him and so he is more diligent and more focused.

Others like Bill Altman have tried *Namasmarana,* the constant repetition of a Name of God that helps to keep them directed toward the Divine. Bill told me that he experimented with different Names until he found one name he could use as a *mantra* that was pleasing to him. Using signs or symbols such as looking for the number 9 has the effect of keeping me thinking about Baba. And one little habit that I have been working to develop, is that of inviting Baba to join me in whatever I am doing and wherever I am going. For instance just before our family gathers for our Christmas Celebration at my home, I do a prayerful meditation wherein I invite Baba to join us that evening and to celebrate with us. I try to picture Him sitting among us when we dedicate a Christmas reading from the Bible or when we are handing out the gifts, and I try to remember, although not always successfully, to thank Him for having joined us, when the celebration is over.

I remember a meeting of Sai devotees at my home where Patty and others had set out food for a pot luck supper. The food was placed on a table and we served ourselves. While in line for the food, I was talking with Ramesh Wadhwani. As we left the line and while I was still talking to Ramesh, he took one step back and away from me, bowed his head over the food and SAI-lently blessed the food dedicating it to the Lord. Although I was surprised at the sudden interruption in our conversation, I have never forgotten the incident and the lesson it taught me. The Lord comes first! Bless the food, then talk.

In addition to the repetition of the Holy Name and the chanting of the *Gayathri Mantra*, Patty listens to or sings *bhajans* as often as she is able. As she drives in to or from work, songs of God or songs of praise to God are constantly on her lips. She feels that they quiet her and center her so that she is less prone to the ups and downs or vagaries of life. The *bhajans* keep her focusing on the God within helping her to understand the answer to her question "Who am I really?" Through her chanting comes the realisation that she and Sai and God are one!

All of these techniques help us to focus on God, but becoming a truly God Conscious person requires **practice, patience and forgiveness**. Repetition of our chosen *sadhana* or spiritual method is essential. Not thoughtless repetition, but a **conscious dedication to practice** over and over the chosen method or methods of keeping God in our hearts and minds. We must **intend** to remember Him always. **Patience** is necessary because living in the Presence of the Lord **takes time** to develop. At first, other people, things and events will get in the way of our consistency, but picking up again, in spite of interruption, is the tool that finally builds the habit. We must not quit. We are building our roadway to Divinity, step by plodding step until finally the goal is reached. Lastly, we must be able to **forgive ourselves** when we fail to remember to pray over our food, or when we over sleep and miss our meditation, or listen to the radio instead of doing *Namasmarana.* Guilt is extra baggage that we can not afford to carry on this journey! When we fail, we must accept the failure and start anew. Over time, with conscious resolve we will be the beneficiaries of Baba's promise:

*"To get God's grace, you have
to engage yourself in sacred action.
Bear in mind the three P's:*

Purity, Patience and Perseverance.

*With these three you are bound
to acquire good health and bliss"*

Sathya Sai Baba
Sanathana Sarathi
Vol 38, July 1995
No. 7, Page 173

CHAPTER 44

YOU HAVE MY HEART!

"Remember, Sai does not live in
structures of stone or brick and mortar!
*He lives in **soft hearts**,*
warm with sympathy
and fragrant with universal love."

Sai Avatar
Volume II
Paragraph 334
Page 163

As Patty and I prepared to travel to Kodaikanal and Sai Baba, I thought that I would attempt to correct my forgetfulness of nine years earlier by bringing a stone from our front yard to India as a sign of the unity between myself and Baba. On the day that we were to begin the journey, I walked into the woods near our home and combed the area for a suitable little rock to take with me. After a few minutes search, I found a red, heart shaped stone just a little larger than a quarter. "How appropriate," I thought. "I can use this stone as a symbol of my 'heart of stone.' " I packed it carefully in one of my traveling bags and we were off.

I am very much a mind person and don't usually experience wide swings of emotion. Very seldom do I cry or get swept away by elation. I observe and recognise other people's hurts and joys and can respond to them, but I am responding with my logical mind. I can empathise and sympathise, because I see the need, but rarely do I feel another's emotions. So, it was with that mind set, that I had thought of myself as one with a "heart of stone." I have always been amazed and somewhat bewildered by those people who can sense another's emotional needs. It seemed to me that I was deficient in the feeling or feminine side of my psyche and I resented my seeming inability to deeply experience emotionally.

Even my initial reaction to Sathya Sai Baba was from my mind. I read every book **about** Him, inquired **of** Him and looked **into** Him, but I didn't experience the loving, deep, emotional feeling that Patty, Charles Gregory and others knew and savoured. When I had travelled to India in 1985, I hoped Baba's Presence and nearness would move me to feel His Love and Grace, but they did not. Intellectually, I knew that Sathya Sai Baba was an Incarnation of Divinity but I didn't feel that truth.

Although my approach to Baba on this trip to Kodai was very devotional, I still was reaching Him through my mind. But then a curious thing happened. Charles Gregory had given me his new book, "Lightwing and the Dreamwalker" to read one evening. I read late into the night and completed all but about six or seven pages before falling to sleep. The next morning I brought the book with me to morning *darshan* and finished the last several pages while waiting for Baba to appear. Those pages describe a loving reaction of a young boy to the needs of his grandfather. When I had finished reading , I began to think of my late grandparents, all of whom had been very close to me, and I began to cry. I wasn't sad; I was't sobbing loudly; it wasn't even obvious to those around me that I was weeping. The tears just warmly and gently journeyed down my cheeks and I didn't want to wipe them away. I remembered each of my grandparents and **experienced** loving them very much. I was **enjoying** the tears and didn't want them to stop. It wasn't that I had lost control; it was just that I was totally experiencing my love for them and the tears were just the outward manifestation of what I was **feeling!**

Where did that delicious feeling come from? I knew that it was not from my mind. It was from deep within and it came naturally. I didn't have to think it or logic it, it just swelled up from my heart. The whole episode was a grace from the *Avatar*. But, as much as I savoured the moment, it never dawned on me that Baba was helping me touch the feminine side of my soul. I didn't realise that my gentle weeping was evidence that even I had a feeling center, a sensitive core. To my way of thinking, my heart was still a heart of stone. And so, I took to carrying the little, red heart shaped stone with me to *darshan* and when Baba walked near, I held the stone in front of my heart and prayed that He "melt my stone heart."

For several days, He never looked in my direction as I held up the stone and repeated my prayer. Then, on our last day at Kodai, at the last *darshan*, I once again held up the stone and asked Him to melt my stone heart. Suddenly, without looking directly at me, He turned away. I felt His anger even though he didn't look at me or speak one word aloud. But, inside my head, I heard Him speak clearly: *"You don't have a heart of stone!"* He said sharply. *"You have My*

Heart!"   I sensed that His words were meant to correct me, not rebuke me.

> " *'I am low, mean, small, useless, poor, sinful, inferior'*
> *--such feelings also are egoistic;*
> *when the ego goes,*
> *you do not feel either*
> *superior **or** inferior.*
> *...self-condemnation is also egoism..."*

Sathya Sai Speaks
Volume III
Page 25

I had been so ready to believe that I couldn't feel; that I couldn't get in touch with my inner caring nature, that I had forgotten one of the principal teachings of the *Sai Avatar*: Sai and God and I are One! I forgot His exhortation to dive deep into myself to find myself. The state of Bliss, the condition of Divine Love is found in all men. Everyone is capable of reaching that Love because it is the Center of our being. I had simply been looking in the wrong place, on the surface, in my mind. I should have been looking deeper into my heart.

> *"When there is a lamp in our house,*
> *why should you go begging for the fire elsewhere?*
> *Why should you go in search of God*
> *when the Lord of Lords is housed in you?*
> *You need not go elsewhere*
> *when you realise that the Lord*
> *is enthroned in your heart."*

Summer Showers in Brindavan 1993
Page 13

What a wonderful revelation! I left that last *darshan* saddened by the thought that we were leaving Baba, Kodai Kanal and India but exhilarated by my newly discovered insight that I could reach my feeling center by directing my attention inward. I felt lighter somehow and relieved that I wasn't an unfeeling automaton programmed only to think.

Upon returning to the United States, Patty and I decided to host a reunion of the American group that had travelled with us to Kodaikanal. Most of our team of eighteen were able to join us. Before dinner, George Condon, an ordained Congregational Minister, facilitated a session where each of us, in turn, shared both our **feelings** and observations of our pilgrimage to Sathya Sai Baba. As each person spoke, the colour, smells and general feel of Kodai came magically to life again. The reminiscences of my fellow travellers kindled a spark in me and I found myself re-experiencing our journey to His Feet. By the time it was my turn to speak, I was thinking that each one of us was tied to the rest by the chord of Baba's love. Even though we were all of different shapes, colours and sizes, there was a oneness that linked us together. That oneness couldn't be found in the way we looked, because we all looked different; it couldn't be found in the way we spoke, because we all talked of our own individual observations; it couldn't be found in our understanding of Baba because we all understood Him differently. It **was** found in the **love** that we felt for Him; it **was** found in our **yearning** for Him; it **was** found in our **hearts**!

> *"Have the Love of God*
> *filling and thrilling your heart;*
> *then you cannot hate any one,*
> *you cannot indulge in unhealthy rivalries,*
> *you will not find fault with any one.*
> *Life becomes soft, sweet and smooth."*

A Recapitulation Of Sathya Sai Baba's
Divine Teaching
page 61

Suddenly, it was clear to me that we, in that room, were **one**! Each of us, deep down was searching for that **self** same Bliss, that **self** same Love, that **self** same Divinity! In truth, we and Sai and God are one! With that realisation, a feeling of love welled up from my heart and the tears began to flow. I tried to express my feelings of love for my brothers and sisters in that room and the more I tried, the more I cried! But I didn't care. I wasn't self conscious. I wanted them each to feel what I was feeling. I wanted them each to experience my joy at being part of their lives and finding them in my heart. I told them through the tears: "I love you all, very much!"

> *"Holding everything within Him,*
> *Illumining everything by His Consciousness,*
> *The Divine (Brahman) is in you*
> *And you are in the Brahman*
> *There is no difference*
> *Between you and Brahman.*
> *What greater truth can I convey*
> *To all of you assembled here?"*

> Sathya Sai Baba
> Quotation introducing
> Baba's Divine Discourse
> of November 23, 1994
> Found in the December 1994 issue
> of <u>Sanathana Sarathi</u>, Volume 37,
> No. 12, Page 309

CHAPTER 45

FOR ALWAYS YOU WILL BE MY PRECIOUS SON

"First you must know your own full address.
Who are you? The Aathman.
Whence did you come? From the Aathman.

Where are you going? To the Aathman itself.
How long can you be here? Until you merge with the Aathman."

The Greatest Adventure
Chapter 1
Page 18
Dr. M.V.N. Murthy

In May of 1994, after we had returned from our pilgrimage to Kodai Kanal, I began the task of expanding the outline which had been blessed by Baba, into this book. By mid March of 1995, Charles and Edith Gregory had completed the critical editing and I had sent a draft to John and Elena Hartgering for final editing. Patty and I had decided to travel again to Kodaikanal on April second in order to bring the book to Baba in hopes that He would bless it and name it. Somehow, everything came together on time and the Hartgerings returned the final product, with a polished format, to us just a few days before a 747 KLM jet liner lifted us into the skies in New York and sped us toward the *Avatar*.

One of the reasons that I was so excited about traveling to India with the book was that many of the people who had helped me in its production were also journeying to the feet of the *Avatar* at the same time. John and Elena Hartgering were flying with us while Charles and Edith Gregory had left two weeks earlier. Tony LoGrasso, who had written the forward, and his wife, Maria, arrived in Prasanthi Nilyam about a week before we began our sojourn. I secretly hoped that Baba was bringing us to India together so that we could all share in the joy of His accepting and blessing the book.

When we arrived in Bombay, we received a telephone call from Tony and Maria who informed us that Baba was at Puttaparthi and that we should come there rather than fly to Madurai and then to Kodaikanal. Tony was not sure when or if Baba would be visiting Kodai, so early the next morning we set off by plane to Bangalore and then taxied to Puttaparthi. We arrived at the *ashram* after *darshan*,

Tony Lograsso, myself and John Hartgering as Baba materialises Vibhuti for John.

I came to see Baba as Father

made arrangements with the accomodations office for a room and caught up with Tony and Maria.

Now, one of the prayerful requests that I had made of Baba while planning this trip, was that I experience Him as Father. In Kodai, I had been blessed to see Him as Mother, so loving and gentle. Now I wanted to observe His Fatherly aspect. I wanted His protection and guidance. I took to repeating a *mantra* in my mind: "You are Father; I am Your son. Please guide me." Soon after I had arrived at Puttaparthi, I was walking up an incline toward the building where we would be living while at the *ashram*. As I reached the top of the hill, I looked up and stared at a sign with a thought from Baba written on it. The sign read:

> *"We Love God*
> *God Is Our Father"*

There are many signs like this one with Sai Baba's teachings on them throughout the *ashram* but I had really not seen them in my mind's eye. They didn't register in my consciousness until I saw this sign addressing God as Father. I felt it was Baba's way of letting me know that He had heard my request and that it would be as Father that I would experience Him on this trip.

Being at Puttparthi instead of Kodaikanal afforded me an opportunity that I had missed when we were last at Prasanthi Nilyam in 1985. At that time we had very little knowledge of the workings of the *ashram*. No one ever explained to me that I could have risen early each morning and been allowed into the *mandir*, the temple dedicated to Sathya Sai Baba and Shirdi Sai Baba to participate in morning prayers. Each morning before the sun rises, devotees sit reverently in the main hall of the *mandir* and intone the original sound of all creation, the "*Om*," twenty-one times and then chant the *Suprabhatam*, a song calling God, the *Avatar*, Sai Baba, to awaken and lend His Glory to a new day. It is also a call to awaken the God within each of us to flourish and shine. I had come to love the *Suprabhatam* at Sai retreats or at other Sai functions and always felt that I had missed something special in not having participated in that call to the Divine when I visited Prasanthi. So it was with joyful eagerness that I arose that first morning and set off to experience the *Omkar* and the *Suprabhatam* in Baba's temple, the *mandir*.

The Seva Dal leaders lined us up in a queue on the marble floor in front of the *mandir*. Towering above us was the new concrete roof that Baba has had constructed to protect devotees from the relentless sun of the Puttaparthi desert while waiting for Baba's *darshan*. Large, lighted chandeliers hang gracefully from this covering and the feel of the place so early in the morning is of peace and holiness. For Patty, the beautiful columns and airiness evoked the feeling of being in a temple in ancient Greece or Atlantis. Finally, we were led into the main hall of the *mandir* where pictures of Shirdi Sai and Sathya Sai frame the altar. On the left is a large statue of Shirdi Baba and on the right, on a raised dais, is Baba's chair. Dominating the rear of the room is a large chariot carrying Arjuna, the warrior of the *Bhagavad Gita* listening to Krishna, Avatar and charioteer, instructing him on his duty.

We sat quietly until the singers began to chant *Omkar*, the Sound of God, twenty-one times. I cannot describe in words that glorious sound echoing in that holy chamber. It seemed to fill every corner, every space and then resound into me and through me. The thrill of my envelopment in that sound as it was sung by the many devotees sitting cross-legged, with eyes closed, raised my spirit in bliss and thanksgiving. The many years of thinking what it would be like to be in the *mandir* at *Omkar* was fulfilled in wonderment at the beauty of that sound. I realized that Baba knew of my earlier disappointment and had called me to Puttaparthi to fulfill my desire for this grace.

Later, we were seated, the men on the right of the marble floor in front of the *mandir* and the women on the left. In an instant, all backs straightened, all heads turned, all eyes widened as that burst of orange-red robe suddenly appeared and Baba walked slowly from His quarters in the newly renovated Poornachandra Hall, through the crowd of ten thousand devotees. I was sitting with Tony LoGrasso as Baba walked within fifteen feet of us three times without looking in our direction. My heart was pounding with excitement. I never felt so expectant at Kodai the year before. Instead of sitting reverently, I found myself turning to follow His every movement and at one point, scurrying across the marble to get closer to Him as He changed direction. Such is the desire to be near the Lord. Yet, Baba seemed to purposefully avert His eyes so as not to look at us. Tony hoped that the feeling of rejection that one feels when Baba seems not to notice us is one way for us to atone for some *karmic* debt. "Especially since He ignored us three times," he said.

Baba has told us often to love His uncertainty. We had made arrangements to stay at Kodaikanal and then found Baba was at Puttaparthi. Patty had a meditation on the plane en route to Bombay that Baba would be at Whitefield. After morning *darshan* word spread that Baba was leaving and sure enough His car was brought up to the Poornachandra and off He sped. To Kodai? We wondered. No, He was on His way to Brindavan, His *ashram* and college at Whitefield near Bangalore. Patty had seen correctly. So, after a stay of less than twenty-four hours at Prasanthi Nilyam, we checked out at the accomodations office and followed Baba to Whitefield much to Patty's delight. The temperature was over 115 degrees at Puttaparthi! When we had arrived in India, I had prayed to Him not to let me miss one *darshan* of Him because of our uncertainty as to where He might be located. He brought us to Puttaparthi for His Grace and after darshan we journeyed to Whitefield. No *darshan* time lost.

Arriving at Whitefield, the LoGrassos, the Hartgerings and Patty and I found lodgings in a group of villas owned by a Dr. Patel. Patty and I were assigned a room on the second floor of one villa. Several days later it struck me that our room number was "F-9." As had occurred at Kodaikanal in 1994, our room number was the number of the *Avatar*. Because I use the number nine to remind me of Sai Baba, I took our room assignment as an indication that Baba welcomed us to Whitefield and his Presence. But if the nine was a symbol then the "F," too, should convey a meaning for me, but for days I could not find the message in that letter. Then, one day I had an insight that the "F" stood for "Father!" I had been calling to Baba as Father and relating to Him as son; the symbol of our room number was perfect. Baba, the *Avatar* and Father had welcomed us and provided for us.

We arrived at Brindavan on April sixth and attended *darshan* on the morning of the seventh. *Darshan* is held at Sai Ramesh Hall within the walls of the college. It is a huge rectangular structure, open on three sides and covered with a high plastic roof held in place by metal trusses. At the main entrance, four or five steps lead up to the marble floor which is divided into large black squares where devotees are seated. Around each square are white marbled aisles so that Baba can walk around and among the devotees giving maximum viewing at *darshan* and bringing Him quite close to those seated in the block that He is near. At the far end of the hall is a raised dais or platform, in the middle of which, stands a large, square, ornate canopy with an onion shaped dome. Under this canopy is a statue of Krishna playing His *Murali* (Indian flute) and Baba's chair. In the afternoon, Baba does not walk among the people, but rather, enters the dais from a rear door, walks across the platform and sits on the chair while six to eight thousand devotees absorb His presence and joyfully sing bhajans to the Lord.

On that first day at Whitefield, I was seated in a front row along an aisle in one of the squares. Baba walked right past me, managing to look to the left and to the right but seemingly oblivious to my presence. It is amazing how He did that, because I was holding up the binder containing the manuscript of this book just inches from His eyes and yet, He appeared not to notice. I was a little embarrassed. It seemed to me that everyone in the Hall could tell that Baba had purposefully ignored me.

The following morning, before *darshan,* I told Patty how I felt when Baba walked past me. Throughout my life I have fought a tendency to believe that I was not good enough. On this trip to India, I was determined to lay this problem at Baba's feet and ask His guidance and support in overcoming this negative view of myself. Needless to say, Baba's inattention to me heightened and accentuated this feeling of insufficiency. But, just talking to Patty about it helped and I set off for morning *darshan* feeling a little better.

Our line was the second line seated in Ramesh Hall that morning. John Hartgering and Tony LoGrasso were seated on either side of me at the back of a square. There was a white marbled aisle directly behind us. Around eight o'clock, all heads turned toward the entrance to Baba's residence as the slow walking, orange robed *Avatar* appeared. He entered the hall at the side and walked along an aisle to the rear of the hall where He gave *darshan* not only to those in the hall, but to those standing or sitting in the large concrete square outside of the hall. Slowly, He moved down the center aisle and walked back toward the front of the Hall. When He reached the aisle behind us, He turned into it and glided in our direction. We all turned around so that we would be facing Him if He approached us. He was taking letters from devotees across the aisle. My heart was racing, as I held up the book and cried out: "Your book, Baba!" He gazed at it with a look of recognition and walked toward me, his hand extended as if to touch the cover. Abruptly, He withdrew His hand. My heart sank. Then He reached forward and touched the book about three times. I was so excited that I am not really sure how many times He tapped the blue binder but tap it He did. He had given the book His blessing.

I looked down and found myself staring at His foot. The Seva Dal leaders had given everyone instructions before Baba came out for *darshan* that we were not to try to touch His feet unless He gave permission. In my mind I asked Him to give me a sign to show His approval that I could take *padnamaskara*, the touching of the feet of the *Avatar*. Immediately, as if hearing my thoughts, he moved His foot toward me and I placed my hand on it.

Suddenly, He turned to John Hartgering and asked him:

"Where are you from?"

John remembered Ramesh Wadhwani's story and so responded: "From you, Swami." Baba leaned toward John and asked again:

"From U.S.A., yes?"

John responded: "Yes, Swami." Immediately, Baba's right hand began that familiar circular motion and in an instant I was watching *vibhuthi* pouring from His palm into John's uplifted hand. I could see the whitish flakes coming directly from His hand. Turning, He moved His hand toward me and I instinctively held up my hand and the *vibhuthi* filled my palm. I was stunned! I had often thought that if Baba made *vibhuthi* for me it wouldn't be impressive. After all, it's only ash, I thought. Well, I was wrong. There I sat, staring into my palm, examing the tiny white flakes that crumbled into fine particles when touched and not knowing what to do next. Thankfully, one of the Seva Dal people with Baba handed Tony LoGrasso a piece of paper for me to wrap the *vibhuthi*. Carefully, I turned my hand and dropped the *vibhuthi* into the paper which Tony folded for me. I ate the remaining ash on my palm and began to cry. It took me a while to regain a sense of my surroundings. Baba, meanwhile, had left our aisle and walked down a side aisle in the direction of the dais. Finally, I turned around still filled with emotion. I had been granted *padnamaskar* and was thrilled that He had blessed the book, but I was dazed and disoriented by His manifestation and presentation to me of the white *vibhuthi* flakes

There are as many reasons why Baba distributes *vibhuthi* as there are people who receive it. I have tried to analyse why Baba would choose me to grant this gift. I had come on this pilgrimage asking Him to grant me self-confidence and praying that my feeling of not ever being enough would dissipate. Often *vibhuthi* is curative and maybe Baba used it to help me believe in my own self worth and ultimate divinity.

Several weeks later, when reflecting on his encounter with Baba that morning, John Hartgering understood the implication of Baba's response, *"U.S.A., yes"* to mean *"You say yes."* Baba had said in 1968:

"If you will accept Me and say 'Yes,'
I too will respond and say, 'Yes, yes, yes.'
If you deny and say 'No,'
I also echo 'No.' "

Samuel Sandweiss, M. D.
The Holy Man and the Psychiatriast
Pages 87-88

Through Baba's Grace, John has adopted that teaching, and made it his special intention to say "Yes!" when the opportunity to serve Baba by serving others arises. In addition to spiritual changes in his personal life, John has said "Yes" to Baba through service work with Habitat for Humanity, the Street Ministry, and community renewal in the inner city of Hartford, Connecticut.

Later that morning, I volunteered for work in the foreign devotees' canteen cutting tomatoes and squash and cucumbers for lunch and dinner. Christine, the lady in charge asked me if I would help bring the green garbage to Baba's compound for use as fertilizer in Baba's garden. A young German devotee and I each took hold of a handle on either side of a large, heavy, plastic garbage container and trundled off toward the gate to Baba's residence. As we walked along, it became apparent to me that what we were doing, bringing garbage for Baba's garden, was a great symbol of what Baba asks us always to do. He wants us to bring our pleasure and pain, our happiness and our sorrow and leave them with Him without regard to endings or consequences. We are to leave all results to Him. We do our best and He does the rest. We bring Him our garbage and He transforms it into new life in the garden that He plants and sows.

"Deliver all your anxieties, troubles, travails and desires
to me,
and in return receive joy, peace and strength of mind
from me."

At The Feet of Sai
R. Lowenberg
Chapter 12
Page 77

That evening, Patty, Maria and Tony LoGrasso and I went to the international *bhajan* at the Sai Deep, a garden in the back of one of the villas at Whitefield. Christiana, a young German woman who lives at Puttaparthi led devotees from all over the world in hymns and *bhajans*. One of the beautiful songs that she sang that night touched me deeply. I felt that the words were from Baba and were addressed directly to my heart. He was encouraging me to realise my self worth and to reject the feeling of not being enough:

How can anyone ever tell you
you are anything less than beautiful?
How can anyone ever tell you
you are less than whole?
How can anyone fail to notice
that your loving is a miracle?
How deeply your connected to my soul.

The song so moved me that when Patty and I returned to our room, we wrote two additional stanzas that expanded on the theme that each of us is worthy and connected to the divine:

Don't let anyone steal your spirit.
Let it soar and fly on high.
Don't let anyone slow your progress
as you touch the sky.

Don't let anyone be mistaken,
we will never be apart.
I'll always live within you, in your heart.

You must seek to find the treasure
that I've left within your soul.
You must know with love unshaken,
you can reach your goal.
You must sense your life eternal
that we are ever one.
For always you will be my precious son.

How comforting were those words. Through them I felt Baba showering His love on me, encouraging me and teaching me that I am lovable, worthy and "good enough," because I am divine. I am His son. I thought that this song would somehow turn me around so that for the rest of this pilgrimage to His Lotus Feet, I would be totally transformed; that I would be self-confident, happy and full of bliss. But it didn't work out that way. Instead, my feelings went on a roller coaster ride, up and down, up and down. On April eleventh after *darshan,* I went back to my room for a short while before going to the canteen to do *seva* (service offered to the Lord) work in the kitchen. I decided to pick up my guitar and play the song, "How can anyone ever tell you," just to relax. I played and sang that song three or four times straight as memories of my father flooded my mind. So much of what I am or am not is colored by my love for my dad and how much I tried to be like him and to satisfy him. I know that my feelings of inadequacy are tied to my perceptions of what I thought I needed to be to gain his approval. Suddenly, I began to cry; not a gentle weeping but an uncontrolled sobbing that racked my body. I cried for about thirty minutes. When I was able to compose myself, I barely had the strength to walk the five feet to reach the water basin to wash my face and refresh myself.

I sat down with the guitar again and started playing the same song once more. This time I was reminded of some loving words my son, Andy had spoken to me just before we began this pilgrimage to Sai Baba. He told me that he thought that I was "a holy man too." Of course, the tears came in torrents again. I knew that Baba was working on me. I was obviously in his washing machine, being cleaned out. I believe the tears were a sign of the beginning of a slow transformation. Baba is not going to wave a magic wand and make me self-confident overnight, but he did touch me deep within my soul and began the process of gradually changing my beliefs and thought patterns from the inside out.

As the days passed, nothing seemed to raise my spirits. Later in the week, I went again to the international devotees *bhajan* at the Sai Deep. I was feeling very lonely. Tony and Maria had left for home the night before. Patty was being blessed with beautiful insights found in deep meditation. She had trouble talking to me about that and would burst into tears when she tried. And Baba seemed to be ignoring me again as He wound His way during *darshan*. So, like a little boy, I was sulking. I decided to sit and listen to the singing but not join in. I sat pouting under a flower arbor while the others sang beautiful songs of praise to God. Suddenly, a flower fell from the trellis over head and landed gently in my hand nestled on my lap. Intuitively, I knew it was a loving gift from the Sai mother but like a petulant child, I wouldn't let His little leela raise my spirit. "It is not enough, Baba," I whispered. "You must talk to me. I need to know consciously that you love me and that I am good enough." That night, I complained so bitterly to Patty of my own feelings of inadequacy, that I made her cry. There was no question that I was very hurt and wounded. In spite of His flowery gift, I had no ability to pull myself up from my feelings of failure and insufficiency.

The next day at the afternoon *bhajans*, I was seated in the front line on the aisle in the second square. Baba came through the door onto the dais from my left and slowly walked to His chair as He usually did for *bhajans*. Somehow, I knew that He would walk past the chair, down the steps and into the crowd of devotees, and He did. He walked up the aisle to my right, not approaching anyone, not taking letters from anyone, not giving *vibhuthi* to anyone or talking to anyone. He simply walked in the very middle of the aisle and looked at the devotees looking at Him. He took a right turn and proceeded down the aisle in front of me. Once again, I held up the book in front of my chest and kept repeating in my mind the prayer: "Baba, please name your book." He turned to me and looked at the book. He raised His eyebrows in a sign of recogniton and He asked me:

"From where did you come?"

I couldn't make out what He had said, so I said, "I'm sorry Baba I didn't hear you." He repeated the question again;

"From where did you come?"

I quickly answered without thinking: "From Connecticut, U.S.A." He gave me a nod of his head and looked right through me. I realised in an instant that I had not responded, "from You, Baba," and I didn't know what to do. He smirked at me and His twinkling eyes seemed to say :

"Aha, I got you!"

Before I could recover, He had walked away from me. My emotions ran havoc. At first, I was disappointed in myself for my unthinking answer, but then I started to laugh as I realised that He had controlled the whole episode. There were so many ways that His question touched me and taught me. First, I had been quite proud that I had answered the same question at Kodaikanal by saying: "From You, Baba." I had loudly told anyone who would listen that I had answered "correctly." Here, Baba was showing me that that answer must be heartfelt and that I have to delve deeper before I can answer with real awareness that He and I are one.

Secondly, His question was really an answer to my constant prayer over the many days of *darshan*, that He name this book. I had asked Him at Kodai the year before, to name it and He had said:

"Not now!"

Several days later, He had approached me and asked me:

"From where did you come?"

As I answered Him then, I didn't make the connection that He was naming the book although Patty and Tony LoGrasso thought that could be one interpretation of His words. And now, again at Brindavan, one year later, He was asking the same question, but this time it came after I had spent days asking Him in my heart to name His book. It felt comfortable to Patty and to me that He was responding to my constant badgering for a name. Baba teaches that we are all divine and that we, as *Atma*, the divine spark, are all part of the divine flame that is *Paramatma*, the Universal Absolute, the Supreme Self, God. When Sathya Sai Baba asks:

"From where did you come?"

He is calling us to recognise that we have come from the Divine and that we are part of the Divine. By giving me that question as the name of this book, He is teaching me that all of my spiritual experiences, in fact, all of the experiences of my life are meant to remind me of the truth that my self has emerged from and is part of the Supreme Self which is :

"...The Absolute from which everything has emanated,
in which all this exists,
into which all this merges,
the yarn of which the cloth, Prakriti (the world
and nature) is formed."

Translations By Baba
Compiled by Homer S. Youngs
Page 113

Baba turned back toward the dais and walked up the steps to take His place on His chair during the singing of bhajans. I did not observe Him take any letters, create *vibhuthi* or talk to anyone other than myself. It seemed to me that the sole reason for His short sojourn was to talk to me. Now, I know that all Baba's actions and words can have many purposes and meanings, but for me, it was the answer to my prayer that He singled me out and spoke to me. I saw that loving gesture as reassurance from the loving Father of all, that I am worthy and sufficient and should not allow myself to feel inadequate. I am His son. I am an emanation of the Divine. Sai and I and God are one.

"I am the embodiment of Love;
Love is my instrument.
There is no creature without Love;
the lowest loves itself at least,
and its self is God."

The Greatest Adventure
Chapter 66
Dr. M.V.N. Murthy
Page 360

AFTERWORD

WHO IS HE...THIS AVATAR?

"Therefore I have come armed with
the fullness of the Power of the Formless God
to correct mankind, raise human consciousness
and put people back on the Right Path of Truth,
Righteousness, Peace and Love to Divinity..."

Kristina Gale-Kumar
The Scriptures Are Fulfilled
Chapter 6
Page 245

The writing of this book, over the past two years, has been a wonderful exercise for me. It has given me the opportunity to examine my life in terms of a spiritual journey. The people and events that were the threads woven through the fabric of my life brought me, inexorably to Bhagavan Sri Sathya Sai Baba, Man of Miracles, Guru, *Avatar*, Form of the Divine. In my opinion, after having walked my walk, He is the singular most intriguing man of God since Jesus Christ. So who is He, really? He claims to be a vertical descent of the Godhead into matter, or in Christian terms, an incarnation of Divinity born into the human family so that humanity can relate to Him. He comes in order to raise mankind's consciousness to a higher level through His miracles, His teachings and His will.

He has multiplied food, created material objects such as rings, crosses, and holy ash out of thin air. He has appeared to many across the miles, indeed, across the oceans! He has made the lame to walk, the deaf to hear, and the blind to see...and...He has raised at least two people from the dead, an elderly American, Walter Cowan of California, and an Indian devotee whose body was putrefying in the hot air of India! Obviously, it is not possible for me to define, describe or fully understand an entity of such immense superhuman power.

Of Himself, He says:

*"In truth, you cannot understand the nature of My Reality
either today, or even after a thousand years of steady austerity
or ardent inquiry even if all mankind joins in that effort.
But, in a short time, you will become cognizant of the bliss
showered by the Divine Principle, which has taken upon Itself
this sacred body and this sacred Name.
Your good fortune which will provide you this chance
is greater than what was available for anchorites, monks,
sages, saints and even personalities
embodying facets of Divine Glory."*

Baba The Breath of Sai
Page 4

It is with an understanding of my limitations on this subject and in humility, that I offer to the reader a short summary of the life of Sathya Sai Baba and my opinion as to what He means in my life. I leave it for each and every reader of my words to make their own inquiry and draw their own conclusions of His meaning in their minds and hearts.

Sathya Sai Baba was born as Satyanarayana Raju on November 23, 1926, between 3 a.m. and 6 a.m. in the small, backward village of Puttaparthi, India. His mother, Easwaramma, a simple, devout Hindu, wife and mother, reported that His conception was not the result of a sexual union, but rather an overshadowing of the Spirit of God, wherein a blue light engulfed her and she conceived.

As a young man, He proved to be an exceptional athlete, actor and gifted author of spiritual dramas. However, He was most recognised for His spiritual knowledge, His loving ways, and His miraculous powers. He often materialised gifts out of thin air, delighting His friends with candies and sweets.

At age 13, His personality changed dramatically. He would go for long periods without speaking or He would recite Holy Scriptures, of which, He had no formal knowledge. His parents tried every conceivable method to "cure" young Sathya, including exorcism and physical remedies which were often painful. Finally, at age 14, He announced that He would no longer be treated as a dependent family member, but in much the same way as Jesus, announced that He must be about the business for which He had come. He would serve His devotees who were *"calling"* for him. His father, having suffered greatly during His son's "illness, " could not endure Sathya's declarations of independence and challenged Him...daring Him to reveal who and what He was. At this, Sathya asked for a spray of flowers, and having been given them, He threw them into the air. As the petals reached the floor, they arranged themselves into the words, "Sai Baba."

The very arrangement was miraculous, of course, but the name, "Sai Baba," sent shock waves through the crowd. Those who knew, realised that Sathya was claiming to be "Sai Baba," a revered Holy Man of the prior nineteenth and early twentieth centuries. That Sai Baba, of Shirdi, India, was worshipped at the time of Sathya's declaration, as an *Avatar*. Sathya claimed that the *Sai Avatar* would actually be born three times: Once as Shirdi Sai Baba in the nineteenth century, again as *Sathya* (meaning "truth") Sai Baba of this century, and finally as *Prema* (meaning "Love") Sai Baba of the twenty-first century.

"He who came as Sai Baba
has now come again as Sathya Sai Baba.
Moreover, the Sais come in a series.
After this there will be another,
Prema Sai,
who will take birth in the Mysore region.'

<u>Sai Avatar</u>
Paragraph 177

From that day on, Sathya Sai Baba has lived a life of miracles, spiritual witness and teachings. His message is that all creation, whether material, intellectual or spiritual, is One; that all of our daily activities should be worship, whether service to others, meditation, work, sports or hobbies. All people should be recognised as Divine and should be treated with reverence, respect and love. Our behaviour in all things should be righteous. But if these truths are His message, why the emphasis on miracles? Why does He display His command over nature and her elements?

Sathya Sai Baba has called His miracles, *leela,* or Divine play. He says that they are relatively unimportant as a part of His Incarnation. They are merely his calling cards, his attention getters.

Yes, they are used to heal, to cure, and to awaken the consciousness of men to rise in a paradigm leap to a broader, more intuitive understanding of the experience of God and His creation, but often, they are meant simply to focus us so that the teaching of the *Sai Avatar* can then be heard.

> *"I am determined to correct you only after*
> *informing you of My credentials.*
> *That is why I am now and then announcing My Nature*
> *by means of miracles; that is, acts which are beyond*
> *human capacity and human understanding.*
> *Not that I am anxious to show off My Powers.*
> *The object is to draw you closer to Me,*
> *to cement your hearts to Me."*

Sathya Sai Speaks
Volume II
Page 118

The Sai miracles are similar to the miracles of Jesus. It is said that Sai Baba has duplicated all of the major miracles of Jesus, as reported in the New Testament. His miraculous activities, in this modern age of science, has solidified my belief in the Piscine Man of God, Jesus Christ. If these miracles can occur in the here and now, similar wonders could have occurred two thousand years ago in a simpler age. Like Jesus commanding the wind and waves of the Sea of Galilee, Sai Baba with a wave of His hand, has reversed the flow of a flooding river and commanded ocean waves lapping on the shore to rise in huge columns of spray and brine. He has changed water into petrol so that stranded motorists could continue their journey. His ability to heal in an instant or over time has been documented and written of in dozens of books. While at Kodai Kanal in 1994, an Australian devotee told me that in an interview, Baba placed his hands on an Australian woman who was dying of cancer and said: *"Cancer is cancelled."* My Australian friend reported her fully cured.

At His *ashram* in Puttaparthi, India, He has been known to materialise holy ash, *vibhuthi,* out of His palms, distributing it among devotees. While at Puttaparthi in 1985, I saw Him wave His hand and spray the seated crowd with it as a material symbol of His Grace and His Love.   At other times He has materialised pounds and pounds of this *vibhuthi* from an upturned urn much too small to hold the volume of ash that spewed from its mouth. Often the *vibhuthi* acts as a medicine, physically healing the ill and it is a constant reminder to mankind that our physical bodies are not permanent. They shall return back to the dust and dirt of the earth, from whence they came.

He has, with a wave of His hand, created lockets, gold chains, mandalas and rings that fit the finger of the recipients perfectly. At the *ashram*, Prasanthi Nilayam, I met an Italian lady who showed me a ring that Baba had materialised for her and explained that it was a perfect fit. She had never met or spoken to Him before and yet, out of ten thousand people gathered there, He simply pulled the ring from the ether, fitting her finger perfectly without any measurement.

One of His most spectacular miracles, when considered over time, was His gift to Dr. John Hislop of California, of a ring with a line drawn on its crest. Sai explained that as He grew older and closer to His death, and therefore, closer to the birth of the third *Sai Avatar*, Prema Sai Baba, the ring given to Hislop would more and more evidence the facial features of Prema Sai Baba. I held that ring in my hand in 1993 and at that time, the line on the ring had multiplied so that the ring carried an image of a bearded man beginning to resemble somewhat, the typical depiction of Jesus Christ.

Another materialisation for Hislop was of a figurine of the crucified Christ on a cross of wood which Sai claimed was made of molecules from the original cross. After having blown into His hands, the cross miraculously appeared, only inches in height, but the figure on the cross is so detailed in its depiction, that the agony of the passion is clearly evident. Hislop had that cross tested and it was found that the wood of the small cross was approximately two thousand years old!

`   In Shelton, Connecticut, and in Manhattan, New York, and in fact, in homes around the world, Sai Baba's ability to command nature over distance has been witnessed daily by literally thousands of people over the past ten years. In these homes, pictures of Sai Baba, Krishna, Christ and other *avatars* and saints, have become covered with the holy ash, *vibhuthi* and with *amrita*, a sweet fluid called the "Nectar of the Gods." The *vibhuthi* or *amrita* appears on some pictures on the glass and on some between the photographs and the glass. It is often widespread with many pictures being part of the miracle.

Some of the questions always asked about Sathya Sai Baba are: "Is He planning to start a new religion or a cult? Does He claim to supersede or replace the God men of the past such as Zoroaster, Buddha, Krishna, Christ or Mohammed?" He himself has answered:

> *"I do not appreciate in the least*
> *the distinction between*
> *the various appearances of God,*
> *Sai, Rama, Krishna, etc.*
> *I do not proclaim that this is more important*
> *or that the other is less important.*
> *Continue your worship of your chosen God*
> *along lines already familiar to you.*
> *Then you will find that you are coming nearer to Me,*
> *for all names are Mine, and all forms are Mine.*
> *There is no need to change your chosen God*
> *and adopt a new One*
> *When you have seen Me and heard Me."*

A Recapitulation of Satya Sai Baba's
Divine Teaching
Page 4

His teaching, then, is not to judge one *Avatar* or one Incarnation over another or even one religion over another. Sai Teaches that each of us must walk his own path up the mountain of spiritual awakening. However, we must be non judgmental of others on other paths or at different levels of our path.

> *"If the dancer trips, he blames the drummer,*
> *as the saying goes.*
> *That is not right in the spiritual field.*
> *You have to climb the peak alone."*

Sathya Sai Speaks
Volume II
Page 106

"Whatever one's religion may be
everyone should cultivate respect for other faiths.
One who does not have such an attitude of tolerance
and respect for other religions
is not a true follower of his own religion
A person without religious tolerance
is like a counterfeit coin
or a flower without fragrance."

Indulal Shah
Spiritual Blueprints of My Journey
Chapter 9
Page 125

Sathya Sai Baba teaches that Divinity should be sought in one's self. Like the message of the Great Pyramid: "Man look within;" like the message of the ancient Greeks: "Man Know thyself," the seeker must search within his own heart for reality. The beginning and end of the journey is the self. Sai stresses that peace and happiness can not be obtained from the outside. He asks us to harmonise ourselves; become one with the God within us. Only then, he explains, can we be truly happy. Baba says: *" I am in there,"* as He points to your breast.

"This kind of constant dwelling
on the indwelling God
will promote Love
for all beings."

Thought For the Day
1008 Gems from the Sri Sai
Manasasarovar
Page 171

To someone like myself, brought up in the Christian tradition, the Divinity of Christ is comfortable...and the possibility of several divine incarnations over time in history is not unbelievable. After all, if it happened once in Jesus Christ, it would be like putting a wall around God to say it could never happen again. So, I am comfortable with the possibility that a vertical descent of divinity and an incarnation of an *Avatar*, could be the explanation not only of Christ, but of many spiritual personages such as Krishna, Buddha, Zoroaster and Sai Baba among others. But I had to question myself to see if I were comfortable with the *Sai Avatar* coming in three lifetimes, in three continuous centuries and being all part of one and the same divine spark? After reflection, I concluded that the answer for me is a resounding "yes!" It is exciting for me to reflect that the Trinity of Christianity, the three aspects of the God of the Hindus, and the three activities of divine energy are mirrored in this *Sai Avatar*. Christians refer to three persons in one God: Father, Son and Holy Spirit. Hindus worship Brahma, Siva and Vishnu and adepts of all religions have recognised the creative, destructive and preservative aspects of God.

Sai Baba of Shirdi recognised by many as an *Avatar*, was, as an old man, revered for His fatherly aspect. When I think of Him, I see Father-Creator-Brahma. Sathya Sai Baba of our age and time calls Himself: "Truth," and claims to be an incarnation of Siva, the destructive aspect of the Hindu Trinity. It is interesting to note that most prophecies, including those of Daniel of the Old Testament, of Nostradamus, of Edgar Cayce, among others, look to the end of this century as a time of great change, spiritual, material, or both. The prophecies have suggested that these changes could occur through war, earth changes, polar shifts, prayer and meditation. Sathya Sai Baba could be the *Avatar* of the end of the age. To me, He is Shiva, the Destroyer or the Holy Spirit.

And lastly, these same prophecies look to a Golden Age, a new millennium, a time of human cooperation and a paradigm leap in spiritual consciousness, an age of love. And the *Sai Avatar* still to come in the next century is to be called: *Prema*, meaning love. Do we find here the Son of God, Vishnu, the Preserver? Is Prema Sai to be the *Avatar* for the New Age? In the Hindu, Prema Sai Baba, will the Jews' search for a Messiah, the Muslim search for the Mahdi, and the Christian yearning for the Second Coming of Christ be fulfilled and harmonised? The answers to these questions may not be easy or obvious, but If Sathya Sai Baba is who He says He is, an Incarnation of Divinity...then truly **spiritual** changes of immense importance are upon us.

"My power is immeasurable, my truth inexplicable,
unfathomable.
I am beyond the reach of the most intensive inquiry
and the most meticulous measurement.
There is nothing I do not see, no where I do not know the way,
no problem I cannot solve
My sufficiency is unconditional.
I am the totality--all of it!"

> Ron Laing
> Sai Baba The Embodiment of Love
> Book 2
> Chapter 2
> Page 142

I believe that Bhagavan Sri Sathya Sai Baba is an *Avatar*, an incarnation of Divinity. His call, like the message of other God-Men who lived in ages past, is for all humanity to live every moment aware of Divinity and for each of us to realise our own divinity. It is my prayer, that I and all mankind will strive to reach that realisation.

"How many are making any sacrifice?
How many are putting Swami's teachings into practice?
Why are you gathered here?
It is all useless unless you practice
at least one of my teachings."

> Sanathana Sarathi
> December 1994
> Volume 37 No. 12
> Page 315

BIBLIOGRAPHY

_____. *Sathya Sai Speaks, Volumes I-XI*.
Tustin, California: Sathya Sai Book Center of America. 1993
_____. *Summer Showers In Brindavan.*
Prasanthi Nilayam, India. Sri Sathya Sai Books and
Publications Trust.
_____.*Spiritual Diary*.
Prasanthi Nilayam: Sri Sathya Sai Books and Publications.
1980.
_____.*Sadhana The Inward Path*. Brindavan, Bangalore,
India: Sri Sathya Sai Education and Publication Foundation.
1976.
_____.*Thought For The Day.*
Prasanthi Nilayam: Sri Sathya Sai Institute of Higher
Learning. 1992.
_____.*Summer Roses On The Blue Mountains*.
Prasanthi Nilayam: Sri Sathya Sai Education & Publication
Foundation. 1976.
_____.*Teachings of Sri Sathya Sai Baba*.
Tustin California: Sathya Sai Book Center of America. 1974.
Baskin, Diana. *Divine Memories of Sathya Sai Baba*.
San Diego, California: Birth Day Publishing Company. 1990.
Bhagavan Sri Sathya Sai Baba. *Chinna Katha.*
Prasanthi Nilayam. Sri Sathya Sai Books and Publications
Trust.
Bock, Janet. *The Jesus Mystery*. Santa Monica, California: Aura
Books.1990.
Bruce, Rita. *Vision of Sai.*
Prasanthi Nilayam, India: Sri Sathya Sai Books and
Publications Trust. 1991.
Devi, Indra. *Sai Baba and Sai Yoga*.
Delhi: The Macmillan Company of India Limited. 1975.
Ganapati, Rs. *Baba: Sathya Sai, Part I*.
Madras, India: Divya Vidya Trust. 1991.
Gandhi, C.L. (Compiled by). *Sai Avatar*.
Calclutta: C.J. Gandhi Welfare Trust for Bhagavan Sri Sathya
Sai Trust.
Gardner, Mark and Barbara. *Sai Baba and You: Practical
Spirituality*.
Santa Barbara, California: Wisdom Works Press. 1990.

Gokak, Vinayak Krishna. *The Advent of Sathya Sai*.
　　Purbadesh Mudran: Sri Sathya Sai Prakashan (N-E Region).
　　1977.
Gunaji, Nagesh Vasudev. *Shri Sai Satcharita or the Wonderful
　　Life and Teachings of Shri Sai Baba*.
　　Bombay, India: Shri Sai Baba Sansthan. 1991.
Hejmadi, D. (Compiled by). *Voice of the Avatar*.
　　Prasanthi Nilayam: Sri Sathya Sai Books and Publications.
Hewlett, Lee and Nataraj, K. (Translated by)
　　An Eastern View of Jesus Christ
　　London.　Sai Publications.　1982.
Hislop, John S. Dr.
　　Conversations With Bhagavan Sri Sathya Sai Baba.
　　Prasanthi Nilayam. Sri Sathya Sai Books and Publications
　　Trust.
Hislop, John S. *My Baba and I*.
　　San Diego, California: Birth Day Publishing Company. 1985.
Irani, Dara. *The First Pilgrimage To Sathya Sai Baba*.
　　Corona, California: TPS Publications. 1982.
Kasturi, N. *Sathya Sai Baba Sathyam Sivam Sundaram Part I.*
　　Tustin, California. American Edition. Sathya Sai Book Center
　　of America 1989.
Kasturi, N. *Sathyam Sivam Sundaram Part IV.*
　　Prasanthi Nilayam. Sri Sathya Sai Books and Publications.
　　1980.
Kasturi, N. *Loving God*.
　　Prasanthi Nilayam, India: Sri Sathya Sai Books and
　　Publications Trust. 1982.
Kasturi, N. *Pathway To Peace*.
　　Prasanthi Nilayam: Sri Sathya Sai Books and Publications
　　Trust. 1985.
Kakade, R.T. and Rao, A. Veerbhadra. *Shirdi to Puttaparthi*.
　　Hyderabad, India: IRA Publications. 1985.
Kanu, Victor. *Sathya Sai Baba God Incarnate*.
　　Prasanthi Nilayam: Sri Sathya Sai Books and Publications
　　Trust.
Krishnamurty, Tumuluru. (Compiled by) *Sai Avatar Volume II*.
　　Prasanthi Nilayam. Published for the Sri Sathya Sai Education
　　and Foundation by C.J. Gandhi Welfare Trust.

Krystal, Phyllis. *The Ultimate Experience.*
    York Beach, Maine: Samuel Weiser, Inc. 1994
Laing, Ron and Mason, Peggy.
    Sai Baba The Embodiment of Love.
    Bath, England: Gateway Books. 1982.
Lowenberg, R. *At The Feet of Sai.*
    Bombay: P.G. Mirchandani for India Book House Pvt. Ltd.
    1983.
Maheshwaranand, Swami.
    Sai Baba and Nara Narayan Gufa Ashram.
    Prasanthi Nilayam: Shri Shantibhai S. Tailor. 1990.
Marwaha, Annemarie. *...And the Greatest is Love.*
    Prasanthi Nilayam: Sri Sathya Sai Books And Publications
    Trust.
Mavinkurve, Brahmanand, Dr.
    Namasmarana A Universal Sadhana.
    Prasanthi Nilayam: Sri Sathya Sai Books and Publications
    Trust.
Mazzoleni, Don Mario. *A Catholic Priest Meets Sai Baba.*
    Faber, Va: Leela Press. 1993
Mc Martin, Grace J. (Compiled by) *A Recapitulation of Baba's*
    Divine Teachings.
    Hyderabad, India: Avon Printing Works.1982.
Mc Martin, Grace J. (Compiled by) *Baba, The Breath of Sai.*
    Hyderabad, India: Avon Printing Works. 1984.
Mc Martin, Grace J. *Seva A Flower At His Feet.*
    Hyderabad, India: Avon Printing Works. 1985.
Miller, Barbara Stoler (A translation by). *The Bhagavad Gita.*
    Bantam Books. 1986.
Murphet, Howard, *Sai Baba Avatar.*
    San Diego California. Birth Day Publishing Company.
    1977.
Murphet, Howard. *Sai Baba Invitation to Glory.*
    Delhi: Macmillan India Limited. 1982
Murphet;, Howard. *Where the Road Ends.*
    Delhi: Macmillan India Limited. 1993
Murthy, M.V.N. *The Greatest Adventure.*
    Prasanthi Nilyam, India:
    Sri Sathya Sai Books and Publications Trust.

Osborne, Arthur. *The Incredible Sai Baba*.
Hyderabad: Orient Longman Limited. 1957.
_____. *Yoga of Action*.
Compiled by Patel, Kirit and Amin, Vijay C.
Parthasarathy, Rangaswami. *God Who Walked On Earth*
New Delhi, India: Sterling Publishers, PVT. Ltd. 1996
Penn, Faith and Penn, Charles. *Sai Ram*.
Tustin, California. Sathya Sai Book Center of America. 1992.
Penn, Charles. *My Beloved.*
Tustin, California: Charles Penn. 1981
Rai, R. Mohan. *Satya Sai Avatar, Glimpses of Divinity*
New Delhi: Sterling Publishers Private Limited. 1987.
Ramarao, N.B.S.
Dreams, Visions & Divine Experiences with Baba.
Madras: Prasanthi Printers. 1992.
Rao, M.N. *Our God and Your Mind*.
Prasanthi Nilayam: M. Srinivas. 1992.
Rigopoulos, Antonio.
The Life and Teachings of Sai Baba of Shirdi
Albany, New York. State University of New York Press. 1993
Rodriguez, Birgitte. *Glimpses of the Divine.*
York Beach, Maine: Samuel Weiser, Inc. 1993.
Ruhela, Satya Pal.
Sri Sathya Sai Baba and The Future of Mankind.
New Delhi: Sai Age Publications. 1991.
Ruhela, S.P. *Sri Shirdi Sai Baba Avatar*. Faridabad: Sai Age
Publications. 1992
Sandweiss, Samuel H. *Sai Baba The Holy Man And The Psychiatrist.*
San Diego, California: Birth Day Publishing Company. 1975.
Shah, Indulal. *Spiritual Blueprints of My Journey*.
Bombay. M.D. Rajan, Typographic for Saria Charities Trust.
1993.
Sinha, Krishna Nandan, *Sai Baba. The Rose Fire of Heaven*.
New Delhi, India: Sterling Publishers, PVT. Ltd. 1996
Thayee, Sri La Sri Shivamma. *My Life With Sri Shirdi Sai Baba*.
Faridabad: Sai Age Publications. 1992.
Thomas, Joy. *Life is a Challenge Meet It*.
Beaumont, California: Ontic Book Publishers 1991.

Warner, Judy. *Transformation of the Heart*.
    York Beach, Maine: Samuel Weiser, Inc.1990.

Periodicals

Sanathana Sarathi
Sri Sathya Sai Books and Publications Trust
Prasanthi Nilayam
Anantapur District
Andhra Pradesh,
Pin Code-515134

Sathya Sai Newsletter, U.S.A.
P.O. Box 660908
Arcadia, California 91066-0908